The Truth About
Armageddon

BY THE SAME AUTHOR

A Basic Semitic Bibliography (Annotated) (1950)
Hebrew Handbook (1951, rev. 1953, 1955)
Amazing Dead Sea Scrolls and the Christian Faith (1956, rev. 1962)
Bibliography of the Dead Sea Scrolls, 1948–1957 (1958)
Great Personalities of the Old Testament (1959)
Great Personalities of the New Testament (1961)
Great Personalities of the Bible (1965; reprint of the two previous titles)
Handbook of New Testament Greek (1964; rev. 1968)
Daily Life in Bible Times (1966)
The Dead Sea Scrolls and the Christian Faith (1972; reprint of 1956 work)
The Dead Sea Scrolls and the New Testament (1972)
Church Alive! An Exposition of Acts (1972)
Handbook of New Testament Greek, 2 vols.
(1973, fully revised and enlarged)
Israel, A Biblical View (1976)
Handbook of Biblical Hebrew, 2 vols. (1978; fully revised and enlarged)
Scripture, Tradition, and Interpretation (with W. W. Gasque, 1978)
Old Testament Survey (with D. A. Hubbard and F. W. Bush, 1982)

Associate Editor, Biblical Geography and Archeology, for the revision of
International Standard Bible Encyclopedia (1961–)

The Truth About
Armageddon

What the Bible Says
About the End Times

William Sanford LaSor

BAKER BOOK HOUSE
Grand Rapids, Michigan 49516

To Fred and Carol,
Lisa, Becky, and Kristin,
this work is lovingly dedicated

Reprinted 1987 by Baker Book House
with permission of copyright owner

Second printing, August 1988

Library of Congress Cataloging in Publication Data

LaSor, William Sanford.
  THE TRUTH ABOUT ARMAGEDDON.

  Bibliography
  Includes indexes.
  1. Eschatology—Biblical teaching. I. Title.
BS680.E8L37 1982   236   82-47748
ISBN 0-8010-5637-3   AACR2

Printed in the United States of America

Contents

Preface   xi

List of Abbreviations   xiv

1. The Present Concern with the End   1
  The Problem   1
  First-Time-Ever Signs   1
  Other Signs of the Times   4
  The Present Task   6
  Notes   8
  Additional Reading   9

2. What Is "The End of the World"?   11
  The Problem   11
  What Does "End" Mean?   11
  The End of What?   13
  The Old Testament Background   15
  The New Testament Idea of the End   18
  Summary   20
  Notes   20
  Additional Reading   22

3. The Present Age   23
  The Problem   23
  What Is an Age?   24
  This Is a Satanic Age   24
  This Is a Revelatory Age   28
  This Is an Age of Human Government   30
  This Is an Age of Redeemable Men and Women   32
  Summary   33
  Notes   33
  Additional Reading   35

4. The People of God   36

The Problem   36
What Does "Chosen" Mean?   36
The Elect   38
The Purpose of Election   41
The Basis of Election   43
One People or Two?   44
Summary   45
Notes   45
Additional Reading   47

5. The Servant of the Lord   49

The Problem   49
The Idea of Servant and Service   49
Implications of Being the Lord's Servant   51
The Sufferings of God's Servants   52
Summary   57
Notes   57
Additional Reading   59

6. The Satanic Character of This Age   60

The Problem   60
The Satanic World System   60
The Person and Nature of Satan   67
Summary   70
Notes   71
Additional Reading   73

7. The Messianic Idea   74

The Problem   74
The Kingdom and the King   74
The Messianic Hope   77
The Messianic Claim of Jesus   81
Summary   85
Notes   86
Additional Reading   87

8. The Second Coming of Christ   90

The Problem   90
The Universal Faith of the Church   91
The Terms Used   94
Jesus' Teaching Concerning His Return   96
The Manner of His Coming   99
Remaining Questions   102
Summary   103
Notes   103
Additional Reading   105

9. The Antichrist   108

The Problem   108
The Origin of the Idea   108
New Testament Figures   111
Summary   116
Notes   117
Additional Reading   118

10. The Great Tribulation   120

The Problem   120
The Scriptural Basis   120
The Nature and Purpose of the Tribulation   126
How Long Will the Tribulation Last?   128
Does the Church Go Through the Tribulation?   130
Summary   132
Notes   132
Additional Reading   134

11. Armageddon   135

The Problem   135
The Day of the Lord   136
Gog of the Land of Magog   137
Other Old Testament Prophecies   140
New Teatament Teachings   143
Summary   146

Notes   *147*
Additional Reading   *149*

12. The Millennium   *150*
The Problem   *150*
Terms and Definitions   *150*
The Biblical Basis   *151*
Development of the Dogma   *159*
Why Should There Be an Earthly Kingdom?   *160*
Summary   *161*
Notes   *161*
Additional Reading   *163*

13. The Resurrection   *165*
The Problem   *165*
What Is "Resurrection"?   *165*
Development of the Idea   *167*
Objections to the Doctrine   *170*
One Resurrection or Two?   *171*
Between Death and Resurrection   *175*
Summary   *177*
Notes   *177*
Additional Reading   *179*

14. The Judgment   *180*
The Problem   *180*
Judgment and Government   *180*
Coming to Grips with Terms   *182*
Is Judgment an Act or a Process?   *184*
The Biblical Doctrine of the Last Judgment   *185*
Some Burning Questions   *190*
Summary   *192*
Notes   *193*
Additional Reading   *194*

15. The New Heavens and the New Earth   *196*

The Problem   *196*
The Biblical Basis of the Doctrine   *196*
Biblical Description of the New Creation   *199*
The Kingdom of God   *203*
Notes   *205*
Additional Reading   *206*

Bibliography   *207*
Subject Index   *211*
Index of Scripture Verses   *221*

Preface

We live in a time of great uncertainty. On the radio this morning a student of world terrorism reported on terrorist training camps of which he claimed to have personal knowledge, and of plans that he had seen for widespread disorder and destruction in the United States when the proper time comes. I have no idea whether he knows what he is talking about, but I do know that the pope, kings, presidents, ambassadors, and consular officials are not safe in any country in the world today.

This is also a time of great excitement over "the end of the world." I discuss this in Chapter 1, but here let me say that my purpose in writing this book is not to add to the fears and uncertainties that I sense in the world, nor to capitalize on the situation by producing more sensationalism.

I believe that the Bible speaks to every age, and especially to times of fear. I am convinced that the prophets and apostles were given revelations from God—not to predict events, but to serve the people of God who live in perilous times. For fifty years I have studied the Bible professionally (I entered theological seminary in 1931), with earned degrees in both the Old and New Testaments, and I have taught and written on both Testaments. I believe both Testaments are inspired by God and both are necessary if we would understand God's message for our day. I am also of the opinion that many eschatological studies (studies of the end time) are written from one-sided positions—either from the Old Testament alone without taking into account how Jesus and the apostles handled those Scriptures, or from the New Testament without understanding the true nature of Old Testament prophecy and without using it as anything but a collection of proof-texts.

My personal bias will be obvious at many points. I receive and accept the Scriptures of the Old and New Testaments as the word of God, the infallible rule of faith and life. My training has grounded me in biblical criticism, and I am well aware of source- and form-critical theories. I am a trained philologian, and I work from Hebrew, Aramaic, and Greek texts, with help from numerous other languages. I mention these things, as the Apostle Paul on occasion boasted of his training, not to glorify myself, but rather to give you, the reader, a certain degree of assurance. If I do not say "Deutero-Isaiah" or " 'J' and 'E,' " it is not because I have not heard of them. And if I quote from the Pastorals as from Paul, it is not from ignorance. After much study I have come to some convictions. This is my faith. If you disagree, that is your faith. I am not trying to impose my convictions on you; rather, I am setting them forth for your consideration. If they are helpful to you, I give God the glory.

I grew up with the *Scofield Reference Bible*. As a seminarian, I felt something of the scorn that some Bible students have for those who use this Bible. Under Professor Otto Piper I was led to study Premillennialism in depth, and my master's thesis on "The Exegetical Basis of Premillennialism" gave me a firm basis for my premillennial beliefs—although I discarded some of the elements of Dispensationalism. For over thirty years I was Professor of Old Testament, and I spent much time in the Prophets. My interest in eschatology led me to examine the end-time prophecies in much greater depth, and my training and previous experience in New Testament enabled me to attempt a synthesis of the eschatology of both Testaments.

With the rash of books that have appeared in the past decade or so on the various subjects connected with the end of the world. I became a bit restive. Emotionalism was more evident that sound scholarship. Claims were made that could not be supported by biblical exegesis. Finally I felt led of God to "get into the act." After giving a series of studies in the adult education program of the Pasadena Presbyterian Church, and repeating (and enlarging) this series for the Homebuilders' Class of the First Presbyterian Church of Hollywood, I put the studies into manuscript form. To Roy M. Carlisle, Editor, I am indebted for his interest in the project and his willingness to accept the manuscript for publication by Harper & Row.

To my beloved wife of many years, Betsy, I would express my gratitude for her support and love—and for a bit of the drudgery of proofreading. For the second time in my literary efforts, I have no one to thank for typing the text, for I did it all by myself with my little computer. All mistakes are therefore mine alone. Thanks be to God, I long ago learned that he is able to take even our imperfections and use them to his glory.

In dedicating this work to our younger son and his family, I have happy memories of traveling many roads with some or all of them in four continents, and none happier than the memories of visiting the lands of the Bible with them. If they are called upon to face times of trouble, I pray that they may find strength from God through this book. And what I pray for them, I pray for you, too! May our blessed Lord hasten the day when every sorrow will be turned to joy, when God shall wipe away all tears, when his will is done on earth as it is in heaven!

WILLIAM SANFORD LASOR

Altadena, California
31 January 1982

List of Abbreviations

A-G (Arndt-Gingrich), *A Greek-English Lexicon of the New Testament*

BDB (Brown-Driver-Briggs), *Hebrew and English Lexicon of the Old Testament*

DAC *Dictionary of the Apostolic Church*

DCG *Dictionary of Christ and the Gospels*

HDB *Hasting's Dictionary of the Bible*

IDB *Interpreter's Dictionary of the Bible*

ISBE *International Standard Bible Encyclopedia*

KJV King James Version

LSJ (Liddell-Scott-Jones), *Greek-English Lexicon*

LXX Septuagint

MT Masoretic text

NASB *New American Standard Bible*

NBD *The New Bible Dictionary*

NIV *New International Version*

NSRB *New Scofield Reference Bible*

NT New Testament

OT Old Testament

RSV Revised Standard Version

SRB *Scofield Reference Bible*

TDNT *Theological Dictionary of the New Testament*

1. The Present Concern with the End

The Problem

There is widespread interest in subjects related to "the end of the world"— or *eschatology*, to give it a theological label. This is not the first time in history that there has been such interest, verging sometimes on fanaticism, but it is the first time that certain cataclysmic events have become a distinct possibility.

In addition to these first-time-ever situations, there are other "signs of the times." To many students of the Bible, particularly to those who are primarily interested in biblical prophecy, these situations and events have combined to lead them to believe that the end is near. Others who are not particularly interested in Bible prophecies have also come to a similar conclusion—but their theories are not our concern in this present study.

It is my conviction that there are prophecies of the end times in the Bible and that these deserve serious attention by all who read the Bible and particularly by those who claim to believe that the Bible is the word of God. It is also my conviction that many foolish or fantastic claims have been made in the name of prophetic study that have, at least in certain circles, tended to make the study of prophecy appear ridiculous.[a] Let's look at some of the signs of the times.

First-Time-Ever Signs

The Possibility of Worldwide Destruction. Since 1947 *The Bulletin of Atomic Scientists* has displayed a clock showing the hands close to midnight. Scientists were expressing concern that the discovery of nuclear fission could bring about the destruction of the civilized world. In 1979 the clock read 11:51. The discovery of nuclear fission, the destruction of an entire city with a single A-bomb, the stockpiling of more than enough nuclear weapons to destroy half the earth, and recently the proliferation of the ability to produce such weapons so that any tinhorn dictator or psychopathic terrorist may soon have power beyond the wildest imagination has many running scared. This is particularly true of the scientists who know the potential of nuclear weapons. Some theologians and biblical students have come to realize that we have entered an age when literal fulfillment of global disaster prophecies such as those found in the book of Revelation[1] is now possible. Little wonder that books and movies are appearing with "Armageddon" or "Apocalypse" in their titles!

Establishment of the State of Israel.   The return of many Jews to Palestine in the closing decades of the nineteenth and the early part of the twentieth centuries, the resurrection of the Hebrew language, the rise of Zionism under the influence of Theodore Herzl, and finally the Holocaust, which caused the immigration of scores of thousands of Jews and resulted in the formation of the State of Israel, not only had political effects in the Middle East but also convinced many Bible students, who had long predicted the return of the Jews to the land of their fathers, that the "times of the Gentiles"[2b] were rapidly drawing to a close, setting the stage for the coming of the Messiah (the Second Coming of Christ). When the Israelis "liberated" Jerusalem in the Six-Day War (1967), some biblical scholars declared that the "times of the Gentiles" had indeed ended. Those who were inclined to be "date setters" tried to calculate the time of the end, and 1984 or other dates in this decade became popular targets.[c]

Oil and Armageddon.   The Middle East (or Near East) has often been the scene of bloody battles, certainly since the time of Sargon of Akkad (mid–third millennium B.C.). Since the formation of the State of Israel in 1948, there has been from time to time a unification of Arab tribes and states in an anti-Zionist attitude that sought to "drive Israel into the sea." Israel's reaction and its surprising military ability exacerbated the hostility of the Arabs, but this wore down to little more than a verbal war with occasional acts of ter-

---

1. E.g., Rev. 8:7–13.   2. Luke 21:24

rorism. Then came the formation of OPEC, the tenfold increase in the price of oil, and the flow of billions of dollars into the oil-producing Arab nations. Economic and political pressures were threatened or applied to the West, and support for Israel, a tiny Jewish island in the vast Arab world, began to weaken. The meddling of Russia in the Middle East, in Syria and Egypt and then in Afghanistan, followed by the collapse of Iran and the opening of the possibility for a Russian takeover of that land have given the Western nations (not to mention Japan, which is also affected) great concern lest their oil supplies be cut off. As a result, it is now possible for the first time in history for something like an Armageddon, the massing of nations against Israel,[3] to take place. Many Bible students have long believed that Gog of the land of Magog[4] refers to Russia, and present events have strengthened their conviction.

Satellites, Computers, and 666. With recent developments in electronics, the invention of highly sophisticated computers, and the placing in earth-orbit of numbers of satellites, the way is now open for the accumulation of vast quantities of information about each one of us. At the same time, by means of satellite communication, immediate dissemination of propaganda is possible. Add to these the use of subliminal thought-control messages, and the prophecy of total economic control has for the first time in history become a possibility. Students of the Bible have long puzzled over the total power of the "beast"[5] and the significance of his "number," which is 666.[6] At least the possibility of such power is now apparent.[d]

The European Common Market and the Revived Roman Empire. Because of the two-pronged pressure of Russian economic and military power to the east of them and that of the United States to the west of them, the nations of western Europe have sought greater security in the formation of a common market, the removal of trade and travel restrictions, and less dependence on the United States. Students of the prophecies of Daniel have long declared that the fourth part of the image, or the fourth kingdom, is the Roman Empire,[7] and that it would be restored in the time of the end, in a

---

3. See Ezek. 38–39, especially 38:2–9.   4. Ezek. 38:2.   5. Rev. 13:11–18.
6. Rev. 13:18.   7. Dan. 2:40.

ten-kingdom form corresponding to the toes of the image.[8] As the Common Market developed, Bible students were looking for the ten parts to emerge; when the tenth nation was admitted, it was possible for the first time since the collapse of the Holy Roman Empire for those who hold to this interpretation to say that Daniel's prophecy is now being fulfilled.[e]

Other Signs of the Times

Wars and Rumors of Wars.   There have been wars in every generation before and since the famed Pax Romana of the first century. To claim that there are more today than in the past is perhaps to claim too much, but to claim that the science of war has reached an all-time high (or low) certainly is true. With the use of nuclear weapons, spy satellites, and computerized weaponry, any war of the future can be beyond our ability to describe, bringing Ezekiel 38–39 and Revelation out of the realm of apocalyptic fantasies and into the realm of the historically possible.

Famines.   The "population explosion," to which environmentalists have called our attention, presents the possibility that before this century is ended the world could run short of food. Pollution of the air, the ground, and particularly the sources of water likewise suggests that we may be destroying our life-support systems on Spaceship Earth. In fact, widespread famine has been predicted by several authors.[f]

Earthquakes.   As with wars, it would be folly to say that there are more earthquakes today than in times past. Perhaps it is simply our increased knowledge of them that has led some to this conclusion. It is correct to say, however, this increase (whether of frequency or intensity, or simply of our knowledge of earthquakes) has become a sign of the times. Predictions that San Francisco will be devastated or that western California will break off and fall into the sea as a result of the next great earthquake are well known.[g] Students of prophecy remind us that the seer of Patmos foretold "a great earthquake such as had never been since men were on the earth" that would destroy the cities of the earth.[9]

False Prophets.   Every generation has had its prophets, many of

---

8. Dan 2:42, 44; cf. 7:24; Rev. 17:12,13,17.   **9.** Rev. 16:18.

whom were proven false. The widespread interest in astrology and a dependence on horoscopes that amounts to a denial of our boasted scientific world-ground, the rise of new religious sects and leaders, some of which are quite bizarre, interest in the occult, in satanology, and even in biblical prophecies all suggest that a large part of the world is ready to listen to almost any prophet. The stage is set, we are being told, for the "false prophet"[10] who will lead many into Satan's false religious system. The establishment of councils of churches, interfaith movements, and religious eclecticism, most of which require either the dilution of biblical doctrine or its denial, are seen by some as signs of the great apostasy that will come on earth.[11h]

The Increase of Knowledge.   Knowledge today is increasing at an exponential rate. To handle this, data banks and retrieval processes are necessary, and future research will require teams of scholars working at computers resembling the Space Center at Houston. Experiments in parapsychology, genetic engineering, test-tube conception, cloning, and the possibility of creating new forms of life, or even of life itself, have thrown fear into some scientists and moralists. Laboratories in space, travel to the planets or even beyond the solar system, the proud boast (expressed or implied) that there are no limits to human knowledge and human conquest add up to the deification of the human being. Daniel's prophecy[12] is being fulfilled. Superman is about to attempt to seize the throne of God[13]

Et Cetera.   The list could be multiplied at great length, and indeed it has been in some of the books that have appeared in the last ten or fifteen years. The vast consumption of fossil fuels, resulting in the production of carbon dioxide at a faster rate than the photosynthesis of the trees we have left standing can convert it back to oxygen and simple sugars, is raising the temperature of the planet, which in turn will result in the melting of the polar ice caps and glaciers, raising the level of the oceans, flooding the coastlands, and submerging the great coastal cities.[i]

Development of nuclear energy, Three Mile Island, and the

---

10. Rev. 19:20.   11. Luke 18:8; 2 Thess. 2:3–4; Rev. 17–18.   12. Dan. 12:4.   13. Dan. 7:25; 11:36; Rev. 13:5–7.

China Syndrome have caused others to talk of a nuclear "burn through" that will cause unbelievable horror. Nuclear laboratories are being accused of causing cancer in persons who work in them. The use of aerosol sprays, we are told, is destroying the protective ozone of the upper atmosphere, greatly increasing the risk of skin cancer. The inability to come up with a solution to the problem of nuclear waste is poisoning our streams, oceans, and ultimately all of us.

The breakdown of the family, the relativization of morals, the terrifying emphasis on sex, particularly unnatural forms of sexual gratification,[14] and the rise of the "me generation"[15] have caused concern not only to those who believe in Judeo-Christian morals, but even to some sociologists. Loss of respect for law and government, widespread terrorism in the home and the classroom, in the city, and even in the nations of the world, so that no life is safe and no government is secure, has led some to conclude that the "man of sin" is about to be revealed, that Antichrist may even now be alive somewhere on this planet.[16]

Others have suggested that the spread of Communism, which defines morality as that which advances the cause, sees the individual as of less value than the society, and seeks to suppress all religion but itself, is a sign of the times. And what of the widespread use of alcohol, marijuana, narcotics, and hallucinogens? Or the increasing number of suicides among teenagers, psychiatrists, and the well-to-do? Or the decline of mother love, with its retinue of abortion, disposal of the newborn children in trash bags, putting children up for adoption, or continual child abuse?[j]

The Present Task

Cartoonists have often portrayed the apocalyptic as a man with ungroomed hair, a wild look in his eyes, strange clothing scarcely covering his bony body, carrying a sign that reads "THE END IS COMING!" Since the days of Amos, and often without understanding the true meaning of his words, self-appointed prophets have declaimed, "Prepare to meet thy God!"[17] Today this message

---

14. Cf. Rom. 1:26,27.   **15.** 2 Tim. 3:2.   **16.** See 2 Thess. 2:3,4,7–12.
17. Amos 4:12.

is no longer the cry of an eccentric, for scientists, philosophers, educators, legislators, politicians, the poor and the rich, laborers and managers—all stand aghast at the rapid changes taking place in our world. "Future shock" is now here. Armageddon is perhaps about to burst out.

With support from so many areas of knowledge, students of the Bible (sometimes with a less than complete knowledge of biblical teachings and little training in biblical exegesis) have gotten into the act. If the world is rushing headlong into some kind of destruction, whether nuclear holocaust or collapse of governments under universal anarchy or just the inability of the human psyche to handle the problems, the Bible must have something to say on the subject. When will the end come? Where and how will it take place? How can we escape? Some join a cult and move to Guyana, or some other place. Some sell their possessions and plan to move to Petra or Arizona. Some are just waiting for Jesus to come and lift them up from the earth before the final battle takes place.

Eschatologies of many sorts are being composed all around us. Some kind of end is coming, they agree. The Bible, from beginning to end, has much to say on this subject. In this work I am seeking to sort out the teachings of the Bible and the positive contributions they offer to our faith. It is not my intention to erect a system, to set dates, or to make spectacular identifications. Nor do I intend to hurl ridicule or invective on those Bible students with whose methods I may differ or with whose conclusions I may disagree. My professional study of the Bible extends over fifty years, and my research has led me to study many books and many points of view. I have learned, I believe, to appreciate the positive contributions regardless of viewpoint, to be humble before biblical teachings where there are complicated problems and various interpretations, and to have strong convictions where the Bible is clear.

Eschatology that is truly biblical must be integrated with other biblical doctrines. For this reason I plan to study the biblical doctrine of the end in the light of other important doctrines. I think my reason will become clear as we proceed with our consideration of this subject.

NOTES

a. Some of these statements are simply poorly expressed truth. For example, J. W. White, in *Re-Entry!* (Minneapolis, MN: World Wide Publications, 1971), states: "The teaching of the second coming of our Lord is dealt with some 1,845 times in the Bible, 318 of these being in the New Testament. The return of the Lord is the dominant theme of 17 Old Testament books" (p. 14). As a matter of fact, the Return of Christ is *not mentioned at all* in the Old Testament. What White probably had in mind was the material concerning the end of the age that was not fulfilled by the first advent of Christ and that requires another advent.

b. The prophecy of the fig tree putting forth its leaves (Matt. 24:32) has also been taken to refer to the restoration of Israel.

c. Some have calculated that "this generation" (Matt. 24:34) began with the formation of the State of Israel in 1948 and, allowing forty years to a generation, would terminate about 1987. If the Great Tribulation, or Daniel's Seventieth Week, were to be subtracted from this figure, the Rapture could occur at any time in the 1980s, the Tribulation could begin in 1984, and the Millennium could begin in 1987 or 1988. I am not offering these as prophetic dates, but simply as an explanation of some of the fervor concerning the end of this age.

d. Once again, fantasy often enters the discussion, as, for example, when it is pointed out that the license plates of Israeli tour buses begin with 666, leaving some of us wondering what possible connection this has with the scriptural passage.

e. See R. Pache, *The Return of Jesus Christ*, pp. 155–158. Written before the formation of the Common Market, this work projects "ten dictators (Rev. 17:12) who shall group themselves into a narrow confederation around one great head to come, the Antichrist" (p. 158). See H. Lindsey, *The Late Great Planet Earth* (Grand Rapids, MI: Zondervan, 1970; New York: Bantam, 1973), pp. 82–86.

f. See W. and P. Paddock, *Famine, 1975* (Boston: Little, Brown, 1967). H. Lindsey quotes the prediction by a geneticist of "a worldwide famine in 1985" in *The Late Great Planet Earth*, p. 90.

g. See C. Gentry, *The Last Days of the Great State of California* (New York: Ballantine, 1975).

h. In all cases, my inclusion of data neither affirms nor denies that I hold the same or a similar position. This is a survey. My own convictions will become clear in subsequent chapters of this work.

i. A report by Lee Dembart in the *Los Angeles Times*, 8 January 1982, p. 1, gives scientific estimates that the melting of the polar ice caps could raise the level of the seas by 18 feet in the next fifty to two hundred years, the result of the "greenhouse effect."

j. E. A. Wynne, in *The Public Interest* (Summer 1981), reports an increase in suicide and homicide rates for white males aged 15–24 of 235 percent and 254 percent respectively since 1955, and for those under 18 from 200 in

1950 to 6500 per 100,000 in 1977, an increase of 3200 percent. From *Evangelical Newsletter* 8,26 (25 Dec. 1981):2.

ADDITIONAL READING

Addresses on the International Prophetic Conference. Boston: Watchword and Truth, 1901.

Beegle, D. M. *Prophecy and Prediction.* Ann Arbor, MI: Pryor Pettingill, 1978.

The Bulletin of Atomic Scientists.

Calder, Nigel. ed. *The World in 1984.* 2 vols. Baltimore, MD: Penguin, 1965.

Chafer, Lewis Sperry. *Signs of the Times.* Chicago: Bible Institute Colportage Association, 1919.

Chalmers, Thomas M. *The Present Condition of Israel in the Light of Prophecy.* Philadelphia: American Society for Prophetic Study, 1923.

"The Deluge of Disastermania." *Time,* 5 March 1979.

Feinberg, Charles L. ed. *Focus on Prophecy.* Westwood, NJ: Revell, 1964.

Fiorenza, E. S. "Eschatology of the NT." *Interpreter's Dictionary of the Bible,* supplementary volume, pp. 271–277.

Gaustad, Edwin S. ed. *The Rise of Adventism: A Commentary on Social and Religious Ferment of Mid-Nineteenth Century America.* New York: Harper & Row, 1974.

Gentry, Curt. *The Last Days of the Great State of California.* New York: Ballantine, 1975.

Guinness, H. Grattan. *The Approaching End of the Age.* New ed. London: Morgan & Scott, 1918.

Ironside, Harry A. *The Lamp of Prophecy or Signs of the Times.* 2d ed. Grand Rapids, MI: Zondervan, 1940.

Israel—Past, Present, and Future. Chicago: Hebrew Mission, 1915.

Kümmel, W. G. *Promise and Fulfillment: The Eschatological Message of Jesus.* Translated by D. M. Barton. 2d Eng. ed. London: SCM, 1961.

Ladd, George E. *The Blessed Hope.* Grand Rapids, MI: Eerdmans, 1956.

――――. "Eschatology." In *ISBE* 2 (1982), 130–143.

LaHaye, Tim. *The Beginning of the End.* Wheaton, IL: Tyndale, 1972.

Lindsell, Harold. *The Gathering Storm: World Events and the Return of Christ.* Wheaton, IL: Tyndale, 1980.

Lindsey, Hal. *The Late Great Planet Earth.* Grand Rapids, MI: Zondervan, 1970; New York: Bantam, 1973.

McConkey, James H. *The End of the Age.* Pittsburgh, PA: Silver, 1919.

Orwell, George. *1984.* New York: New American Library, 1949.

Paddock, W. and F. *Famine, 1975.* Boston: Little, Brown, 1967.

Pettingill, William L. ed. *Light on Prophecy: Proceedings and Addresses at the Philadelphia Prophetic Conference, May 28–30, 1918.* New York: Christian Herald, 1918.

Pettingill, William L. *God's Prophecies for Plain People.* Wilmington, DE: Just-a-Word, 1923.

Pierson, Robert H. *Good-bye, Planet Earth.* Mountain View, CA: Pacific Press, 1976.

Sale-Harrison, L. *The League of Nations*. Harrisburg, PA; Evangelical Press, 1930.

————. *The Coming Great Northern Confederacy*. New York: Loizeaux Bros., n.d.

Scofield, C. I. *What Do the Prophets Say?* Philadelphia: Sunday School Times, 1918.

Thielecke, H. "Signs of the End." In *Evangelical Faith*. Translated by G. W. Bromiley. Grand Rapids, MI: Eerdmans, 1982. Vol. 3, pp. 433–435.

Toffler, Alvin. *Future Shock*. New York: Bantam, 1970.

————. *The Third Wave*. New York: Bantam, 1981. Chap. 27.

Trumbell, Charles G. ed. *How I Came To Believe in Our Lord's Return and Why I Believe the Lord's Return Is Near*. Chicago: Bible Institute Colportage Association, 1934.

Ward, Hiley H. *Religion 2001 A.D.* Garden City, NY: Doubleday, 1975.

White, J. W. *Re-Entry!* Minneapolis, MN: World Wide Publications, 1971.

Wilson, Dwight. *Armageddon Now!* Grand Rapids, MI: Baker, 1977.

Wood, Leon J. *The Bible and Future Events*. Grand Rapids, MI: Zondervan, 1973.

Woodson, Leslie H. *Population, Pollution, and Prophecy*. Old Tappan, NJ: Revell, 1973.

2. What Is "The End of the World"?

The Problem

"The end of the world" is a common expression. It is found in secular as well as religious writings.[a] Unfortunately, it is often interpreted or understood to mean the end of all existence, or at least the end of all material existence: the dropping of the cosmic curtain on the last act on the stage called Earth.

It is essential, if we are to understand the biblical doctrines of the end, to know the biblical meanings of the words "end" and "world," especially as the words are used by the individual authors in context. It is not enough to say "End means end, and world means world." In no literature, including the Bible, can we force such conclusions. Words derive specificity from context.[b] Some may not enjoy the study of words, but vocabulary control is a prerequisite for the study of any subject, whether it be chemistry or cooking, psychology or cybernetics. Theological and biblical studies are no exception. We therefore turn to the study of words concerning the end.

What Does "End" Mean?

Eschatos. The Greek word *eschatos,* from which we have the word "eschatology" (the study of doctrines pertaining to the end), means "end." But this definition needs elaboration, for the word can be used of (a) position, (b) space, or (c) time. "The first shall be last (*eschatoi,* "last ones") and the last first"[1] indicates rank or position. "Unto the end (*eschatou,* "last part") of the earth.[2] refers to space. "Children, it is the last (*eschatē*) hour"[3] has to do with time.[c]

---

1. Matt. 19:30.   2. Acts 1:8.   3. 1 John 2:18.

The Greek word *eschatos* is used to translate the Hebrew word *qēṣ*, which has the same range of meanings. From the root meaning "to cut (off)" it develops the idea of the end of space ("the end of the earth"[4]) or of time ("the end has come"[5]).

But even the temporal idea of "the last (hour/day/time)" has to be more carefully defined. When John said, "It is the last hour,"[6] he may have thought the end was near, but when we read this verse and apply it to the present day, we are giving it a somewhat different meaning. We make a mental transfer that moves first from John's day to the entire age, and then to a present application. The author of Hebrews can say that God has spoken to us by a Son "in these last days,"[7] where he is contrasting the present age with the days of old when God spoke "by the prophets." Peter shows further complexity of the term when he uses it on the one hand to say that Christ "was made manifest at the end of times,"[8] referring to the advent that had already taken place, while on the other hand he speaks of "a salvation ready to be revealed in the last time,"[9] referring to the future advent.[d]

Telos.   The Greeks had another word for "end," *telos,* and in some ways it is more significant for this study. In fact, we might prefer to speak of "teleology" rather than "eschatology," for *telos* has more of the idea of "completion, goal." When Paul says "Christ is the end (*telos*) of the law,"[10] does he mean that the law has ceased to exist—one possibility—or that it has realized its purpose in Christ? Commentaries discuss the problem at some length. When Christ says, "And if Satan has risen up against himself and is divided, he cannot stand, but is coming to an end (*telos*),"[11] the meaning is that Satan will cease to exist, not that he will achieve his purpose. But when Paul says "the end (*telos*) of the preaching is love,"[12] he is clearly using the word in the sense of "goal, purpose, intended result."[e]

We have not yet considered other words and expressions, but we can already see that "the end of the world" can mean the achievement of its intended purpose as well as, or perhaps rather than, the cessation of its existence.

---

4. Isa. 48:20   5. Amos 8:2.   6. 1 John 2:18.   7. Heb. 1:2.   8. 1 Pet. 1:20.   9. 1 Pet. 1:5.   10. Rom. 10:4.   11. Mark 3:26.   12. 1 Tim. 1:5.

The End of What?

Just as there are various words and meanings for "end," so there are also a number for "world." We are perhaps familiar with the alternate expression "the end of the *age,*" so we must consider this word also, and raise the question of whether "world" and "age" are interchangeable, or whether they have distinctions that must be observed.

World.   The Greek word *kosmos,* from which we get such words as "cosmonaut," "cosmic," "cosmetic," and so forth, means "order, arrangement, beauty, adornment."[f] In the New Testament the word is used: (a) of the universe, the sum of all created beings and things; (b) of the abode of men, the planet earth, the theater of history; and (c) of humanity, the fallen creation, the theater of salvation.[g] "The God who made the world (*kosmon*) and everything in it"[13] refers clearly to the whole creation. "For all the nations of the world seek these things"[14] would seem to refer to this planet, or possibly a designated part of the planet where there are "nations." But when Paul speaks of "the wisdom of this world"[15] and "the spirit of the world,"[16] distinguishing them from "the wisdom of God"[17] and "the Spirit of God,"[18] he is using the word "world" to refer to fallen humanity.[h]

It is in this third sense that the expression "the end of the world" is used.[i] The "world," as we shall see in Chapter 3, exists from the fall of humanity to the end of this age. But the fallen world includes not only humanity, but the "whole creation."[19] God is therefore never referred to as "King of the Kosmos."[j] Rather, this world is under another ruler, "the prince of this world."[20]

The Church is not "of this world,"[21] yet it must live in the world. Paul recognized the problem in using the word when he clarified the meaning of his advice "not to associate with immoral men." He did not mean, he explains, "the immoral of the world . . . since then you would need to go out of the world,"[22] but rather "those inside the church."[23] Christians "shine as lights in the

---

13. Acts 17:24.   **14.** Luke 12:30.   **15.** 1 Cor. 1:20.   **16.** 1 Cor. 2:12.
17. 1 Cor. 1:21.   **18.** 1 Cor. 2:11f.   **19.** Cf. Rom. 8:19–22.   **20.** John 14:30.   **21.** John 17:14.   **22.** 1 Cor. 5:9–10.   **23.** 1 Cor. 5:12.

world."[24] In the age to come, this "world" is replaced by the Kingdom of God.[25]

The Greek word *oikoumenē*, "world," from which we get "(o)ecumenical" and related words, is also used in the New Testament. It can mean either "the (whole) earth" or "the (political) world, the Roman Empire."[k] The word occurs in the statement, "And this gospel of the kingdom will be preached throughout the whole world (*oikoumenē*), as a testimony to all nations,"[26] where the context indicates that it refers to the inhabited earth. On the other hand, in Agabus' prophecy of a famine "over all the world (*oikoumenēn*)"[27] the reference is most probably to the Roman Empire.[27] When the Thessalonians refer to Paul and Silas as "men who have turned the world upside down,"[28] the term has to be limited to that portion of the empire that had felt the effects of apostolic preaching. In Hebrews 2:5, the expression "the world (*oikoumenēn*) to come" seems to be equivalent to "the age to come," although it may indicate a limitation to the earthly part (the messianic reign) of that age. Paul avoids using the word *oikoumenē* except when he quotes Psalm 18:4.[29]

Age. The Greek word *aiōn*, from which we get "eon (aeon)," basically means "time, lifetime, generation, long time, age, for ever."[l] The philosophical concept of "eternity" as distinct from "time" was probably unknown in the Old Testament, and perhaps also in the New. The expression "the age of the ages"[30] approaches the idea of "eternal," and hence it is possible to speak of God as *aiōnios*.[31] But in common biblical usage, an "age" can (must?) have an end, and the expression "this age" is practically synonymous with "this world." This age has its cares ("the cares of the world [*aiōnos*]"[32]) and it will come to an end ("the close of the age"[33]).

In the Old Testament the word most frequently translated into Greek *aiōn* is the Hebrew ʿôlām, "long duration, antiquity, futurity."[m] It can be used of the distant past ("days of old"[34]) or the

---

24. Phil. 2:15.   25. Cf. Matt. 25:34.   26. Matt. 24:14.   27. Acts 11:28; cf. Luke 2:1.   28. Acts 17:6.   29. Rom. 10:18.   30. Heb. 1:8; Ps. 44:6.   31. Rom. 16:26.   32. Matt. 13:22.   33. Matt 13:39.   34. Isa. 63:9.

undefined future ("a slave for ever"[35]). When it is used in connection with God's promises, this word approaches the idea of "eternal" ("an everlasting covenant"[36])."

So far our study indicates that the term "world" in the Bible often conveys the idea of a period of time or a system within that period. It had a beginning, and it will have an end or goal. But we must pursue this idea further, for it is central to the study of biblical eschatology.

This Age and the Age to Come.   The Jews of the Intertestamental Period developed the concept of "this age" (*hāʿôlām hazzeʰ*) and "the age to come" (*haʿôlām habbāʰ*).° This idea is found also in the New Testament,[37] and the origin of the expression "the end of the world" is to be traced to this Judeo-Christian concept. As understood by both Jews and early Christians, this world (or age) will end and will be replaced by the age to come.ᵖ

It is perhaps an oversimplification to speak of "this age" and "the age to come," as if there were to be only two ages. Expressions such as "to all the ages,"[38] "to the ages of the ages,"[39] and "to all the generations of the age of the ages"[40] suggest that there may be more things in heaven and earth than are dreamt of in our philosophy.

In any event, the expressions "this age" and "the age to come" are not found in the Old Testament, and since both Judaism and New Testament Christianity are based on the Jewish scriptures, we must ask where the idea of the two (or more) ages originated.

The Old Testament Background

Studies in Christian eschatology often begin with the New Testament. The Old Testament is then used as a sort of religious attic where all sorts of relics from the past are found. From time to time, Christian scholars poke around in this attic, hoping to find something that will be useful for their purposes. In most cases this has amounted to "proof-texting,"—taking passages partially or entirely removed from context to prove doctrines that are found (or believed to be found) in the New Testament.

This method ignores historical developments. The New Testa-

---

35. Deut. 15:17.   36. Gen. 90:6; cf. 2 Sam. 7:13ff.   37. See Matt. 12:
32.   38. Jude v. 25.   39. Gal. 1:5.   40. Eph. 3.21.

ment writers were Jews, except for Luke, and he was greatly influenced by the Jewish ideas of Paul. Every presentation of a doctrinal concept, whether by Jesus or by any of his followers, had to be
capable of scriptural support—which means support of the Old
Testament. Jesus made it clear that he did not come "to abolish
the law and the prophets" but rather to "fulfill" them.[41] (We shall
have occasion to examine the meaning of "fulfillment" of
scriptures at a later point.) What scriptures support the idea of the
two ages?

"In the Latter Days."   The expression *b^e'aḥărît hayyāmîm*, "in
the end (latter part) of the days" is important.[q] When Jacob gave
his final blessing, he gathered about him his sons, saying, "that I may
tell you what shall befall you in days to come."[42] Moses foretells a
future apostasy in the land, to be followed by a scattering of Israel
and then a return, including the statement, "All these things shall
come upon you in the latter days."[43] Isaiah says, "It shall come to
pass in the latter days that the mountain of the house of the Lord
shall be established as the highest of the mountains."[44] Hosea,
speaking of a future repentance of Israel, says "and they shall come
in fear to the Lord and to his goodness in the latter days.[45] Jeremiah
uses the expression several times in connection with events that were
to take place "in the latter days."[46] Ezekiel prophesies of a war of Gog
against Israel "in the latter days.[47] (earlier he uses an alternate
expression, "in the latter years"[48]).[r]

The idea of "the latter days" is expressed in other terms, principally those including the words "day" or "days." Since these are
very common words, the study of them becomes quite difficult.

"Behold, Days Are Coming."   The phrase *hinnê^h yāmîm bā'îm*,
"behold, (the) days are coming," is significant for our study.[s] The
expression has to do with any future event, not necessarily one that
is eschatological. Amos[49] and Isaiah[50] for example, use it with
reference to the exile to come (sixth century B.C.). Jeremiah uses it
in connection with his prophecy of the change of the name
"Topheth" to "Valley of Slaughter."[51] Joel uses a more complex

---

41. Matt. 5:17.   42. Gen. 49:1.   43. Deut. 4:30; cf. 31:29.   44. Isa.
2:2; Mic. 4:1.   45. Hos. 3:5.   46. Jer. 23:20; 30:24; 48:47; 49:39.
47. Ezek. 38:16.   48. Ezek. 38:8.   49. Amos 4:2.   50. Isa. 39:6.
51. Jer. 7:32.

form of the expression, "For behold, in those days and at that time, when I restore the fortunes of Judah and Jerusalem . . ."[52] Study of the passages will show that it gradually came to be used of an end-time event or series of events.[53]

"In That Day"; "In Those Days." These phrases can be used of the past or the future. They can be used in ordinary speech or in prophetic passages that have to do with end-time events. Because of the high frequency of occurrence of these expressions, study is very tedious, and I have made only a representative selection of passages that I find helpful in understanding the subject at hand. Hosea foresees an idyllic age when all living things are brought into a covenant, when war is abolished, and when peace, righteousness, justice, covenant-love (*ḥésed*), and mercy are characteristics of the time.[34] Joel speaks of a day when "the mountains shall drip sweet wine, and the hills shall flow with milk, and all the stream beds of Judah shall flow with water";[55] the context makes this indisputably an end-time prophecy. Micah foresees a day when the Lord will gather those who have been afflicted and establish his eternal reign on Zion.[56]

Isaiah is particularly rich in statements referring to "that day." "The branch of the Lord [a messianic expression] shall be fruitful and glorious."[57] The "remnant" will return.[58] "The root of Jesse [another messianic expression] shall stand as an ensign to the peoples; him shall the nations seek."[59] Jeremiah gives similar prophecies,[60] as does Joel.[61] By way of contrast, "that day" will also be a time when the Lord's wrath is revealed against his foes and the foes of his people.[62]

Synthesis. From this brief survey we can see that by the end of the Old Testament period the material was available from which the doctrine of two ages could be developed. The present time was a period when the world was divided into two groups: the people of God (Israelites, Jews) and the nations (Gentiles). The people of God were disobedient, becoming apostate, deserving of punishment, and

---

52. Joel 3:1 (MT 4:1).   53. Cf. Amos 8:11 with 9:13, and Jer. 30:3, 31:31–34 with 7:32.   54. Hos. 2:18–20 (MT 16–18).   55. Joel 3:18 (MT 4:18).   56. Mic. 4:6.   57. Isa. 4:2.   58. Isa. 10:20.   59. Isa. 11:10,11; cf. 19:19,24 (MT 23).   60. Cf. Jer. 3:16–18.   61. Cf. Joel 3:1,2 (MT 4:1,2).   62. Cf. Ezek. 38:14,18–23; Zech. 12:3–8.

yet were the objects of God's covenant-love (*ḥéseḏ*). They will therefore be punished, but a remnant will be preserved. They will be scattered to the nations, but a remnant will be regathered to the land. As for the nations, they will be judged by God for their hostility to him and to his people. Yet, they too will come to serve him, for they will come to Jerusalem to learn of him from his people. And so there was established the idea of an end of this present age of unrighteousness, and the beginning of a new age of righteousness.

This concept is much more complex, as further study will show. There is the matter of sin, its nature and its origin (Chapter 3). This leads to the presentation of God's saving purpose, the election, the covenant (Chapter 4), the kingdom and its king (Chapters 7 and 12). These ideas lead to the development of the concept of Satan on the one hand (Chapter 6) and the Messiah on the other (Chapter 7). The conflict leads ultimately to the final attempt of the anti-God forces to destroy God's people (Chapters 9 and 11) and the final action of God against this "Gog" (Chapters 8, 10, 11, and 14). The days to come promise all sorts of blessings, material and spiritual, temporal and eternal (Chapters 12, 13, and 15). Biblical eschatology simply cannot be studied apart from this age-long redemptive purpose of God.'

The New Testament Idea of the End

The Jewish people, during the period that followed the close of the Old Testament revelation, developed in many ways the ideas found in the Old Testament, including the two ages, the messianic king and his kingdom, angelology and satanology, and the apocalyptic "Son of Man." Various elaborations of these and other subjects can be found in the apocryphal and pseudepigraphical writings of the Intertestamental Period, in the sectarian materials from Qumran, and in the New Testament. To make such a statement is not a denial of divine revelation, but an effort to understand more of the ways in which God has made himself and his purpose known. The New Testament, including the teachings of Jesus, gives ample evidence that the ideas and writings of the Intertestamental Period were an accepted part of the revelatory process of God.ᵘ

Process. The New Testament views the "end" as a process as well as a result. To Paul "the end of the ages" had come on his generation.[63] To the author of Hebrews, it was already the "last days."[64] Peter did not hesitate to claim that Joel's prophecy of "the last days" was being fulfilled on the day of Pentecost,[65] and he stated that Christ "was made manifest at the end of times."[66] John wrote "it is the last hour."[67] Therefore it is possible to look upon the present age as the "end" toward which redemptive history was moving and of which the prophets prophesied. Many have observed, however, that this present age falls far short of the splendors, much less the righteousness and peace promised by the prophets.[v]

Result. The New Testament looks forward to an "end" in the future. The resurrection—at least that of the dead to whom Paul refers—will take place "at the last trumpet."[68] The "last enemy," death, is not conquered until the "end," when Christ will have put all enemies under his feet.[69] The reign of Christ, according to Paul, is already a fact,[70] but it is in process toward its goal.

It is in the teachings of Christ himself that we find the clearest references to an end still in the future. The "parables of the kingdom"[71] make it clear that fulfillment of prophecy had already begun. "Truly, I say to you, many prophets and righteous men longed to see what you see, and did not see it, and to hear what you hear, and did not hear it.[72] But there is also a future "close of the age,"[73] when the evil will be separated from the righteous,[74] the wicked to be cast into "the furnace of fire,"[75] and the righteous to "shine like the sun in the kingdom of their Father."[76] Likewise, the "Olivet Discourse"[77] includes clear references to events that must take place before the "end of the age."[78] The Last Supper contains a reference to "that day when I drink it new with you in my Father's kingdom."[79] In the postresurrection appearance on the Mount of Olives, Jesus refused to set the time of the establishment of his kingdom,[80] and the two "men" who appeared "in white robes" stated that "this Jesus, who was taken up from you into

---

63. 1 Cor. 10:11. **64.** Heb. 1:2. **65.** Acts 2:16,17. **66.** 1 Pet. 1:20. **67.** 1 John 2:18. **68.** 1 Cor. 15:52. **69.** 1 Cor. 15:24–26. **70.** 1 Cor. 15:27. **71.** Matt. 13. **72.** Matt. 13:17; cf. 13:18–23. **73.** Matt. 13:39,49. **74.** Matt. 13:41,49. **75.** Matt. 13:42,50. **76.** Matt. 13:43. **77.** Matt. 24 and parallels. **78.** Cf. Matt. 24:6,14,29–32. **79.** Matt. 26: 29. **80.** Acts 1:6–8.

heaven, will come in the same way as you saw him go into heaven.[81] This belief in the return of Christ to establish his kingdom became a burning hope in the early Church. So "the end of the age" took on a more specific meaning, pointing toward a future event or series of events connected with the Second Advent of Christ."

Summary

The Bible does look forward to the "end," but it is not the cessation of existence. Rather, it is the achievement of the redemptive goal toward which God has been working ever since the fall of humanity. The term does not specifically mean the end of the material world, but rather the end of the present world-system, the moving from the present age into the age to come. This has effects upon the material world, upon the political systems of the world, upon the lack of justice and peace in the present, resulting in the righteousness and harmony of the world to come. Components of this process, and details of what has been revealed concerning the result, will be the subjects of later chapters.

NOTES

a. C. Hodge includes in *Systematic Theology* (New York: Scribner, Armstrong, 1874) a section entitled "The End of the World" (3: 851). Hodge argues that the "end" is intended in a literal sense: the destruction of this world by fire, followed by a palingenesis, or creation of new heavens and a new earth (pp. 852–855).

b. What, for example, does a Frenchman mean when he says *tout le monde* (literally, "all the world")? In a restricted situation he may be referring simply to the few members of a committee. The idiom *tout le monde* is approximately the equivalent of our "everybody."

c. The various ways of translating a single Greek word remind us of the limitations imposed if we work only from English (or other modern) translations. The different endings on the Greek word are inflectional morphemes.

d. For further study, see *TDNT* 2: 697f.; O. Cullmann, *Christ and Time* (Philadelphia: Westminster, 1964), pp. 50–60. J. Barr, in *Semantics of Biblical Language* (London: Oxford University Press, 1961), has criticized both *TWNT* (the German original of *TDNT*) and Cullmann for the study of words out of context. While much of what Barr says is true, and indeed had been said by some of us long before his book appeared, it is also true

---

81. Acts 1:11.

that contexts consist of words: both words and contexts must be studied, as I regularly do and am attempting to do in this study.

e. TDNT 8: 49–56.

f. LSJ 1: 985.

g. A-G, pp. 446–448. In the Old Testament the same range of ideas is found. For "universe" the expression "heaven and earth" (Gen. 1:2) is generally used. For the planet earth, either *tēḇēl,* "world, the planet," or *'ereṣ,* "earth," is used (cf. 1 Sam. 2:8, where both words are used in poetic parallelism). For human habitation or its inhabitants, *'ereṣ* is the common term. Nowhere in the Old Testament is matter considered to be evil and therefore to be done away, hence we should not expect to find such a view in the New Testament—contrary to the theories of those who would try to make the New Testament a product of the Greek world.

h. Or possibly to the satanic cause of the Fall, the prince of this world; see Chapter 3, below.

i. As we shall see in Chapter 15, there is possibly also a reference to the end of the present physical earth.

j. "Creation" here refers principally to this earth; see Chapter 15, below. The expression "This is my Father's world" is a bit of sentimentality without sound biblical support. "Nature red in tooth and claw" presents a more accurate picture but fails to take into consideration the redemptive purpose of God.

k. A-G, pp. 563f.

l. LSJ 1: 45.

m. BDB, pp. 761ff.

n. That the word did not fully convey the idea of eternity seems to demonstrated by the fact that it occurs in the plural, "everlasting salvation," literally "a salvation of ages," or is joined with *wā'ēd,* "and ever" ("the Lord is king for ever and ever," Ps. 10:16), when something more than "age-long" is intended.

o. See G. F. Moore, *Judaism in the First Centuries of the Christian Era,* 2: 378ff.; see also the entries in his index under "World to Come." The "Intertestamental Period"—a term not used by Jews, who prefer to speak of "the Second Commonwealth" or "the Second Temple"—is roughly the last two or three centuries of the pre-Christian era and the first century of our era.

p. The earliest occurrence of the expression "the world to come" is found in Enoch 71:15. In Jewish teachings, the messianic age is the closing portion of *this* age and is distinct from the age to come (Sanhedrin 99a; Berakot 34b, etc.). However, this distinction seems to be a later development, replacing an earlier lack of such distinction. Cf. Moore, *Judaism,* 2: 378; J. Klausner, *The Messianic Idea in Israel,* pp. 408–419, especially p. 409.

q. It is listed fourteen times in Mandelkern's Concordance.

r. Because the phrase is translated in various ways, study of the subject is difficult without access to either a Hebrew or a Hebrew-English concordance.

s. BDB, p. 400, 7c, indicates twenty references, fourteen of which are in Jeremiah.

t. Cf. G. Vos, *The Pauline Eschatology*, pp. 42–61. Attempts to separate eschatology, and particularly "apocalyptic eschatology," from "prophetic" religion have resulted in the cutting up of the Prophets into fragments, the excision of the element of hope from Prophets of "gloom and doom," the loss of an Old Testament biblical theology, and all too often, the dismissal of the Old Testament as divine revelation. "The end from the beginning" is not only a description of God's knowledge; it is his plan, and the revelation of his redemptive plan must be studied in the same way.

u. I did not say "part of the word of God." The canonical Scriptures were recognized by Jews, including Jesus and the apostles, as having divine authority, whereas the other writings were not so considered. This distinction underlies the concept of canon.

v. The truth in "realized eschatology" is based on the New Testament teachings that the end is already here. The error in the system is to fail to realize that the process has an end, also clearly taught in the New Testament.

w. Cf. *TDNT* 2: 697–698.

ADDITIONAL READING

Barr, James. *The Biblical Words for Time.* 1962.

Cullmann, Oscar. *Christ and Time.* Translated by Floyd V. Filson. Rev. ed. Philadelphia: Westminster, 1964.

Erickson, Millard J. *Contemporary Options in Eschatology.* Grand Rapids, MI: Baker, 1977.

Guinness, H. Grattan. *History Unveiling Prophecy, or Time as an Interpreter.* New York: Revell, 1905.

Gunkel, H. *Schöpfung und Chaos in Urzeit und Endzeit.* Göttingen: Vandenhoeck & Ruprecht, 1922.

Moltmann, Jurgen. "Theology as Eschatology." In *The Future of Hope: Theology as Eschatology*, edited by F. Herzog. New York: Herder and Herder, 1970.

Rist, M. "Eschatology of the Apoc. and Pseudep." *IDB* 2: 133–135.

3. The Present Age

The Problem

Unless we understand the nature of the present age as it is described in the Bible, we shall have difficulty understanding why it stands under a curse and must be brought to an end. Those who see the present as an age of progress under the control of human beings who, given enough time and resources, can solve its problems will of course see no validity in the previous statement. To them biblical eschatology is "pessimism," meaning that it has given up on the human race. If we do not accept the biblical doctrine that the material world was made by the Creator and was "good," we shall have difficulty in understanding the biblical teachings concerning the redemption of the material earth and all it contains, and the idea of bodily resurrection will appear as nonsense. Those who believe that matter is evil usually are philosophical idealists or cosmic Dualists. If we reject the doctrine of Satan and other creatures who are not human beings but who have power and influence over human beings in this age, we shall be unable to understand the cosmic dimensions of the struggle between sin and righteousness and of the deepest nature of the temptations of Jesus.

I propose therefore to discuss the present age as I understand the biblical teachings that are relevant. It is my belief that the biblical view of history is linear, progressing from the expulsion from Eden to the entrance into the Holy City. I do not accept the theory that it is circular or cyclical, that humankind returns to the original creation-condition (the return to Eden), or that human (and other) beings go through endless reincarnations. There was an age (or an eternity) before, and there will be an age after; history has a beginning and an end. The figure might be described as helical, for the progress often recalls situations in the past and uses them as types or examples of the "better" that is to come. The line can be described as undular, for the progress is not straight-line; rather there are successes and failures (or in more biblical terms, apostasies and repentances), each of which becomes an opportunity for divine revelation. But biblical history is clearly linear.

What Is an Age?

An "age" can be defined as the period of time during which a being or thing exists, is used, or has influence. Thus we may speak of "the age of Shakespeare," "the Bronze Age," or "the age of chivalry." The concept is somewhat indefinite, particularly while the age is in existence, and there are overlapping elements. For example, it was possible within this century to find aborigines in Australia living in the Stone Age (i.e., the period when tools were made largely of stone) at the same time that other inhabitants of the land were far advanced in the Iron Age. Future anthropologists may decide that the Iron Age has already ended and has been succeeded by the Plastic Age. Still, it is possible to compare one age with another (e.g., the modern age in music with that of the "three B's") and recognize specific characteristics.

According to the biblical presentation, this present age may be defined as the period from the entrance of sin and death into the human race to the conquest over sin and death. It was preceded by an idyllic age of innocence in the Garden, and it will be followed by the age of righteousness in the Kingdom of God. We must therefore study the characteristics of this age.

This Is a Satanic Age

I am using the word "satanic" in its most general sense. The Hebrew word śāṭān meant "adversary" and was particularly used in the sense of an adversary of God or of the people of God. This present age is characterized by opposition to the law of God, to the revealed will of God, to those who seek to follow God's will, and ultimately to God himself.

Creation.   In the beginning, God created the heavens and the earth,[1] the material space-time continuum that we occupy.[a] God created "the Adam" as the last act of creation, and, viewing his

---

1. Gen. 1:1.

work, God was satisfied. "And God saw everything that he had made, and behold, it was very good."[2]

According to Genesis 1:27, "God created the Adam in his own image; in the image of God he created him: male and female he created them."[b] It is therefore somewhat less than correct to speak of "man" (meaning the male) as "in the image of God," and no more satisfactory to speak of woman in the same way. The image of God is reflected in the "male and female" creation. The attributes of God include motherly as well as fatherly qualities.[c] The need of a "help-meet" for the male is stated,[3] but translations generally fail to bring out the meaning of the Hebrew, which is something like, "I will make for him a helper like his complement," or that which completes what he is lacking. The word ʿēzer, "helper," should not be given a menial connotation, for God himself is described using the same term, "our help."[4]

But to use the idea of "the image of God" solely to point out the complementarity of male and female is to lose an even more important doctrine, namely that God is a community of persons.[d] The significance of this doctrine in the study of eschatology should not be ignored. The ultimate goal of God's redemptive activity is not to have a great number of rugged individuals sitting on separate clouds, but a community, expressed in this age by Israel and the Church, and in the age to come by the Holy City. The figure of the Church as the body of Christ[5] is significant. Eschatology cannot be limited to individual salvation and resurrection, but must include also the complete redemption and integration of the various members that constitute the body.

Fall. The perfect conditions under which the Adamic couple lived are only hinted at in the creation story. The provisions of the Garden were esthetically as well as nutritionally satisfying,[6] and the couple was blissfully innocent.[7] But this did not continue forever.[e] A satanic element is introduced. God had placed in the Garden "the tree of the knowledge of good and evil,"[f] and had commanded the Adam not to eat of it, adding "for in the day that you eat of it you shall die."[8] The adversary serpent said,[g] "You will not die," and

---

2. Gen. 1:31. 3. Gen. 2:18. 4. Ps. 33:20. 5. 1 Cor. 12.
6. Gen. 2:9. 7. Gen. 2:25. 8. Gen. 2:17.

suggested that God was in fact withholding from the couple the means of becoming like him.[9]

The woman yielded to the temptation and ate of the fruit. She in turn tempted her husband, and he ate,[10] and with that action innocence was lost.[11] This event is referred to in biblical theology as the Fall. It becomes an important biblical doctrine, more so in the New Testament than in the Old, and is still remembered in the end time.[12] The human creature had fallen from the high estate in which he and she had been created.

Effects of the Fall. In the Genesis account, the outline of results is presented briefly in 3:14–19, sometimes referred to as "the curse," although the word is actually used only with reference to the serpent[13] and the ground.[14] The great lessons of the story are often obscured by modern caricatures of the biblical story.[h] The fact that the ancient people of God saw something more, some divine authority that led to canonizing the account, cannot be easily dismissed. Because Israel and the Church recognized the deeper theological implications, this did not become another archeological relic like the Gilgamesh Epic.

God had said, "In the day that you eat of it you shall die."[15] But now God is speaking of future generations that would experience the hostility of the adversary,[16] of childbearing,[17] of toil "all the days of your life,"[18] and of a return to the earth only after these other events had occurred.[19] At the same time, there is a termination of the fellowship that had existed between God and the Adamic couple.[20] Accordingly, the term "death" takes on a complex meaning, including on the one hand the end of physical life ("to dust you shall return"), and on the other the loss of access to means of eternal life.[21] As if to underscore this dual nature of human beings, the genealogy of Adam repeatedly includes the words "and he died,"[22] while at the same time it is broken by the reference to Enoch who "walked with God; and he was not, for

---

9. Gen. 3:4–5.   10. Gen. 3:6.   11. Gen. 3:7.   12. Cf. Rev. 12:9.
13. Gen. 3:14.   14. Gen. 3:17.   15. Gen. 2:17.   16. Gen. 3:15.
17. Gen. 3:16.   18. Gen. 3:17.   19. Gen. 3:19.   20. Gen. 3:23,24.
21. Gen. 3:22,24.   22. Gen. 5:5,8,11,14,17,19,21,31.

God took him,"[23] providing a reason to hope for something more than death.

The cursing of the ground, the basis of the source of food for humankind, introduces another element of the satanic. Whereas the trees of the Garden "were good for food,"[24] suggesting that Adam and Eve needed only to reach out, pick, and eat, now the ground is to bring forth "thorns and thistles," and the "plants of the field," which would provide the sustenance, will henceforth be found in a hostile environment that requires toil and sweat.[25] Doubtless it was with this in mind that the apostle Paul spoke of the "bondage of decay" of creation, and of its "groaning in travail."[26] The prophets, in their visions of a coming day, foresaw a natural habitat freed from these hostile elements.[27]

The revelation of the person and work of Satan is not given at this point in Scripture. In fact, it is not given to any great extent until the teachings of Jesus. Nevertheless, the basis for a doctrine of Satanology is found here. For one thing, the suggestion that led to the Fall came from outside the human race. The Adam was created in God's image, and in God's person there is no temptation to sin. Further, the serpent exhibits not only an effort to tempt the human pair, but even to thwart God's purpose in creation. There is therefore a cosmic dimension, which we shall study later (Chapter 6), according to which more than the fall of humanity is indicated. God is confronted by a spirit of rebellion, a satanic attempt that contravenes God's command and suggests to the Adam that God is small and selfish.[28]

The present age, then, is the age in which God confronts this rebellion.[i] A hint of this fact is given in the words to the serpent: "I will put enmity between you and the woman, and between your seed and her seed; he shall bruise your head, and you shall bruise his heel."[29] Sometimes referred to as the "protevangelium" (the earliest form of the gospel) and a messianic prophecy, this statement is hardly either. It is, however, a declaration of the ongoing conflict, with a suggestion of victory over the serpent ("he [the woman's seed] shall bruise your [the serpent's] head"). It is therefore a soteriological

---

23. Gen. 5:24.   24. Gen. 2:9.   25. Gen. 2:18,19.   26. Rom. 8:21, 22.   27. Cf. Isa. 55:13.   28. Gen. 3:3,5.   29. Gen. 3:15.

prophecy and contains a hint of eschatology. God has not surrendered to the serpent-adversary; rather, God has pronounced his doom.

This Is a Revelatory Age

The Bible portrays Yahweh as the God who is active in history and who makes known to his servants the significance of those acts.[30] This age, then, might be called the age of revelation, or more precisely, of redemptive revelation, for the ultimate purpose of revelation is not simply the satisfaction of curiosity but the salvation of creation.

Revelation. The term "revelation" can be understood in various ways. To some, "the revelation of God" is an objective genitive: it means what men have come to know about God. To others, it is a subjective genitive: it means what God has revealed. To the one, God is the object of our search; to the other, God is the subject, and revelation comes from him. If we understand Genesis 3:24 to mean that humans were henceforth barred from access to the ultimate solution of their problems ("the tree of life," of which he might eat and live for ever),[31] then the human search for God is fruitless. The Bible presents God as stooping, condescending, searching for, in order to find and save the fallen creation.

Election. The first stage in this revelatory activity was the choosing of a people to whom God could make himself known, and through whom he could reveal himself to the rest of humankind. The biblical doctrine of election properly begins with Abram (Abraham), continues through Isaac and Jacob (Israel) and the Israelites, and ultimately involves David and the Davidic throne, centering on the "son of David" whose throne shall be forever. The purpose of election is the blessing of the nations.[32]

Saving Acts. The first great redemptive act of God was the deliverance of the Israelites from Egyptian bondage.[j] This becomes a paradigm of "redemption," the basis of the law, the constant motif of the Prophets, and finally the source of terminology used in the New Testament (e.g., "Christ our Passover").[33] The history of the people of God is a constant experience of redemptive activity,

---

30. Cf. Amos 3:7.   31. Gen. 3:22.   32. Gen. 12:3.   33. 1 Cor. 5:7.

whether in mighty acts such as the defeat of the inhabitants of Canaan in the days of Joshua and the withholding of rain in the days of Elijah, or in the recital of those acts in the liturgy or in the revelations to the prophets.[34] Thus the Israelites came to believe that God was not only the judge of the nations,[35] but that he also disposed of them according to his will.[36] Finally God sent his son, who made God known by his person, his words, and his works, and who then died on Calvary to atone for our sins, who rose for our justification, and who promised to come again to complete the redemptive activity of God.

Natural Revelation. God also revealed something of his nature and his purpose in nature. He sent the rain on the just and the unjust, or he withheld it for a season.[37] He thundered from Zion; the earth trembled. He sent the scorching east wind, or the devastating hordes of locusts. He gave the fruits in their seasons, and blessed his people with abundance of rain. He set the sun in the heavens and the stars in their courses. The people of God came to see God active everywhere in nature, rewarding obedience and punishing disobedience.[k]

Holiness. The concept of "holy" becomes an important revelation of God. At first the term simply conveyed the idea of separation. God is in heaven and human beings on earth.[38] His thoughts are not our thoughts.[39] God was on the top of Sinai, and even the ground before the mountain was holy and could not be penetrated by the Israelites.[40] God sat between the cherubim and could not be approached by anyone save the high priest, and then only on the Day of Atonement.[41] Gradually God conveyed the idea that this separateness involves moral and religious behavior. God's "otherness" is integral with his nature, and the holiness of his people is related to his revealed will. To be holy as he is holy is to become like him.[42] In the New Testament the doctrine of sanctification is an elaboration of the teachings of the prophets,[43l] and the ultimate outcome is the New Jerusalem, the "holy city,"[44] in which is nothing

---

34. Cf. Ps. 135; Jer. 1:4–10; Ezek. 2:1–8; Amos 3:7. 35. Cf. Amos 1:3–2:3.
36. Amos 6:2; 9:7. 37. Cf. 1 Kings 17:1. 38. Eccles. 5:2. 39. Isa. 55:8. 40. Cf. Exod. 19:12–24. 41. Lev. 16. 42. Cf. Lev. 19:2.
43. Cf. 2 Cor 3:17,18; 1 Thess. 4:3. 44. Rev. 21:2.

unclean.[45] The terrible acts of God, portrayed in Revelation, serve to remove the unclean and the purify the earth, preparing it for the redemption of the whole creation.

This Is an Age of Human Government

This age is characterized by human government; the age to come will be the Kingdom of God.[m] The Old Testament introduces the idea of human government soon after the expulsion from Eden, and then moves on to the ideal kingdom of righteousness and peace under the "son of David."

Prior to the Flood.   The first city was built by Cain.[46] The satanic quality had already been demonstrated in the Cain and Abel story,[47] and Cain's separation from his parents and family was part of the punishment. The story of the city closes with the taunt-song of Lamech.[48] The characteristic of the period leading up to Noah appears to have been something akin to anarchy.[49n]

Prior to the Israelite Monarchy.   The "Table of Nations"[50] serves to introduce the grouping of peoples into petty states.[o] The "Tower of Babel" account[51] suggests that the division of humankind into separate peoples was a judicial act of God.[52] We might also infer that it was a redemptive act, whereby God frustrated a satanic effort to embrace all humankind under a godless system.[p]

The kingdoms of the Mesopotamian plain, the Levant, Asia Minor, northern Africa, and the Mediterranean islands are fairly well known to us from archeological evidence, including vast quantities of written materials.[q] By the time the Israelites were established in the land of the Canaanites, there had already been sufficient experience, whether by habitation or contact with merchants or oppression by military forces, that the Israelites could demand to have a king "to govern us like all the nations."[53] God acceded to their request.[54]

The Time of the Prophets.   With the installation of the Israelite monarchy, God began to reveal his will through a succession of prophets. At first these men (and a small number of women) were chiefly advisors to the king on religious matters—which included the

---

45. Rev. 21:27.   **46.** Gen. 4:18.   **47.** Gen. 4:8–12.   **48.** Gen. 4:23, 24.   **49.** Gen. 6:5–6.   **50.** Gen. 10.   **51.** Gen. 11.   **52.** Gen. 11:6–8.   **53.** 1 Sam. 8:5.   **54.** 1 Sam. 8:9.

interrelationships of human individuals and groups. Reading the Prophets we become aware of the fact that the religious practices of the Canaanite peoples were invading Israel, and idolatry with abominable practices became a prominent target of prophetic preaching. Later, as idolatry took a greater hold on the kings, priests, and people—with the support of false prophets—the prophets of Yahweh spoke of punishment to come and finally of God's rejection of his people and his decision to scatter them to the nations.

But there was another element in the prophetic message. Saul, the first king, had been "rejected" by Yahweh, and David succeeded him.[55] Later in his reign, David planned to build "a house for the lord,"[56] but God vetoed the idea. Instead, he said that David's "son" would build the house.[57] The prophecy of David's son and the house he would build continued long after Solomon had built the temple, indeed even after Solomon's temple had been destroyed.[58]

Daniel's Vision of Kingdoms.   In the prophecy of Daniel the judgment of the kingdoms of the world is foretold. Beginning with the neo-Babylonian kingdom of Nebuchadnezzar, seen as the head of gold,[59] successive kingdoms are revealed by other parts of the image. "In the days of those kings," continues Daniel, referring to the ten kingdoms represented by the toes of the image,[60] "the God of heaven will set up a kingdom which shall never be destroyed. . . . It shall break in pieces all these kingdoms and bring them to an end, and it shall stand for ever."[61]

The Satanic Nature of the Kingdoms.   Since the kingdoms of the world are almost without exception presented in Scripture as worshiping false gods (the reference to Cyrus in Isaiah 44:28; 45:1 seems to be the only exception), we may draw an initial inference that they are satanic, that is, opposed to God. This inference gains support from other facts. The kingdoms of the world oppose the people of God, whether led by Pharaoh in the days of Moses, or Ahab and Jezebel in the days of Elijah, or Haman in the days of Mordecai and Esther, or Nero in the days of Peter and Paul. Satan offered Jesus

---

55. 1 Sam. 15:28; 2 Sam. 5:3.   **56.** 2 Sam. 7:2.   **57.** 2 Sam. 7:13.
58. Cf. Zech. 12:7ff.; 13:1.   **59.** Dan. 2:38.   **60.** Dan. 2:43.   **61.** Dan. 2:45.

"all the kingdoms of the world,"[62] and Jesus did not deny that Satan held title to them. The kingdoms of this world maintain their existence by might and oppression, as Jesus recognized when he said, "If my kingdom were of this world, my servants would fight."[63] Likewise Paul recognized this truth when he advised the Romans to "be subject to the governing authorities,[64] for the ruler "does not bear the sword in vain."[65] In the end time, the kingdoms of this world are ruled by one who comes from heaven, whose name is The Word of God,[66] who is "King of kings and Lord of lords."[67]

This Is an Age of Redeemable Men and Women

It is unbiblical to limit the application of biblical doctrines to human individuals, for God intended to establish a community, a holy city, a kingdom of righteousness and peace. At the same time, it is contrary to biblical intent to apply the judicial sections only to Satan, world kingdoms, and people we don't like. The Bible is a very personal book, and the Kingdom for which we hope and pray will be made up of individual men and women and boys and girls who have been redeemed by the blood of the Lamb.[68]

The Adamic Nature.   We are God's creatures. But we are not by nature his children. He is rarely called "Father" in the Old Testament, and then only by his people, the redeemed.[69] When God drove Adam from the Garden and barred the way of return, he symbolically declared that we have no claim on him. The history of the human race is a record of unbroken sin. We are children of the earth, earthy. We lie and cheat, hurt and destroy, kill and steal, lust and fornicate. The rich are insatiable in greed, and the poor and defenseless are downtrodden. The powerful demand and seize ever more power. James summarizes it in a few words: "What causes wars, and what causes fightings among you? Is it not your passions that are at war in your members? You desire and do not have; so you kill. And you covet and cannot obtain; so you fight and wage war."[70] The human heart is the source of evil; it must be replaced by a new heart. The human will is satanic; it must be transformed and conformed to

---

62. Matt. 4:8.   **63.** John 18:36.   **64.** Rom. 13:1.   **65.** Rom. 13:4.
66. Rev. 19:13-15.   **67.** Rev. 19:16.   **68.** Cf. Rev. 5:9-10.   **69.** Isa.
63:16; 64:8-9; Jer. 31:9.   **70.** James 4:1,2.

the will of God. How this redemption is to be accomplished is the story of the Bible.

The People of God. One of the great themes of the Bible is the doctrine of the grace of God. Just as God sought his fallen creatures in the Garden of Eden,[71] so he has condescended graciously to rescue the fallen throughout this age. We shall develop the theme of the people of God in the next chapter; for the moment we must note that the "elect" in this age enjoy no free ride. The people of God are subject to satanic temptations and pressures. They sin and repent. They are often guilty of the same sins as the "Gentiles." The only difference is their faith in God.

Summary

This age is a period of satanic confusion, in which humans think they are lords of the planet, masters of their fate, and captains of their souls. They have moments when they catch visions of something better, when they long to be better than they are, to be swinging on a star. They look at the world about them and know that all is not right. Thinking that they have the ability to rectify matters, they blunder from one attempt to another. Sometimes they tire of the struggle and shout, "Stop the world, I want to get off!"

But if this is a satanic age, it is also—thanks be to God—a redemptive age. God has never given up on his original purpose in creating us. He will not destroy our freedom of choice. He will not force us to exchange our present bondage to Satan for bondage to an intractable God. His method is love. In various times and ways he has made himself known through the prophets, and finally through the Son. He knows that we shall willingly surrender to him only because we have come to know his redeeming love. We shall learn to love our fellow sinners only when we come to realize that while we were yet sinners, he loved us and gave his son for our salvation.

NOTES

a. For our present purpose, we are concerned with the human race; therefore the question of the age of the universe, the nature of this planet prior to

71. Gen. 3:8–9.

the appearance of the Adamic being, and related subjects lie beyond the present discussion.

b. I have deliberately translated literally for two reasons: (1) "the Adam" in the earlier part of the story is the name of the male-female creation, and therefore not to be taken as a sex or gender distinction; and (2) the complementarity of male and female is a very important, if often overlooked, doctrine of Scripture, which has taken on greater significance in these days of "unisex."

c. The word for "compassion" (*raḥămîm*) and cognate words, often used of God, are derived from the word for "womb" (*reḥem*) and could be described as the love of the mother for the child.

d. It is possible that the plural form ʾĕlōhîm ("God") is intended to express this community of persons. Since the word when used to refer to God is regularly used with singular and not plural verbs or modifiers, it cannot be taken as a plural. And since the "plural of majesty" is never used of Israelite kings, I cannot accept this form as such. To go beyond this, however, and argue for a doctrine of the Trinity cannot be based solely on the plural form ʾĕlōhîm.

e. The length of this period of innocence cannot be determined from biblical data. To me, it seems unrealistic to suppose that Adam was created on Friday afternoon and fell the following week, or conversely to suppose that the age of bliss continued for years.

f. The phrase in Hebrew is very difficult both syntactically and hermeneutically. I take it to mean some quality of God himself (Gen. 3:5,22), in the moral realm (good-evil is probably a merism, i.e., a figure of speech in which opposites or extremes are used to denote an entire category), that was to be withheld from Adam, at least for a probationary period.

g. It is unnecessary to discuss the power of speech attributed to the serpent. The first chapters of Genesis belong to *Urzeit*, the period before the historical, and language used to present divine revelation may be described as suprahistorical.

h. Another suggestion is that the account is etiological, to answer the questions, "Why do serpents crawl on their bellies?" "Why do women have pain in childbirth?" "Why are there weeds?" "Why do people die?" and so forth.

i. One of the Hebrew words for "sin" (*peša*ʿ) means "rebellion," although it is usually translated "transgression."

j. I have not included Noah in this discussion because the Bible rarely refers to him, while often referring to Abraham or Israel. This does not imply that I do not accept the biblical teachings in chapters 4–11 of Genesis. The simple fact is that Noah is mentioned only about eight times in the rest of the Old Testament, and in the New Testament only in Matthew 24:37; Luke 17:27; Hebrews 11:7; 1 Peter 3:20; and 2 Peter 2:5—never in doctrinal discussions such as Romans 4 or Galatians 3.

k. Some scholars object to the term "natural revelation." To me, the idea is biblical and the term is not objectionable so long as we do not use it to the

.exclusion of special revelation, which is concerned more with God's redemptive activity.

l. For a good discussion, see "Sanctification," *NBD*, pp. 1139–1141.

m. In a sense, as we shall see later (Chapter 15), the Kingdom of God always exists, and in another sense it has come with the first advent of Jesus Christ. In its perfect stage, however, it belongs to the age to come (cf. Heb. 9:26–28).

n. One of the values of Dispensationalism, often overlooked, has been its staking out of the epochs of divine revelatory activity. I hope to develop this in a forthcoming work, *Epochal Events of the Bible: An Introduction to Biblical Theology.* I am not, however, a Dispensationalist.

o. Those not familiar with Hebrew word formation may need an explanation, for many of the names in this passage are gentilics (names of peoples) ending in -*îm* (Gen. 10:13), while others have become the actual names of states (cf. v. 6).

p. Indeed, the suggestion has been made that the "tower with its top in the heavens" (Gen. 11:4) was the beginning of the Babylonian religious system (centering on astrology), the end of which is pronounced in Revelation 17–18. See H. Lindsey, *The Late Great Planet Earth* (Grand Rapids, MI: Zondervan, 1970; New York: Bantam, 1973), chap. 10; A. Hislop, *The Two Babylons,* 4th ed. (London: A. & C. Black, 1929). I find this position intriguing, but difficult to support exegetically.

q. See W. S. LaSor, "Libraries," *ISBE* rev. ed., vol. 3, scheduled for publication in 1983.

ADDITIONAL READING

Andrews, S. J. *Christianity and Antichristianity in Their Final Conflict.* Chicago: Bible Institute Colportage Association, 1898.

English, E. S. *Companion to the New Scofield Reference Bible.* New York: Oxford University Press, 1972. Pp. 47–52.

Gaebelein, Arno C. *The Conflict of the Ages.* New York: "Our Hope," 1933.

Grounds, Vernon C. *Revolution and the Christian Faith.* Philadelphia: Lippincott, 1971.

―――. *Evangelicalism and Social Responsibility.* Scottsdale, PA: Herald Press, 1969.

Lyons, Arthur. *The Second Coming: Satanism in America.* New York: Dodd, Mead, 1970.

ponēros, TDNT 6: 546–562.

Rowley, H. H. *Darius the Mede and the Four World Empires in the Book of Daniel.* Cardiff: University of Wales Press, 1935.

Rust, E. C. *Nature and Man in Biblical Thought.* London: Lutterworth, 1953.

Smith, Wilbur M. *The Time Periods of Prophecy.* Philadelphia: American Bible Conference Association, 1935.

4. The People of God

The Problem

The Jews are sometimes called "the Chosen People."[a] Christians also claim to be "God's people,"[1] "chosen of God,"[2] "heirs of God and fellow heirs with Christ."[3] Sometimes the term "the new Israel" is used of the Church, although only with problematical scriptural warrant.[b]

This poses a problem, particularly in eschatology. Is there only *one* people of God, or are there *two*? Has God rejected the Jews because they did not accept Jesus as their Messiah and replaced them with the Christian Church? Or are there two peoples of God, included in separate covenants, the one an earthly and the other a heavenly people?[c] Is the church a "parenthesis"[d] in the time line of Israel, a mystery not revealed prior to Christ and the apostles, an irruption in the redemption history of Israel until the time when the Church is raptured from earth? These are important questions, and many works representing several viewpoints have been written on the subject. I propose to examine the theories and the relevant Scripture passages.

What Does "Chosen" Mean?

The biblical doctrine of *election* is much misunderstood. According to a common view, God chooses some human beings and gives them free passes into heaven; the rest are consigned to hell. No attempt is made to understand the person of God, what he is like, what his purpose is in election, or other significant elements of the doctrine. The interrelationship between God's sovereignty and his omniscience (or foreknowledge), both of which are integral with his person and therefore cannot be dealt with separately, is sometimes reduced by emphasizing one element and downplaying the

---

1. Cf. 1 Pet. 2:9–10.   2. 1 Pet. 2:4; cf. Col. 3:12.   3. Rom. 8:17.

other. The distinctives of "Calvinism" and "Arminianism" witness to the inability even of theologians to compress the biblical teachings on election into a completely satisfactory system. And as for the relevance of the cosmic conflict between God and Satan, the satanic nature of this age and its effect upon human choices—this is rarely mentioned in studies on election.

Terminology. The words "elect" and "chosen" are translations of the Hebrew *bāḥar* and its derivatives and of the Greek *eklegomai* and its derivatives. The words are completely interchangeable, as are the verb forms "to elect" and "to choose." When we elect a president, we choose that person for the office.

G. E. Mendenhall states that for the Hebrew and Greek words there are no synonyms.ᵉ This statement, however, needs some qualification, for the words "to love" and "beloved" sometimes serve to express the idea of election. Thus Matthew can speak of "my servant whom I have chosen, my beloved with whom my soul is well pleased."⁴ Likewise Paul can write, "as regards the election they are beloved for the sake of their forefathers."⁵ It is in this sense that "love/hate" is used, as for example in the statement "Jacob I loved, but Esau I hated."⁶ Another term used somewhat synonymously is "call," as in the statement, "I have called you by name, you are mine,"⁷ or again, in a reference to Abraham, "when he was but one [i.e., a single individual, not yet a 'great nation'] I called him."⁸ The Greek translators of the Old Testament used *eklegomai* and derived forms meaning "to choose, elect, election" to translate the Hebrew words.ᶠ Yet another word with synonymous overtones is "servant," used frequently in Isaiah 41–53 (cf. "O Jacob, my servant, Israel whom I have chosen"⁹). We shall consider this in Chapter 5.

Some feeling for the significance of the Hebrew words may be found in the following observations. The Hebrew root *bḥr,* "choose," gives rise to such words as *bāḥûr,* "young man, youth," and *mibḥār,* "choicest, best." The words are positive, and do not convey the meaning of rejecting what is not choice. Likewise, the Greek words stress the idea of selection or preference, with no explicit suggestion of reprobation.ᵍ

---

4. Matt. 12:18, with some modification of Isa. 42:1.   **5.** Rom. 11:28.
6. Rom. 9:13; cf. Mal. 1:2–3.   **7.** Isa. 43:1; cf. Isa. 43:6.   **8.** Isa. 51:2.
9. Isa. 44:1.

The Elect

The Election of Israel.   Divine election began with the call of Abraham.[10h] God is henceforth known as "the God of Abraham."[11] He made a covenant with Abraham that became an important element in biblical religion.[12] The Israelites were known as "the seed of Abraham.[13j] Paul stresses the point that the covenant with Abraham was not later annulled[14] and builds a long argument on the faith of Abraham and its implications.[15]

The promise to Abraham included at least four elements:

(1) The blessing to Abraham was to be not only to him, but also to his descendants, and even "to all nations." This extensive effect is asserted several times[16] and is used by Paul to include Gentiles who believe.[17]

(2) The descendants of Abraham were to be innumerable, "as the dust of the earth,"[18] "as the stars of heaven,"[19] and "as the sand which is on the seashore."[20j] If there is a bit of hyperbole in these statements, they nevertheless contraindicate the view that there are few that will be saved.

(3) This progeny ("seed") was to include "a multitude of nations" (the word is *gôyîm*, "gentiles")[21] and God told Abraham, "kings shall come forth from you."[22] That other kings than those of Israel would be included is suggested in the promise concerning Ishmael.[23]

(4) The covenant included the promise of the land.[24] This is described in several passages as "the land of Canaan,"[25] and its extent is described as "from the river of Egypt to the great river, the river Euphrates," with the occupants of that time named.[26] The descendants of Abraham were to "be sojourners in a land that is not theirs," but they would return to this land.[27] The promise that Abraham's descendants would become a great nation was repeated

---

10. Gen. 12:2,3.   11. Gen. 26:24; Exod. 3:15; Ps. 47:9; Matt. 22:32. 12. Gen. 17:7; Lev. 26:42; 1 Chron. 16:16; Acts 7:8.   13. Ps. 105:6; Isa. 41:8; Matt. 3:9; cf. Heb. 2:6.   14. Gal. 3:17.   15. Rom. 4:1–25.   16. Gen. 12:3; 18:18; 22:17,18; 26:4; 28:14.   17. Cf. Rom. 4:17; Gal. 3:8.   18. Gen. 13:16.   19. Gen. 15:5.   20. Gen. 17:5.   21. Gen. 17:5; cf. Rom. 4:16, 17.   22. Gen. 17:6.   23. Gen. 17:20.   24. Gen. 13:14–17. 25. Gen. 12:5; 17:8.   26. Gen. 15:18–20.   27. Gen. 15:16.

to Jacob, when he was about to enter Egypt,[28] and the promise of the land was still meaningful when Joseph was on his deathbed.[29] This promise was repeated to Moses.[30] A detailed description of the extent of this promised land is given in Numbers 34:1–12.

The covenant with Abraham was to be continued through his son Isaac, and not through Ishmael ("As for Ishmael, . . . I will bless him. . . . But I will establish my covenant with Isaac"[31]). This is important in the present discussion, for Arabs often maintain that as children of Abraham they have as much claim to Palestine as the Jews do. The covenant was to continue through Jacob and not Esau.[32k]

Some Names. It may be helpful for us to get some names straight, for they are frequently misused. As a descendant of Shem, Abraham was a *Semite*. Later he was referred to as a *Hebrew*.[33] He was not a "Jew," for that term did not come into use until many centuries later. His grandson Jacob was called *Israel*,[34] a name that came to be used for the nation,[35] the Northern Kingdom,[36] the faithful remnant,[37] and (according to one interpretation) the Christian Church.[38] It is extremely important for us to study the context of passages containing the word "Israel," especially when using them in studies on "prophecy" (eschatology). The twelve sons of Jacob were called the *sons of Israel*, which can also be expressed by the term *Israelites*.[1] The citizens of the modern State of Israel are *Israelis* and not "Israelites," and the converse is true.[m]

The Southern Kingdom was *Judah*.[39] The Judeans were taken into captivity by the Babylonians and came to be known as *Jews*.[40] The statement is sometimes made that the term "Jew" is to be distinguished from "Israelite," that Jesus was not a Jew, and that the promises made to Abraham do not apply to the Jews. This is contrary to the clear teachings of the New Testament, where Jesus is called "King of the Jews,"[41] Paul refers to "Jews" as distinguished from "Gentiles,"[42] and speaks of his "fellow Jews" as the people

---

28. Gen. 46:3.   **29.** Gen. 50:24.   **30.** Exod. 3:6–8; 6:8; 33:1,2.
31. Gen. 17:19–21.   **32.** Gen. 28:13, 14; cf. Mal. 1:2,3.   **33.** Gen. 40:15;
Exod. 3:18.   **34.** Gen. 32:28.   **35.** 1 Sam. 7:7.   **36.** 1 Kings 12:19;
Amos 7:8,9.   **37.** Zeph. 3:14; cf. Zeph. 2:7,9.   **38.** Gal. 6:16.   **39.** Cf.
2 Kings 18:1.   **40.** Esther 2:5; Zech. 8:23.   **41.** Matt. 2:2; 27:19.
42. Rom. 2:17–24.

whom God has not rejected.[43] The proper term for this people is "Jew."[n]

A *Gentile* is anyone who is not a Jew. However, the word *gôy*, "gentile, nation," originally could be applied to Abraham,[44] and the plural *gôyîm*, "gentiles, nations," could be used of all nations,[45] including Judah and Israel,[46] although in the majority of cases it meant non-Israelites.

The Election of the Church. The word "church" first appears in the New Testament in the words of Jesus to Peter, "I tell you, you are Peter, and on this rock I will build my church."[47o] The Greek word for "church" is *ekklēsia*, from which we get such words as "ecclesiastical," "Ecclesiastes," and so forth.

Two common arguments centering around this word deserve a brief comment. (1) The word *ekklēsia*, we are sometimes told, means "called out ones," since it is composed of the elements *ek*, "out," and *kaleō*, "to call."[p] The Church, therefore, is composed of those who are "called out of" the world. However, even if this statement is true concerning the elements of the word, in historic usage the word simply meant "assembly, gathering."[q] The simple fact is that Jesus did not take his Church out of the world and did not ask his Father to do so.[48]

(2) We are also sometimes told that the word "church" does not occur in the Old Testament. It was a "mystery,"[r] not revealed until the time of Christ and the apostles. This argument is based on English translations. The Old Testament is mostly in Hebrew, but there was a Greek translation in common use in the days of the apostles. In fact, they seem to quote from the Greek Old Testament more than from the Hebrew (as indicated by passages where the two differ somewhat). The word *ekklēsia* does occur in the Greek Old Testament and is regularly used to translate the Hebrew *qāhāl*, "congregation." As far as the use of words applies, we may conclude that "congregation," used of Israel, and "church," used of the New Testament Church, convey the same idea. The problem admittedly concerns more than just the words that are used.

The Church is an election, a divine choice. Jesus told his disci-

---

43. Rom. 11:13; cf. Rom. 11:1.   **44.** Gen. 12:2.   **45.** Exod. 34:10.
46. Ezek. 35:10; 37:22.   **47.** Matt. 16:18.   **48.** John 17:15.

ples, as they moved from the Upper Room to Gethsemane, "You did not choose me, but I chose you and appointed you that you should go and bear fruit."[49] Whether referring to the group or to the component individuals, Paul spoke of "the elect,"[50] as did Peter[51] and John.[52] This choosing was "before the foundation of the world"[53] and is clearly connected with the eternal redemptive purpose of God.[54] Paul looked upon the Gentiles as "alienated from the commonwealth of Israel,"[55] who were, in the words of Hosea, "not my people"[56] but who have now become "my people." This was the result of God's mercy.[57]

Elect Persons. The words "elect" and "chosen" are applied also to individuals in both Testaments. In this work I have not devoted much space to this subject, since the teachings that raise problems in eschatology have to do mainly with Israel and the Church. Abraham,[58] Moses,[59] David,[60] and Solomon[61] are among those who are chosen. More significant for our study is the use of the term for the king,[62] (especially the type of the messianic king[63]), for the servant,[64] and for the location of the throne, Jerusalem or Zion.[65]

The Purpose of Election

To Receive God's Revelations. The "elect" is a person or a community of persons to whom God has given or is giving a special revelation, and through whom God will reveal himself to other nations or peoples. This is established at the very beginning, for when God called Abram he said "in you all the families of the earth will be blessed."[66] Election in the biblical sense always has a purpose or mission: Abraham was to be the source of blessing to the nations;[67] the disciples of Jesus were chosen to be sent out to preach and cast out demons.[68] Israel was to be a "kingdom of priests,"[69] and since priests are mediators, the figure implies that this "kingdom" was to mediate between God and the nations, in other words, to make known God's will to the Gentiles, and to represent the Gentiles

49. John 15:16.　**50.** Rom. 8:33; Col. 3:12; Titus 1:1.　**51.** 1 Pet. 1:2.
52. 2 John 13.　**53.** Eph. 1:4.　**54.** Eph. 1:7,10.　**55.** Eph. 2:12.
56. Rom. 9:25; cf. Hos. 2:23.　**57.** Rom. 9:15; 11:32.　**58.** Neh. 9:7.
59. Ps. 106:23.　**60.** Ps. 78:70.　**61.** 1 Chron. 28:10.　**62.** 2 Sam. 17:1; 1 Chron. 28:5.　**63.** 1 Chron. 28:6,7.　**64.** Isa. 42:1.　**65.** 1 Kings 14:21; Ps. 132:13.　**66.** Gen. 12:3, RSV mg.　**67.** Gen. 18:18.　**68.** Mark 3:14,15.　**69.** Exod. 19:5,6; cf. Rev. 1:5,6.

before God. The prophet Joel saw the fulfillment of this concept of Israel in the outpouring of God's Spirit resulting in everyone becoming a prophet,[70] and since a prophet is supposed to proclaim God's message to someone, the implication is that sons and daughters and even male and female servants would fulfill that purpose. The prophets and Jesus faulted Israel for failure to accomplish its mission. Election is never an end in itself; it is always a means to an end.

To Bear His Name. When King Saul failed to carry out the mission God had committed to him, the prophet Samuel was charged to say to him, "Has the Lord as great delight in burnt offerings and sacrifices, as in obeying the voice of the Lord?"[71] Isaiah proclaimed the Lord's message: "Sons I have reared and brought up, but they have rebelled against me."[72] Israel was a blind and disobedient servant,[73] but there was an Israelite who was not rebellious,[74] and there was a servant whose perfect obedience accomplished the salvation of his people.[75]

Jesus also requires obedience of his followers. "By this my Father is glorified, that you bear much fruit, and so prove to be my disciples."[76] "This is my commandment, that you love one another as I have loved you."[77] In his selection of his followers, he said, "You did not choose me, but I chose you and appointed you that you should go and bear fruit."[78t] The fulfillment of the promises of God is in part designed to show his greatness and holiness "in the eyes of many nations."[79] A study of the place given in the Scriptures to God's "name" is very helpful.

To Suffer. There is purpose in the sufferings of the people of God. This is not a popular doctrine, for none of us likes to suffer. But study of the people of God in the Bible will quickly show that suffering is their common lot. This results from satanic hostility to God and his people.[80] It also has redemptive value. We shall study more on this subject in Chapters 5 and 10. For the moment, note that the future glorification of the people of God is linked with their suffering.[81]

---

70. Joel 2.28,29 (MT 3:1,2).   71. 1 Sam. 15:22.   72. Isa. 1:2.
73. Isa. 42:19.   74. Isa. 50:5.   75. Isa. 53:11,12.   76. John 15:8.
77. John 15:12.   78. John 15:16.   79. Ezek. 38:20; cf. Ezek. 39:21–23.
80. Cf. Job 1:6–12; 2:1–5.   81. Rom. 8:17,18; Phil. 1:29.

The Basis of Election

The Sovereignty of God.   A basic truth that must always be guarded from denial or dilution is the sovereignty of God. He is the Creator and is not accountable to any being for his decisions. This could easily degenerate into a doctrine of divine caprice except for the fact that God's will is integral with his entire person, including his wisdom and his love. What he determines to do is based on omniscience (his knowledge of all creation and all creatures, the end from the beginning) and on his everlasting love. Jeremiah portrays God as the "potter" with absolute power to determine what he will make of the clay,[82] but even in this very same passage, God declares his sovereign right to "repent of the evil" that he intended to do to a nation if that nation repents[83] or to "repent of the good" if the nation does evil.[84] No statement of the doctrine of God's sovereignty can destroy his sovereignty.

The Sovereignty of Humankind.   Alongside the truth of God's sovereignty must be placed the biblical teaching that man was created "a little less than God,"[85] with a will of his own. Some would insist that humankind lost free will in the Fall and has ever since been in bondage to sin. This observation is valid. Yet, at the same time, every man or woman is fully accountable for the choices he or she makes. We cannot blame our sins on our forefathers. Ezekiel spoke at length on the attitude of his day, that "the fathers have eaten sour grapes, and the children's teeth are set on edge,"[86] and made it clear that we are responsible for our own choices.[87] Nor can we put the blame on Satan[88] or God.[89] At the same time, we need to remember that the sovereignty of God includes his redemptive will." "I have no pleasure in the death of any one, says the Lord God."[90]

Divine Grace.   The redemptive purpose of God operates by his grace, and the covenant he has made with his people is a covenant of grace." Divine grace operates by God's sovereign will. Paul, using the figure of the potter and the clay, says, "What if God, desiring to show his wrath and to make known his power, has endured with

---

82. Jer. 18:2–6.   **83.** Jer. 18:7,8.   **84.** Jer. 18:9, 10.   **85.** Ps. 8:5, lit.
86. Ezek. 18:2.   **87.** Ezek. 18:5–32.   **88.** Cf. Gen. 3:13.   **89.** Cf. James
1:13.   **90.** Ezek. 18:32.

much patience the vessels of wrath made for destruction, in order to make known the riches of his glory for the vessels of mercy, which he has prepared beforehand for glory, even us whom he has called, not from the Jews only but also from the Gentiles?"[91] He goes on, however, to quote Joel, "every one who calls upon the name of the Lord will be saved,"[92] thereby preserving something of human freedom of choice. To many, this is a paradox—a seeming contradiction. If God is sovereign, then humans are merely pawns. If humans have free will, then God cannot be sovereign. The Scriptures, however, maintain both truths—which in itself is an illustration of grace.

One People or Two?

One God.   The God of Jesus and the apostles, therefore the God of the Christian Church, is the God of Abraham.[93] Paul argues that the covenant with Abraham was not annulled by later covenants.[94] In fact, this covenant was for the uncircumcised as well as for the circumcised.[95] The old Marcionite heresy, sometimes quoted even today, that the Jehovah of the Old Testament is not the God and Father of Jesus Christ, is still a heresy and must be repudiated.

One Plan of Salvation.   In his dispute with Judaizers (i.e., those who insisted that Gentiles had to become Jews in order to be saved), Paul did not argue that the Old Testament had been replaced by the New. Rather, he based his argument on his faith that the covenant God made with Abraham was still in effect and indeed included the Gentiles.[96] The author of the epistle to the Hebrews seems at times to be repudiating the old covenant, but a closer study of the tightly knit argument will show that he is indeed building the new on the old. The ritual elements of the Old Testament are "copies of the heavenly things."[97] The argument in Hebrews is not "the first was wrong," but rather "the new is better."[98]

One Body.   In a carefully worded passage, where Paul distinguishes Jews ("we") and Gentiles ("you"), he declares that both were

---

91. Rom. 9:22–24.   **92.** Rom. 10:13, quoting Joel 2:32 (MT 3:5).   **93.** Cf. Matt. 22:32; Acts 7:2.   **94.** Gal. 3:15,18.   **95.** Rom. 4:9–12.   **96.** Rom. 4:9–12.   **97.** Heb. 9:23.   **98.** Heb. 8:6.

"dead through trespasses."[99] The Gentiles were "alienated from the commonwealth of Israel," and therefore "strangers to the covenants of promise, having no hope and without God in the world."[100] God's redemptive purpose was "to reconcile us both to God in one body,"[101] so that "through him [Christ Jesus[102]] we both have access in one Spirit to the Father."[103]

In the long passage on the status of the Jew,[104] Paul portrays some of the Jews as branches broken from the vine,[105] later to be regrafted into the same vine,[106] while the Gentiles are "a wild olive shoot" that has been "grafted in their place."[107] It is significant that Paul does not present a picture of two olive trees, or of a second tree replacing the first, but of a single "root" that supports both the natural branches and the wild shoot.[108]

Summary

There is only one redemptive plan of salvation in the Bible, one covenant of grace, and one people of God. This was hinted at in the Garden,[109] stated first in the covenant with Abraham,[110] and elaborated on by Moses and the prophets. It was proclaimed by Jesus[111] and became a major tenet in the doctrinal writings of Paul.

God, who is himself a community of persons, has willed to thwart the satanic purpose that sets one human being against another, nation against nation, and the entire creation against God, and to bring about a harmony of creation, a oneness of the people of God that can be likened to a human body, of which Christ is the head and every member is necessary, or to change the figure, like a bride which is joined to the bridegroom to become "one flesh."[112]

NOTES

a. A. J. Toynbee in *A Study of History*, abridgement of vols. 1–4 by D. C. Somervell (New York: Oxford University Press, 1947), says, somewhat caustically, "The Jews suffered from the illusion that they were not *a* but *the* 'chosen people' " (p. 37). For further comments on "this idolization of an ephemeral self" see pp. 310f. Some modern Jews, expressing perhaps more truth than they realized, have said, "We're tired of suffering; let

99. Eph. 2:1,5.   100. Eph. 2:12.   101. Eph. 2:16.   102. Eph. 2:13.
103. Eph. 2:18.   104. Rom. 9–11.   105. Rom. 11:17.   106. Rom.
11:24.   107. Rom. 11:17.   108. Rom. 11:18.   109. Gen. 3:15.
110. Gen. 12:3.   111. Cf. John 10:16.   112. Eph. 5:29–31.

someone else be the 'Chosen People' for a while." Seymour Siegel, in "The Meaning of Israel in Jewish Thought," quotes a Yiddish poetess: "Merciful God, choose another people,/We are weary from dying." See M. H. Tanenbaum, M. R. Wilson, and A. J. Rudin, eds., *Evangelicals and Jews in Conversation on Scripture, Theology, and History* (Grand Rapids, MI: Baker, 1978), p. 113.

b. See E. P. Clowney, "The New Israel," in C. E. Armerding and W. W. Gasque, eds., *Dreams, Oracles, and Visions*, pp. 207–220. An opposite view is taken by P. E. Leonard in the same volume, pp. 228–229.

c. See P. E. Leonard, *Dreams, Oracles, and Visions*, p. 228.

d. See R. Pache, *The Return of Jesus Christ*, p. 122. I believe the term "parenthesis" was first used by J. N. Darby, but I have not located the source.

e. G. E. Mendenhall, "Election," *IDB* 2:76; cf. *TDNT* 4: 146.

f. Cf. *TDNT* 4: 145.

g. "Nowhere in the NT is *eklegesthai* explicitly contrasted with reprobation. . . . [It] is not adapted to serve as the basis of a dogma of election and reprobation" (*TDNT* 4: 175).

h. See Chapter 3, note j.

i. This is sometimes obscured by translation, where "seed" is translated "descendants." As Paul pointed out, "seed" is singular (Gal. 3:16), but just as we use the singular "seed" when we speak of either sowing seed or the offspring, so the Hebrew *zéra'* is regularly used in the singular (BDB, pp. 282f.). Paul saw significance in this as it pertained to Christ, and we may likewise see relevance in the fact that Christ is the summation of election, the gathering together of the promises that God made to the elect.

j. To suggest that this implies two peoples, the earthly Israel (dust of the earth) and the heavenly Church (stars of heaven) is certainly reading into the text. On this basis, there should be a third people, the sand on the seashore—who are they?

k. I am not anti-Arab. However, Edom (= Esau) comes in for some rather rough treatment in the Bible. Arabs, in Christ, have all the blessings that are promised to other Christians through Abraham, but not because they can claim physical descent (cf. John 8:31–39).

l. The use of the Hebrew gentilic ending *-î*, pl. *-îm*, rendered in English as *-ite(s)*, often means "sons/descendants of," as can be seen in the Table of Nations (Gen. 10), or the RSV translation, e.g., of "sons of Heth" as "Hittites" (Gen. 23:3ff.).

m. H. Lindsell, for example, uses "Israeli" to apply to the Israelites delivered from Egyptian bondage; see *The Gathering Storm: World Events and the Return of Christ* (Wheaton, IL: Tyndale, 1980), p. 38.

n. Giving the term "Jew" a pejorative sense is the result of anti-Jewish feelings in the Christian Church. Jews are not ashamed to refer to themselves or to each other as "Jews," and Christians should not hesitate to use the word in a similar manner. It is hardly correct to refer to a modern Jew as a "Hebrew," and the term "Hebrew Christian" should be discarded as meaningless.

o. We need not here enter into the discussion of what this means, which can be found in any commentary on the passage, and in many articles on "Peter" in Bible dictionaries. In my opinion, the argument that *petros*, "Peter," is masculine, while *petra*, "rock," is feminine is of little value. If Jesus was speaking Aramaic (or Hebrew)—and why would he be speaking Greek on this occasion?—there would have been no distinction in gender in the word for "rock."

p. Cf. *Scofield Reference Bible*, p. 1021, n.2 (modified in the *New Scofield Reference Bible*); H. A. Ironside, *Lectures on the Book of Revelation*, pp. 37–38.

q. For evidence of historic use, see LSJ 1: 509, and for biblical use see *TDNT* 3: 491ff.

r. See *SRB*, p. 1252, n.1.

s. I have discussed the identification of these "servants" in *Israel: A Biblical View* (Grand Rapids, MI: Eerdmans, 1976), chap. 1. There is, I recognize, a wide difference of opinion on this matter.

t. The statement of G. Schrenk is worth noting: "Election is fulfilled only in obedience. Hence we do not have a static doctrine of election, but a dynamic theology which is oriented to the right attitude of the elect. . . . It establishes decision" (*TDNT* 4: 187).

u. J. Daane, in *The Freedom of God* (Grand Rapids, MI: Eerdmans, 1973), says it well: "God's election must produce what it elects. And it does" (p. 101).

v. It would take a book to define "grace." Put very simply, it is the holy God's will to redeem his sinful and rebellious creatures—with all that is implied theologically in the accomplishment of this will: the decree, love, revelation, forbearance, forgiveness, atonement, and so forth. Cf. "Grace," *NBD*, pp. 491–493; "Grace," *IDB* 2: 463–468; *TDNT* 9: 372–402.

ADDITIONAL READING

Bromiley, G. W. "Call, Calling." *ISBE* 1 (1979): 580–582.

———. "Church." *ISBE* 1 (1979): 693–696.

Brunner, Emil. *The Christian Doctrine of the Church, Faith, and the Consummation*. Philadelphia: Westminster, 1962.

Campbell, Roderick. *Israel and the New Covenant*. Philadelphia: Presbyterian and Reformed, 1954.

Daane, James. *The Freedom of God*. Grand Rapids, MI: Eerdmans, 1973.

Davies, W. D. "Paul and the People of Israel." *New Testament Studies* 24 (1978): 4–39.

DeHaan, Richard. *Israel and the Nations of Prophecy*. Grand Rapids, MI: Zondervan, 1971.

Ellison, H. L. *The Mystery of Israel*. Exeter: Paternoster, 1968.

Jeremias, Joachim. *Jesus' Promise to the Nations*. Naperville, IL: Allenson, 1958.

Kellogg, Samuel H. *The Jews, or Prediction and Fulfilment*. New York: Randolph, n.d.

LaRondelle, Hans K. "Is the Church Spiritual Israel?" *Ministry* 54,9 (Sept. 1981): 17–19.

LaSor, William Sanford. *Israel, A Biblical View.* Grand Rapids, MI: Eerdmans, 1976.

Rees, T. "Choose." *ISBE* 1 (1979): 650–652.

Rengstorf, K. H. *doulos, TDNT* 2: 261–280.

Rowley, H. H. *The Servant of the Lord and Other Essays.* (Oxford: Basil Blackwell, 1965). Pp. 1–93.

Rowley, H. H. *The Biblical Doctrine of Election.* London: Lutterworth, 1950.

Sale-Harrison, L. *Palestine: God's Monument of Prophecy.* Harrisburg, PA: Evangelical Press, 1933.

Smith, J. M. P. "The Chosen People." *American Journal of Semitic Languages* 45 (1928–29): 73ff.

Wright, G. E. *The Old Testament Against Its Environment.* London: SCM, 1950. Pp. 46–54.

5. The Servant of the Lord

The Problem

In the previous chapter we learned something about the biblical concept of election. This raises the question, Why did God create the Adam in the first place, if by his foreknowledge God knew that humankind would fall? And after the Fall, why did God choose to work through an election to accomplish the redemption of creation?

In the "Babylonian Genesis" man was created to be the slave of the gods: "Upon him shall the services of the gods be imposed that they may be at rest."[a] Death was allotted to humankind; immortality was the sole property of the gods.[b] It has been suggested that the Babylonian stories are the origin of the Bible stories, and the Bible does in fact speak of the human as a "servant."

There is, however, a basic difference that has not always been pointed out. Adam was not created to do the menial tasks of God, but to have lordship over the earth.[1] Immortality was not denied to Adam, but it was made contingent upon obedience,[2] and only when the Adamic pair disobeyed the expressed will of God was the way to the tree of life barred.[3] As for the idea that the human being was created to be a servant of God, or more accurately, that the elect persons were chosen to be God's servants—well, this needs further study, which is our present concern.

The Idea of Servant and Service

The Greek Concept. To the Greeks, servitude (or slavery) was something degrading and reprehensible. The word *doulos*, "servant, slave," and its related verb forms were used often in a derogatory way, and slaves were looked upon as chattels that could be bought and sold, beaten, and even put to death at the will of the master.

---

1. Gen. 1:28.   2. Gen. 2:17.   3. Gen. 3:22,23.

Possibly this is the reason behind the preference of the Septuagint translators for the Greek word *pais*, "child, servant," rather than *doulos*, to represent the Hebrew *'ebed*.[c] Later, the attitude in the Greek world was modified, and by New Testament times Greek slaves were often honored and intelligent members of the household, tutors of young sons, physicians to the family, and the like.[d] In the New Testament the word *doulos* is borne proudly by Paul,[4] James,[5] Jude,[6] and indeed by all the apostles.[7] And whereas the term is not generally used of Christ, Paul, in his great passage on the *kenosis* (the "emptying" of his divine nature), stated that Christ Jesus, who was in the form of God, "emptied himself, taking the form of a servant (*doulos*)."[8e]

The Hebrew Concept.   The word *'ebed* apparently never had the bad connotation associated with the earlier use of the Greek word *doulos*. The root idea of the Hebrew word is *work* or *service*, and the cognate languages show something of this basic meaning.[f]

An *'ebed* could be a household servant—like Joseph in Potiphar's house[9]—or a Hebrew who had been bought because of some obligation,[10] or a Gentile.[11] In the case of a Hebrew slave, he was to be set free after six years of service,[12] or under other circumstances in the year of Jubilee.[13] The Sabbath laws applied to servants in the household[14] (in Deuteronomy 5:14-15 this commandment has the additional clause, "you shall remember that you were a servant in the land of Egypt"); and the non-Israelite servant could in effect become an Israelite by circumcision and thus enjoy the privileges of the people of Yahweh.[15]

More significant for our study, however, is the position of the *'ebed* as a servant or worshiper of God. All Israelites who worshiped the Lord, and especially his prophets, were called "servants."[16] Thus, worshiping the Lord and serving him became parallel, almost synonymous, terms: "You shall worship the Lord your God, and him only shall you serve."[17] The idea of Israel as the Lord's servant is placed alongside the concept of the election of

---

4. Rom. 1:1, etc.   5. James 1:1.   6. Jude v. 1.   7. Acts 4:29.
8. Phil. 2:7.   9. Gen. 39:37.   10. Exod. 21:2; Deut. 12:15-18.
11. Lev. 25:44.   12. Deut. 15:12ff.   13. Lev. 25:40.   14. Exod.
20:10.   15. Cf. Exod. 12:44; Deut. 12:12.   16. 2 Kings 9:7; Isa. 54:17;
Amos 3:7.   17. Matt. 4:10, quoting Deut. 6:13.

Israel.[18] Thus Isaiah says, "you whom I took from the ends of the earth, and called from its farthest corners, saying to you, 'You are my servant, I have chosen you and not cast you off.' "[19]

Implications of Being the Lord's Servant

Obedience. It is axiomatic that a servant is expected to obey his or her master. The terms used of the master indicate as much, for the master, in the Hebrew language, is *'ăḏôn,* "lord," and *ba'al,* "owner." The master may be lord of a household, like Joseph who had been put in charge of Pharaoh's house,[20] or even of a nation.[21] The term *'ăḏôn* could be used of the king, equivalent to "his majesty,"[22] or it could be used of Yahweh.[23] In fact, this word, with the suffix for "my" (*'ăḏônāy*) came to be used by the Jews whenever the divine name for Yahweh (the tetragrammaton) appears in the text, and was regularly translated into Greek as *kurios,* "Lord"— although *kurios* commonly meant "lord, sir."

The term *ba'al,* "owner," was used not only of the servant-master relationship, but also of the husband-wife relationship.[g] However, the term *ba'al* was also used for the Canaanite deity, known to us as "Baal," and therefore carried an evil connotation to the prophets of Yahweh. Accordingly, Hosea could look forward to the day when penitent Israelites would call Yahweh "my Man [= Husband]" and not "my Baal." "For," says Yahweh, "I will remove the names of the Baals from her mouth."[24h]

Under a somewhat distorted view of the Old Testament Law, we have sometimes been told that as Christians we are "not under law but under grace." This has occasionally been carried to extremes in a form of antinomianism, saying "I can do anything at all, for I am saved by grace."[i] Jesus said, "Why do you call me 'Lord Lord,' and not do what I tell you?"[25] And again, "You call me Master[j] and Lord; and you are right, for so I am. . . . I have given you an example,-that you also should do as I have done to you. . . . A servant is not greater than his master."[26] Judgment was pronounced on Israel because of disobedience, because Israel had traded one "husband" for another,

---

18. Isa. 41:8. 19. Isa. 41:9. 20. Gen. 45:8. 21. Gen. 45:9.
22. Jer. 22:18. 23. Exod. 23:17. 24. Hos. 2:17 (MT 18). 25. Luke 6:46. 26. John 13:13–16.

which is called "harlotry,"[27] because Israel unlike stupid beasts did not know its owner and master.[28] Jesus summed it up in the Parable of the Vineyard: "The kingdom of God will be taken away from you and given to a nation producing the fruits of it."[29]

Service.   An obedient servant serves his or her master. But in biblical imagery, what does "service" mean? Jesus expressed one form of service, which most of us would agree is the deepest, when he said, "For the Son of man also came not to be served but to serve, and to give his life as a ransom for many."[30] There is, I believe, a redemptive dimension in all service, which we shall discuss below.

But there are many lesser forms of service. Paul, writing to the Corinthians, pictures the Church as the body of Christ composed of individual members,[31] not all of equal honor but all essential to the well-being of the body.[32] Paul names several spiritual "gifts" that are given to the various members of this body, including not only "gifts of healing," "working of miracles," and "various kinds of tongues," but also "faith."[33] These are "varieties of service."[34]

Perhaps the highest form of service and certainly the most endless—although the fact is often forgotten—is worship. The worship of false gods was the greatest sin of the Israelites, and when they refused to repent of this sin they were driven from their land. Satan offered Jesus "all the kingdoms of the world and the glory of them" if Jesus would fall down and worship him.[35] One of the features of the last days will be the enforced worship of the beast.[36] Contrasted with false worship is the oft-repeated picture of the heavenly hosts worshiping God.[37] In the age to come the redeemed will join this heavenly praise: "his servants shall worship him."[38]

The Sufferings of God's Servants

The Bible teaches and history corroborates the doctrine that God's servants in this present age undergo suffering. An age-old question is, "Why do the righteous suffer?" An easy answer is, "They must have done something wrong,"[39] the error of which can be shown by asking a second question: "Then why do the wicked

---

27. Hos. 2:2–6; 4:15.   28. Isa. 1:2,3.   29. Matt. 21:43.   30. Mark 10:45.   31. 1 Cor. 12:27.   32. 1 Cor. 12:21–26.   33. 1 Cor. 12:9,10. 34. 1 Cor. 12:5.   35. Matt. 4:8,9.   36. Rev. 13:12.   37. Cf. Isa. 6:2,3; Luke 2:13,14; Rev. 4:8–11.   38. Rev. 22:3.   39. Job 8:1–4; 11:4–6.

live to old age and grow rich?"[40] But the problem is deeper and far more complex than simple platitudes.

The Problem of Evil.   Suffering is the result of evil. This is not the simple statement that it appears to be. There are at least two kinds of evil: natural and moral. Natural evils include earthquakes, violent storms, famines, epidemic diseases, and the like. They are active in inanimate and subhuman nature, but they also affect human beings. Jesus included at least some of them among the signs of the times.[41] Moral evils are the attitudes and actions of human beings that affect other beings adversely.[k] This distinction is not explicitly set forth in the Bible,[l] but it is implicit.

God creates evil.[42] The people of the Old Testament did not shrink from this idea, as many moderns do. They never attempted to off-load the problem of evil to other gods, or even to Satan. Likewise in the New Testament, even the crucifixion of Christ, done by the hands of lawless men, was by the definite plan and foreknowledge of God.[43] Both moral and natural evils come into being in God's counsel. Humans did not originate evil; it was there before the Fall in Eden.[44] But the Adamic pair, with clear warning, elected to accept the evil choice and so came under bondage to evil. Accordingly, we frequently find expressions such as "enslaved to sin,"[45] "slaves to the elemental beings of the universe,"[46] and "slaves to various passions and pleasures."[47]

The Bible presents the idea of a personified Evil (One), otherwise called "Satan" or "the Devil." This will be discussed more fully in Chapter 6. Jesus was tempted by Satan[48] and taught his disciples to pray "Deliver us from the evil one."[49m] Although this Evil One has great power, he can do nothing without divine permission.[50] To say that the evil suggestion in Eden did not originate in the human being does not shift the ultimate responsibility from God to Satan, for God created Satan.

Kinds of Suffering.   There are at least three kinds of suffering: disciplinary, purifying, and glorifying.[n] Due to considerable overlapping, each of these categories could be subdivided, but since our

---

40. Cf. Job 21:7.   **41.** Matt. 24:7,8.   **42.** Isa. 45:7; Amos 3:6.
43. Acts 2:23.   **44.** Gen. 3:14,15; cf. Ezek. 28:13–15; John 8:44.
45. Rom. 6:6.   **46.** Gal. 4:3; cf. 4:8,9.   **47.** Titus 3:3.   **48.** Matt. 4:1–11.   **49.** Matt. 6:13; cf. John 17:15.   **50.** Cf. Job 1:7–12; 2:6; Luke 22:31,32.

purpose here is not to examine the subject of suffering in depth, but rather to recognize its significance in eschatology, I have attempted to keep our study simple.

Disciplinary Suffering.   Disciplinary suffering comes as a result of disobedience.[51] It may be called "punishment."[52] The distinction is sometimes made that "punishment" is visited upon those who are not God's people, whereas "chastening" is administered to those who seek to serve him. "Happy is the man whom God reproves; therefore despise not the chastening of the Almighty."[53] This distinction, although helpful, does not have scriptural support.[54]

The Hebrew verb *yāsar* and its derivative noun *mûsār* illustrate the complex nature of discipline. The Psalmist can cry, "O Lord, rebuke me not in thy anger, nor chasten me in thy wrath,"[55] indicating that the discipline ("chasten me") can be an expression of God's anger or wrath.° This punitive idea is found in Hosea, where Yahweh says he will "chastise" the priests, the king, and the house of Israel.[56b] But, since the Old Testament is principally concerned with Israel as God's "son," discipline is to be better understood as the training of the son by the father. Israel is "wayward,"[57] and the Lord had warned his people through Moses that "as a man disciplines his son, the Lord your God disciplines you"[58] (cf. Jer. 6:8, where the RSV reads "be warned" for "be instructed").

Punitive punishment of the surrounding nations may be looked upon as disciplinary, in the sense of instructional or revelational, for Israel. The judgments on Egypt's pharaoh and gods[59] were certainly intended for Israel's discipline (instruction), else why would God have revealed this to Moses, and why would the people of God have incorporated this revelation in their Scriptures?[60]

Purificatory Suffering.   Purifying (or sanctifying) suffering results in correction of the people of God.[61] This is the "chastening" that we are told not to despise.[62] But it is also described in such terms

---

51. Deut. 31:17; 1 Kings 14:10; 2 Kings 21:12.   **52.** Lev. 26:41; Ezek. 14:10.   **53.** Job 5:17; cf. Heb. 12:6,7.   **54.** Cf. Ps. 149:7; 2 Cor. 2:6. **55.** Ps. 6:1 (MT 2).   **56.** Hos. 5:2.   **57.** Hos 10:10.   **58.** Deut. 8:5. **59.** Exod. 12:12.   **60.** Cf. Deut. 11:2–7.   **61.** 1 Pet. 4:1,2; 5:10. **62.** Prov. 3:11; Heb. 12:5.

as "a refiner's fire" and "fullers' soap,"[63] and Isaiah can tell God's people "that her warfare is ended, that her iniquity is pardoned, that she has received from the Lord's hand double for all her sins."[64]

No hard-and-fast line can be drawn between the punishment of God's people for their sins and the purifying of them, for the one is intended to lead to the other. If God's intention in discipline is not to cast off or destroy, but rather to chasten and redeem, then all such discipline will produce some sanctification. Judgment, we are told, begins with the household of God.[65] We must keep this revealed truth in mind when we come to the discussion of the Rapture and the Tribulation.

Glorificatory Suffering. Suffering that works to the glory of God[66] is perhaps the most difficult to understand. The "suffering servant" of Isaiah comes to mind, although attempts to identify him have not achieved unanimity. In Isaiah 49–50 it appears to be the prophet himself who is speaking.[q] His task from before his birth was "to bring back Jacob"[67] and to be "as a light to the nations."[68] But regardless of our identification of this servant, we note that his obedience[69] led to suffering and shame.[70] Again, in chapter 53, the unnamed servant (who is not the prophet, as the pronouns indicate[r]) suffers shame[71] and even death.[72] But his "chastisement" (*mûsār*) led to "our peace,"[73] and in his death, which was "the will of the Lord,"[74] he made "many to be accounted righteous."[75] Christians as a general rule see this servant as a prophetic portrayal of Jesus; it is more accurate to say that Jesus, in his humiliation and agony and death on the cross, fulfilled the prophecy, gave it a fullness of meaning that results only when literature becomes life and visions become reality.

But there is yet more in this concept of glorificatory suffering. The suffering of God's people has redemptive significance. I must be very careful how I state this, for I do not want to give the slightest suggestion that the death of Christ is not sufficient to atone for the sins of the world.[76] On the other hand, unless I believe that the suffering of the people of God has enduring

---

63. Mal. 3:2.   64. Isa. 40:1,2.   65. Cf. 1 Pet. 4:17.   66. 1 Pet. 1:6,7; 4:14; Col. 1:24.   67. Isa. 49:5.   68. Isa. 49:6.   69. Isa. 50:5. 70. Isa. 50:6.   71. Isa. 52:14,15; 53:4–7.   72. Isa. 52:8,9.   73. Isa. 52:5.   74. Isa. 52:10.   75. Isa. 52:11.   76. Cf. Heb. 10:14.

significance I have no answer for the Jew who asks me, "How can you believe in a God who allowed the Holocaust?" or for the scoffer who asks, "How can a righteous God allow the Christians of Poland (or Czechoslovakia, or Hungary, or China) to suffer?"

In the letter to the church at Colossae Paul says, "Now I rejoice in my sufferings for your sake, and in my flesh I complete what is lacking in Christ's afflictions for the sake of his body, that is the church."[77] This is an amazing statement. Paul suffered "for your sake"—that is, for the sake of the Church. He completed "what is lacking in Christ's afflictions" for the sake of the Church. To the Philippians he wrote, "I want you to know, brethren, that what has happened to me has really served to advance the gospel."[78] He praises the "God of all comfort, who comforts us in all our affliction, so that we may be able to comfort those who are in any affliction, with the comfort with which we ourselves are comforted by God."[79] He goes on to say, "For as we share abundantly in Christ's sufferings, so through Christ we share abundantly in comfort too. If we are afflicted, it is for your comfort and salvation."[80] "We are children of God," Paul wrote to the Romans, "and if children, then heirs, heirs of God and fellow heirs with Christ, provided we suffer with him that we may also be glorified with him."[81]

Personally, I do not believe in the concept of a storehouse of merit, or works of supererogation—that is, doing something more than is required, so that the "credit" can be applied to the account of someone who owes more than he or she can pay. When I have done all, I am still an unprofitable servant.[82] I rather think that the apostle Paul would be in general agreement.[83] Therefore I must try to understand these amazing statements of his against the background of the perfect sacrifice of Christ. If the chastisement of Israel could work to the glory of God's name among the nations,[84] although the forgiveness of Israel's sins was not the result of its suffering, then in like manner the suffering of the righteous redounds to God's glory.

---

77. Col. 1:24.   **78.** Phil. 1:12.   **79.** 2 Cor. 1:3,4.   **80.** 2 Cor. 1:5,6.
81. Rom. 8:16,17.   **82.** Cf. Luke 17:10.   **83.** Rom. 3:23,24.
84. Ezek. 36:36.

Summary

The story of the prophet Hosea may serve to summarize our study. He was led by God to marry a wife of harlotry.[85] By the time her infidelity was established, it is possible that one or two of the children (Lo-Ammi, "Not my kid," and perhaps Lo-ruhama, "Unloved") were not fathered by Hosea. This introduction to the story can have significance only if the material in the following chapter parallels the story of Gomer. She went after her lovers,[86] forgetting her husband. Then the Lord told Hosea to take her back in love, "even as the Lord loves the people of Israel, though they turn to other gods."[87] We concern ourselves at great length with the problems of Hosea and his wife. God seems to be saying to Hosea: This is the story of my life. I loved Israel and took her to be mine, and she was unfaithful. But I loved her with an everlasting love, therefore I redeemed her.[c]

The problem of suffering is God's problem, too. As long as his creation lies in the bondage of decay, as long as his people forget him and go whoring after other gods, as long as satanic dominion of this planet continues because of the infidelity of God's people, God suffers. He sent his son into this world to suffer. The Church, which is his body, "an extension of the Incarnation," likewise must suffer until the last enemy is defeated.

"A servant is not greater than his master. If they have persecuted me, they will persecute you."[88]

NOTES

a. The *Enuma Elish*, tablet 6, line 6; see A. Heidel, *The Babylonian Genesis*, 2d ed. (Chicago: University of Chicago Press, 1951), p. 46; *Ancient Near Eastern Texts*, ed. J. B. Pritchard (Princeton, NJ: Princeton University Press, 1950), p. 68.

b. Gilgamesh Epic, Old Babylonian Version, tablet 10, col. 3, lines 1–5; see *Ancient Near Eastern Texts*, ed. Pritchard, p. 90.

c. Cf. *TDNT* 2: 261–280. The Hebrew word 'ebed is pronounced approximately "evved."

d. See J. Hatfield, *A History of Ancient Greece*, rev. A. Aymard, trans. A. C. Harrison, ed. E. H. Goddard (Edinburgh: Oliver & Boyd, 1966), see refs. in index under "slavery." See also C. E. Robinson, *Hellas: A Short History*

---

85. Hos. 1:2,3. **86.** Hos. 2:5. **87.** Hos. 3:1. **88.** John 15:20.

of Ancient Greece (Boston: Beacon Press, 1948), pp. 125f.; J. Carcopino, Daily Life in Ancient Rome, trans. H. T. Rowell (New Haven, CT: Yale University Press, 1960), pp. 56–61; J. S. Clemens, "Slave, Slavery, DAC 2: 509–512. The most complete work on slavery is reputed to be H. Wallon, Histoire de l'esclavage dans l'antiquité, 2d ed., 3 vols. (Paris, 1879), but I have not had access to it. See also J. B. Lightfoot, St. Paul's Epistles to the Colossians and to Philemon, 3d ed. (London: Macmillan, 1884), pp. 320ff.

e. The author of Hebrews, drawing on Psalm 40:6–8 (MT 7–9), likewise presents Christ as coming into the world as a slave, if the expression in verse 6, "ears thou hast cut for me," refers to the sign of voluntary servitude of Exodus 21:6. Cf. Hebrews 10:5–9.

f. In Aramaic, 'bd is the root of the common verb "to do, make," while in Arabic the verb means "to obey, worship" and is used in such names as Abdullah ("servant/worshiper of Allah"). The Phoenician cognate, meaning "vassal," has a derogatory sense, but this may have been the result of maritime contacts with the earlier Greek world.

g. In these days of struggle for equality of the sexes, this idea may be quite objectionable. However, in antiquity the husband was lord of his wife, and in many societies she was little more than a chattel. The Israelites came to have a higher view, and in the New Testament the redemptive goal of oneness of male and female is set forth (Gal. 3:28; cf. Eph. 5:21–33, the point of which, vv. 31–33, is often obscured by putting emphasis on v. 22).

h. For the same reason, names compounded with -baal were often read with -bosheth, "shame," instead; cf. Ishbaal and Ishbosheth.

i. A well-known Bible scholar, stressing this idea, once told a seminary audience, "I could be in bed with a harlot when the Lord comes, and I would be taken to heaven." Such a position fails to reckon with the implications of Romans 8:13; 13:9, or Philippians 2:14–16.

j. The Greek word didaskalos means "master, teacher" and is usually translated "teacher" in the RSV. In this context, "master" is preferable.

k. For an excellent discussion see D. R. Dungan, "Evil," ISBE 2 (1929): 1041f.

l. The Greek words kakos and ponēros do not make this distinction; see TNDT 3: 469–484; 4: 546–562.

m. There is no general agreement on this translation. The form ponērou in both Matthew 6:13 and John 17:15 can be either masculine or neuter. I have chosen to translate it as a masculine substantive in the light of Matthew 4:11 and Luke 22:31.

n. J. A. Sanders states: "There are some eight solutions found in the Old Testament to the problem of suffering. Briefly, sufferings are retributive, disciplinary, revelational, probational, illusory (or transitory), mysterious (only God has Wisdom), eschatological, or meaningless." See Suffering as Divine Discipline in the Old Testament and Post-Biblical Judaism (Colgate Rochester Divinity School Bulletin 28 [Nov. 1955], special issue), p. 1. Sanders cites H. W. Robinson, Suffering Human and Divine (New York: Macmillan, 1939).

o. For a discussion of these words, see Chapter 14.
p. The RSV follows the suggested emendation in *Biblia Hebraica Stuttgartensia*, which is based on the reading in LXX.
q. See W. S. LaSor, *Israel: A Biblical View* (Grand Rapids, MI: Eerdmans, 1976), pp. 22–25.
r. Ibid., pp. 26–27.
s. I do not propose to deal with the questions of interpretation or of morality, since there is a deeper truth. Studies of these other problems have been dealt with at length in books and commentaries.
t. Israel is sometimes a "son" and masculine pronouns are used; at other times a "girl" (Ezek. 23) or "wife" (Hos. 2) and feminine pronouns are used. We must never let such details obscure the main lessons.

ADDITIONAL READING

Lindblom, J. *The Servant Songs.* Lund: Universitets Årsskrift, 1951.
Neubauer, Ad. ed. *The Fifty-third Chapter of Isaiah according to the Jewish Interpreters.* 2 vols. 1876. Reprint. New York: KTAV, 1969.
North, C. R. *The Suffering Servant in Deutero-Isaiah.* London: Oxford University Press, 1948.
Rengstorf, K. H. *doulos, TDNT* 2: 261–280.
Rowley, H. H. *The Servant of the Lord, and Other Essays on the Old Testament.* 2d ed. Oxford: Basil Blackwell, 1965. Pp. 3–93.
Young, Edward J. " 'Of Whom Speaketh the Prophet This?' " *Westminster Theological Journal* 11 (1948/49): 133ff.
Zimmerli, W., and Jeremias, J. *The Servant of God.* 2d ed. London: SCM, 1965.

6. The Satanic Character
of This Age

The Problem

Several times I have used the word "satanic" and referred to "Satan." This raises the question of interpretation. What does the Bible mean when it refers to "Satan" or the "Devil"?

"You don't really believe in the Devil, do you?" If you were asked this question, how would you reply? An easy answer might be, "How else can you explain anyone wanting to shoot the pope?" Or perhaps, "What other reason is there for my sweet, innocent child getting into such terrible trouble?" The Christian can answer: "Jesus believed in the Devil, and I accept Jesus' word for it."

From the temptation of the Adamic couple in the Garden of Eden[1] to the casting of the Devil and his hosts into the lake of fire,[2] Satan is either mentioned or implied many times.[a] The bulk of the teachings are from Jesus and Paul. Likewise, the casting out of demons is limited almost entirely to the Gospels and Acts.[b] It is entirely incorrect to say that belief in Satan and demons is a superstition carried over from the Old Testament or invented in the Middle Ages. These are biblical doctrines, part of God's revelation.

The Satanic World System

In our study of the term "world" as used in the Bible, we saw that it is sometimes used to indicate a system that is hostile to God's revelatory-redemptive work. On his last night Jesus said to his disciples: "If the world hates you, know that it has hated me before it hated you. If you were of the world, the world would love its own; but because you are not of the world, but I chose you out

---

1. Gen. 3:1–15.   2. Rev. 20:1–10.

of the world, therefore the world hates you."[3] It is clear that the "world," as the term is used here, is hostile to Jesus Christ, and that the hostility toward his followers stems from this fact—note the words "because" and "therefore." This hostility to Jesus and his followers is satanic, in the basic meaning of the word, that is, "adverse."

The Terms Used. The words *satan, satanas,* "adversary, Satan," came into the Greek language through the Septuagint and were borrowed from Hebrew. The Hebrew word *śāṭān* originally meant simply "adversary, accuser." There was a legal use of the word, evident in Zechariah 3:1, where Joshua the high priest is standing before the angel of the Lord, "and Satan is standing at his right hand to accuse him." The same figure is found in Job.[4] The Hebrew word was sometimes translated into the Greek word *diabolos,* "slanderer, adversary, Devil."[5] Our words "satanic" and "diabolical" have come from these Greek words.[c]

Since these terms, like many words that have become proper names, were no longer fully descriptive, synonyms were frequently used, and from these we can get some idea of what was in the minds of those who spoke about Satan or the Devil. In the New Testament the following terms may be helpful: *drakōn,* "dragon"; *echthros,* "enemy"; *katēgōr,* "accuser"; *ophis,* "serpent"; *ponēros,* "evil (one)"; and *peirazōn,* "tempter."

The term "dragon" occurs thirteen times, all in Revelation 12, 13, 16, and 20.[d] In the Septuagint, *drakōn* was used to translate the Hebrew words for "Leviathan" (*liwyāṭān*[6]) and "sea monster" (*tannîn*[7]), and the term is used in a prophecy against Egypt.[8] The imagery is sometimes traced to the Assyrians, Babylonians, or Persians, where the dragon is portrayed in art and used in mythology. In Revelation, however, the dragon is identified as "that ancient serpent," who is called the Devil and Satan, the deceiver of the whole world"[9] and is further called the "accuser of our brethren . . . who accuses them day and night before our God."[10c] He is the "enemy" with power[11] over whom Jesus has given his disciples authority, the "enemy" who sowed weeds among the

---

3. John 15:18,19. **4.** Job 1:6ff.; 2:1ff. **5.** Cf. 1 Chron. 21:1; Job 1:6. **6.** Job 3:8. **7.** Job 7:12. **8.** Ezek. 29:3; 32:2. **9.** Rev. 12:9; cf. 20:2. **10.** Rev. 12:10. **11.** Luke 10:19.

wheat,[12] defined by Jesus as "the Devil."[13] He is the "tempter"[14] ("the devil"[15]) who attempted to thwart the mission of Jesus at its very outset. Paul was concerned that "somehow the tempter had tempted" the Christians at Thessalonica,[16] rendering Paul's work of no avail.

Even more illuminating are several statements used about Satan. Jesus called him (or her?!) "the ruler [*archōn*] of this world,"[17] who had no power over Jesus.[18] He further stated of the Devil: "He was a murderer from the beginning, and has nothing to do with the truth, because there is no truth in him. When he lies, he speaks according to his own nature, for he is a liar and the father of lies."[19] Paul referred to Satan as "the god of this world" who "has blinded the minds of the unbelievers, to keep them from seeing the light of the gospel of the glory of Christ."[20] He also spoke of Satan as "the prince of the power of the air,"[21] "the spirit that is now at work in the sons of disobedience."

A term that needs more than passing notice is "Beelzebul" (or Beelzebub).[g] It would seem that Jesus had been called "Beelzebul,"[22] and the context ("the master of the house") appears to lend support to the explanation that *z^ebûl* meant "dwelling"—one of the seven heavens, according to one theory, hence a heavenly dwelling.[h] The Pharisees had charged that Jesus cast out demons "only by Beelzebul, the prince of demons."[23] Jesus replied that this would imply that Satan's kingdom was divided against itself, and added, "But if it is by the Spirit of God that I cast out demons, then the kingdom of God has come upon you."[24]

Satan's Purpose. It is obvious from the names and expressions used of him that Satan is opposed to God and that this opposition is expressed in this "world" or age by involving human beings. When the Adamic race was first created, the satanic objective was at once exhibited: it was to lead the human beings to distrust God and to disobey his command.[25] When Jesus began his earthly ministry, Satan immediately attempted to destroy that ministry, first by

---

12. Matt. 13:25,29.　　13. Matt. 13:39.　　14. Matt. 4:4.　　15. Matt. 4:2.　　16. 1 Thess. 3:5.　　17. John 12:31; 14:30; 16:11.　　18. John 14:30. 19. John 8:44.　　20. 2 Cor. 4:4.　　21. Eph. 2:2.　　22. Matt. 10:25. 23. Matt. 12:24; cf. Mark 3:22; Luke 11:15.　　24. Matt. 12:28.　　25. Cf. Gen. 3:4.

suggesting that Jesus should use his power for selfish purposes (to satisfy his physical hunger,[26] and to attract attention by a spectacular feat[27]), and then by offering Jesus all the kingdoms of the world in exchange for Jesus' devotion.[28] At the end of Jesus' earthly ministry, Satan entered into Judas Iscariot, leading him to betray Jesus and thereby bringing about the death of Jesus.[29] According to other scriptures, which we shall study in more detail, at the end of this age Satan will increase his opposition exponentially in one last frenzied attempt to destroy God's redemptive work.

Satan's M. O.   The terminology used about Satan reveals something also of his *modus operandi* (method of operating). It is a tragedy that the Church has devoted so little attention to scriptural details about Satan and has preferred either to remain silent on the subject or to develop its dogmas from Milton's *Paradise Lost*, medieval passion plays, or other mythologies. Even this fact can be viewed as a satanic operation, for Satan operates chiefly by deception.

Since the human being is rarely (if ever) tempted by a recognized evil, the satanic choice is presented as a good. The means of obtaining that good may be evil, as when a robber, in order to obtain the good life, uses force to take away money or other goods from the rightful owner; or in the larger sphere, as when a nation, in order to raise the standard of living or provide *Lebensraum* (space for living) for its people, takes over the territory of another people, whether by military force or by international treaty. The satanic temptation as presented to the Adamic pair was not couched in a suggestion that they should revolt against God, but rather it was in the fruit of a tree "that was good for food," a "delight to the eyes," and "desired to make one wise"—and incidentally, forbidden to them by God, with the hint that God was depriving them of something good.[30] Thus Paul, speaking of "false apostles, deceitful workmen," can compare them to Satan, who "disguises himself as an angel of light."[31]

Satan is not only the Deceiver; he is also the Accuser. In the introduction to the book of Job, Satan is presented as one of the

---

26. Matt. 4:3.   27. Matt. 4:6.   28. Matt. 4:8,9.   29. Luke 22:3; John 13:17.   30. Gen. 3:4–6.   31. 2 Cor. 11:14.

"sons of God,"[32] who appears before God to imply false accusations against Job. Satan does not say bluntly, "Job is a hypocrite!"; rather, he asks, "Does Job fear God for nought?" suggesting that Job's devotion to God is with a selfish motive. There is another point to the story, for it reveals to us something of God's use of the satanic to test his elect. We considered this when we were discussing the meaning of suffering.

Lest we jump to the false assumption that the story of Job is an ancient bit of mythology, we should note that Jesus also recognized this prerogative of Satan when he said to Peter, "Simon, Simon, behold, Satan demanded to have you, that he might sift you like wheat."[33] Jesus added, "but I have prayed for you, that your faith might not fail."[34] In the account of the casting down of Satan to the earth, Satan is called "the accuser of our brethren . . . who accuses them day and night before our God."[35] It is possibly with this view of satanic activity that Paul speaks of the Spirit who "intercedes for the saints"[36] (note that this is in the context of redemption waiting to be completed). The epistle to the Hebrews portrays Jesus as a high priest who continually makes intercession to God for those who draw near to God through him.[37]

It should be obvious that the intention of these accounts is not to teach that God is apt to fall for Satan's methods. If God is all-knowing, as the Bible presents him and as the Church believes, he knows when Satan's charges are lying accusations. There must be other reasons, then, for including these revelations. I suggest that from them we learn (1) that Satan is not omniscient and does not know what God knows; (2) that our trials are sometimes Satan-induced, to prove our faithfulness and to reveal the intercessory nature of our Savior; and (3) that we need ever to be on our guard against Satan's wiles, lest his accusations contain more truth than falsehood. He "prowls around like a roaring lion, seeking some one to devour"[38] —as Peter learned through experience.

Satan's Sphere.   We are mistaken if we believe that Satan is only concerned with individuals like you and me. It is not without good reason that he is called "the god of this age,"[39] "the ruler of this

---

* **32.** Job 1:6; 2:1.   **33.** Luke 22:31.   **34.** Luke 22:32.   **35.** Rev. 12:10.
36. Rom. 8:27.   **37.** Heb. 7:25.   **38.** 1 Pet. 5:8.   **39.** 2 Cor. 4:4.

world,"[40] and "the ruler of the power of the air."[41] When he offered Jesus "all the kingdoms of the world and the glory of them"[42] (Luke 4:6 adds "for it has been delivered to me"), it was no idle claim. The governments of this world, in their gross materialism and their use of deception and force, are basically satanic.

In Daniel's interpretation of Nebuchadnezzar's dream,[43] and again in Daniel's dream of the four beasts,[44] we learn something of the kingdoms of this world. We learn even more from the daily news, but in this case without divine explanation through one of God's appointed prophets. The image in the dream in Daniel 2 portrays a succession of world kingdoms,[45] which are destroyed by a stone "cut from a mountain by no human hand."[46] In place of the human kingdoms is established a kingdom to be set up by the God of heaven.[47]

We must not overlook the fact that the man-made kingdoms do not develop or evolve into the Kingdom of God. Before God's kingdom can be established, they must be destroyed. Likewise in the dream of the four beasts from the sea, which represent "four kings who shall arise out of the earth,"[48] they are not portrayed as beneficent, but as terrible. The fourth beast especially is described as "exceedingly terrible,"[49] that "shall devour the whole earth, and trample it down, and break it to pieces."[50] One of the "horns" of this beast, interpreted as a king,[51] "made war with the saints and prevailed over them,"[52] and in addition blasphemed against the Most High, attempting to "wear out the saints of the Most High."[53] He prevailed "for a time, two times, and half a time," generally interpreted to mean three-and-a-half years, but in any event a short period of limited duration, following which the dominion of the beasts was taken away and dominion was given to "one like a son of man" who came "with the clouds of heaven."[54] The use of this imagery in Revelation 13, 16, and 20 indicates that the kingdoms and the kings of this world are not for ever, but are limited to and characterized by this present satanic age.

Satan's Agents. According to a statement in Revelation, "War

---

40. John 12:31, etc.   41. Eph. 2:2.   42. Matt. 4:8.   43. Dan. 2.
44. Dan. 7.   45. Dan. 2:38,39.   46. Dan. 2:45.   47. Dan. 2:44.
48. Dan. 7:17.   49. Dan. 7:19.   50. Dan. 7:23.   51. Dan. 7:24.
52. Dan. 7:21.   53. Dan. 7:25.   54. Dan. 7:12-14.

arose in heaven, Michael and his angels fighting against the dragon; and the dragon and his angels fought."[55] The dragon was defeated, and he and his angels were thrown down to earth.[56] Paul speaks of his "thorn in the flesh" as "a messenger[i] of Satan."[57] The expression "the ruler (or prince) of the power of the air"[58] suggests that Satan has control over a host of agents, called "angels" (or "messengers"). This idea is amplified in the passage where Paul exhorts the Ephesians to "put on the whole armor of God," stating that "we are not contending against flesh and blood [i.e., mortals of this world], but against the principalities, against the powers, against the world rulers of this present darkness, against the spiritual hosts of wickedness in the heavenly places."[59] Each of the terms used can be applied to human officials—*archas*, "rulers, authorities"; *exousias*, "authorities, officials"; *kosmokratōras*, "world-rulers"[j]—but the complete statement, opening with the words "not against flesh and blood" and closing with "spiritual hosts of wickedness in heavenly places," requires us to interpret these as nonearthly or spirit beings.

Peter speaks of angels who "sinned" and were cast into *Tartarus* (translated "hell" in RSV) to await judgment.[60] Jude also speaks of "angels that did not keep their own position" who have been kept in chains awaiting the judgment.[61] These are sometimes referred to as the "fallen angels" who serve Satan, but this does not have substantial support from Scripture.[k]

The Bible also mentions "demons." The word *daimōn* seems to be avoided in the New Testament, occurring only once[62] in the best manuscripts, possibly because of its connotations.[l] The word *daimonion* is used frequently,[m] usually in cases of demon possession[n] (as a rule carefully distinguished from normal illness or disease). In Paul's writings, demons are associated with idolatry and sorcery,[63] an idea which is also found in Revelation.[64] There does not appear to be any scriptural identification of Satan's "angels" with demons, but demons are obviously included in satanic activities.[o]

Satan also has human agents. Judas Iscariot has already been mentioned earlier in the chapter, and it would be tempting to include others such as Nero and Hitler—but this is going beyond

55. Rev. 12:7.   **56.** Rev. 12:9.   **57.** 2 Cor. 12:7.   **58.** Eph. 2:2.
59. Eph. 6:12.   **60.** 2 Pet. 2:4.   **61.** Jude v. 6.   **62.** Matt. 8:31.
63. 1 Cor. 10:19–21; cf. Gal. 5:20.   **64.** Rev. 9:20; 21:8; 22:15.

biblical revelation. We are certainly warned in Scripture against the Devil's temptations, and Paul refers to "false prophets, deceitful workmen, disguising themselves as apostles of Christ," adding that since Satan "disguises himself as an angel of light," it "is not strange if his servants also disguise themselves as servants of righteousness."[65p]

The Person and Nature of Satan

There is no systematic presentation of Satanology in the Bible. We can only construct a Satanology by gathering together various scriptural passages, and this is done at considerable risk. For one thing, the terms that are used are not always beyond differences of interpretation. Again, some of the passages are in figurative language, which always presents hermeneutical problems. Then, too, we have been so conditioned by Milton, mythology, and medieval mystery plays that we sometimes overlook important scriptural teachings while searching for scriptural support for the views we espouse. Yet, if Satan is as important as indicated by Jesus, Paul, and the Revelator, the Church should at least try to produce a study of the scriptural doctrine of Satan.

Satan Is a Person, Not a Force.   There can be no question about the New Testament concept of Satan. On the basis of our "scientific" or "enlightened" system of thought we may deny that Satan is a person, and we may try to explain the New Testament teachings as the product of a superstitious age (was it any more so than the present day of astrological forecasts, horoscopes, witchcraft, and Satan worship?). But it must be admitted that in the New Testament, as T. H. Gaster remarks, "Satan appears invariably as a distinctive personality. He is represented as entering into men and as the responsible author (not merely the personification) of their evil deeds and passions."[q] For those of us who accept the Bible as the rule of faith, this should settle the matter. Because of Satan's methods of operation, however, we must admit that he appears more frequently as a force or an influence, particularly in our Western "civilization."[r]

Satan Is a Creature, Not a God.   The Bible does not present

---

65. 2 Cor. 11:13–15.

a cosmological dualism, such as is found in Zoroastrianism. In such a dualism there are two coeval deities (i.e., they have both existed from the beginning) engaged in a struggle for victory.[5] To the contrary, in the Bible God is presented as the Creator of all beings and things.[66] He is the only God and there is no other.[67] Satan is one of the "sons of God."[68] This expression can be used of human beings[69] as well as heavenly beings, but the context in Job is clearly nonearthly.[70] Satan and the demons are presented as having superhuman knowledge, so that they recognized Jesus even before his disciples knew his true nature and purpose.[71] But Satan continues to the end, seemingly unaware that victory has already eluded him and that both he and his plan are doomed.

There are some difficult passages in Scripture that seem to teach that Satan's power extends even to the death of the human being. Paul, writing to the Corinthian church concerning a man involved in gross immorality, advises them "to deliver this man to Satan for the destruction of the flesh, that his spirit may be saved in the day of the Lord Jesus."[72] He tells Timothy that "certain persons have made shipwreck of their faith, among them Hymenaeus and Alexander, whom I have delivered to Satan that they may learn not to blaspheme."[73] Do such passages mean that Satan can put human beings to death? Hebrews 2:14 seems to support this interpretation. Speaking of the incarnate and crucified One, the author says, "that through death he might destroy him who has the power of death, that is, the devil."[74] Further support may be found in Job, where God tells Satan, "Behold, he is in your power; only spare his life."[75] Did Jesus have Satan in mind when he said, "Do not fear those who kill the body but cannot kill the soul; rather fear him who can destroy both soul and body in hell"[76]? A study of the commentaries will show that there is no unanimity of interpretation on this matter.

Satan Is Superhuman, but Finite.   From what we have studied so far, it is clear that Satan is something more than a human being: a spirit being among the heavenly beings about whom we know so little. His power is great. But he is a finite being, with a beginning

---

66. Gen. 1:1,31; Isa. 44:24.   **67.** Isa. 45:18.   **68.** Job 1:6; 2:1.
69. Ps. 82:6.   **70.** Job 1:7; 2:2.   **71.** Cf. Matt. 4:3,6; 8:29.   **72.** 1 Cor. 5:5.   **73.** 1 Tim 1:20.   **74.** Heb. 2:14.   **75.** Job 2:6.   **76.** Matt. 10.28.

(when he was created by God) and an end (when he will be cast into the lake of fire). He has access to earth, and has (or had) access to God in heaven,[1] but he could not be in both places at the same time.[77] In the end time of this age, according to scriptures that we shall study (Chapters 9 and 10), he engages in a frenzy of activity in an all-out attempt to destroy God's redemptive work. This activity apparently includes conferring superhuman power on certain individuals[78] so that they can perform "great signs"[79] and even "give breath to the image of the beast so that the image of the beast should even speak."[80]

Isaiah 14 and Ezekiel 28.   Attempts to write a Satanology sometimes include material from Isaiah 14 and Ezekiel 28. We must therefore examine these passages.

In a taunt-song directed against the "king of Babylon,"[81] Isaiah includes the following passage:

How you are fallen from heaven, O Day Star,[4] son of Dawn!
    How you are cut down to the ground, you who laid the nations
    low!
You said in your heart, "I will ascend to heaven;
    above the stars of God I will set my throne on high; . . .
    I will make myself like the Most High."
But you are brought down to Sheol,
    to the depths of the Pit.[82]

The prophet Ezekiel was given a message for the "prince of Tyre,"[83] followed by a lamentation over him.[84] These passages include the following:

Because your heart is proud, and you have said, "I am a god,
    I sit in the seat of the gods, in the heart of the seas," . . .
Will you still say, "I am a god,"
    in the presence of those who slay you . . . ?"[85]

You were signet of perfection, full of wisdom and perfect in beauty.
    You were in Eden, the garden of God;
    every precious stone was your covering, . . .
On the day that you were created they were prepared.

---

77. Cf. Job 1:6,7.   78. Cf. Rev. 13:4,7,12–15.   79. Rev. 13:13.
80. Rev. 13:15.   81. Isa. 14:4.   82. Isa. 14:12–15.   83. Ezek. 28:2–10.
84. Ezek. 28:11–19.   85. Ezek. 28:2–9.

With an anointed guardian cherub I placed you;
  you were on the holy mountain of God;
  in the midst of the stones of fire you walked.
You were blameless in your ways from the day you were created,
  till iniquity was found in you . . .
so I cast you as a profane thing from the mountain of God. . . .[86]

On the basis of straightforward exegesis there can be no question that these passages were meant for their own times and for the persons addressed. There is no indication that they were intended to be descriptions of Satan, and any attempt to build an elaborate system that includes a Satan-ruled, gem-studded paradise that existed between verses 1 and 2 of Genesis 1 is more in the realm of fantasy than biblical study.

At the same time, all scholars admit that there is something more in these passages than descriptions of the king of Babylon and the prince of Tyre. One scholar speaks of "the use of mythological material," "material derived from Canaanite myths."[v] Another writes: "Here we are transported from earth to paradise, from contemporary history to the origin of things. The sin and fall of a state on the Mediterranean coast are the reflection here below of a primal sin and fall in which the spirit of man as such is involved."[w]

Personally, I see something akin to a *sensus plenior*[x] ("fuller meaning") in these passages, the result of the action of God's Spirit on the prophets, so that whether they were using Canaanite mythology or simply writing what they felt God was saying through them, there is a deeper meaning[87] that describes the satanic character of these human rulers. But to use such passages to build a doctrine of Satan is most precarious.

Summary

The redemptive and revelatory work of God in this age is opposed by a satanic spirit being who has great power but who is a finite creature. This satanic being seeks to distort God's revelation, frustrate God's redemptive plan, deceive God's people, and control the kingdoms of the world. In the end time his efforts toward these

---

86. Ezek. 28:11–16.   **87.** 1 Pet. 1:12.

ends will be greatly multiplied, but they will be of short duration, as we shall learn in later chapters.

NOTES

a. The word *diabolos*, "Devil," occurs thirty-seven times in the New Testament: thirteen times in the Gospels, eight times in Paul, and five times in Revelation. The word *satanas*, "Satan," occurs thirty-six times in the New Testament: sixteen times in the Gospels, ten times in Paul, and eight times in Revelation according to Robert Morgenthaler, *Statistik des neutestamentlichen Wortschatzes*. Zurich: Gotthelf-Verlag, 1958), pp. 87, 140. The word *śāṭān*, "adversary, Satan," occurs in the Old Testament thirty-three times, but only in Job (twelve times), 1 Chronicles 21:1, and Zechariah 3:1–2 does the word clearly refer to Satan.

b. See *IDB* Supplement, p. 225. Terms used are: *daimonion*, "demon"; *pneuma akatharton*, "unclean spirit"; *pneuma ponēros*, "evil spirit" (only in Luke 7:21); *pneuma*, "spirit" (only in Mark 9:17); and *daimōn*, "demon" (only in Matt. 8:31). See the excellent article by D. E. Aune, "Demon; Demonology," *ISBE* 1 (1979): 919–923.

c. For *diabolos* see *TDNT* 2: 71–81, especially 79f. For *satanas* see *TDNT* 7: 151–163.

d. This is called "the key image for Satan in the whole book" (*TDNT* 2: 282).

e. This statement closely approximates the basic meaning of *diabolos*, "slanderer."

f. Out of deference to those who object to the exclusive use of male terms when referring to God, I suppose we should allow this option for Satan also. I am offering no new doctrine concerning the sex of Satan.

g. The form *beelzebub* comes from the Latin Vulgate, possibly influenced by the Hebrew words in 2 Kings 1:2 (*ba'al z^ebûb*). Beelzebub has been explained as meaning "lord of flies." See T. H. Gaster, "Beelzebul," *IDB* 1: 374. The form *beelzebul* may be traced to the Ugaritic *zbl b'l*, "Prince Baal," giving the meaning "prince" for the second part of the Greek name. Others have traced it to late Hebrew and Syriac, where it means "dung, feces," and have rendered Beelzebul as *defoecator*, "defecator" (or a nastier word which children and others who have not quite grown up love to use).

h. Gaster rejects this etymology as having no support in cognate languages, *IDB* 1: 374. On the other hand, D. E. Aune accepts it, *ISBE* 1 (1979): 447.

i. The Greek word *aggelos* has been taken over into English as "angel." Basically it means "messenger," as translated by the RSV in this passage.

j. The term *kosmokratōr* is generally used of world-ruling gods, but it is also applied to the emperor Caracalla (A-G, p. 446).

k. Still more problematic is the identification of the "sons of God" of Genesis 6:2 with "fallen angels." An elaborate system has been built by various authors through the ages, who have speculated that the sexless angels (cf. Matt. 22:30) burned with lust and had to enter into human bodies to be able to satisfy that lust. We do much better to stop where the scriptural revelation stops.

l. *Daimōn* in Greek usage carried the idea of deities, demiurges, and spirits of the dead ("shades"). (*TDNT* 2: 2).

m. The word *daimonion* occurs sixty-three times in the New Testament: forty-seven times in the Synoptics, six times in John, five times in Paul, three times in Revelation, once each in Acts and Hebrews. The usage in Acts (17:18), "deities," is in the mouths of the Athenians and has a Greek, rather than New Testament, connotation.

n. Demon possession has become a popular theme in modern novels and films. More recently, it has become the basis of defense in the trial of a nineteen-year-old person charged with stabbing his landlord. The judge (an Irish Catholic) branded the defense strategy "irrelevant," but the lawyers plan to enter evidence by five Catholic priests who conducted "deliverance rituals" designed to drive demons from the defendant's body and have read into the record definitions of demonic possession from Roman Catholic encyclopedias of theology. See *Evangelical Newsletter* (Philadelphia: Evangelical Ministries) 8,24 (27 Nov. 1981): 1. To me, this is reminiscent of the plot in *Miracle on 34th Street*, where the court is called upon to prove the existence of Santa Claus.

o. The whole subject of free will in angels, involving the possibility of their ability to "fall," to the best of my knowledge has not been adequately explored. The same is true concerning the fall of Satan; see below.

p. Along this same line, some of the parables of Jesus need more careful study. In the Parable of the Wheat and the Tares, for example, "the good seed means the sons of the kingdom" and the tares "are the sons of the evil one," which were sown by the Devil (Matt. 13:38–39). Does this mean that Satan actually puts human agents into the kingdom process? In a similar way, the Parable of the Sower, as given in Mark, uses the expressions "these are *the ones sown* upon rocky ground" (Mark 4:16), "others are *the ones sown* among thorns" (v. 18), and "those are *the ones sown* on good ground" (v. 20), suggesting that the human individuals are sown "where the word is sown" (v. 15). This is clearly different than the wording in Matthew, and commentaries in general dismiss the difference and exegete Mark in the same manner as they do Matthew.

q. T. H. Gaster, "Satan," *IDB* 4: 227.

r. Missionaries have long reported observations of demon possession in lands dominated by animism. Could the rise of demon possession—or belief in it—in the West be the result of importing oriental philosophical and religious beliefs?

s. In Zoroastrianism they are Ahura Mazda (Ormazd, the god of light) and Angra Mainyu (Ahriman, the god of darkness). See E. Herzfeld, *Zoroaster and His World*, 2 vols. (Princeton, NJ: Princeton University Press, 1947) 1: 308–315; J. H. Moulton, "Zoroastrianism," *HDB* 4: 988–994; B. S. Easton, "Zoroastrianism," *ISBE* (1929) 5: 3157–3158; M. J. Dresden,

"Persia, History and Religion of," *IDB* 3: 745–746; W. S. LaSor, "Zoroastrianism," *Baker's Dictionary of Theology* (Grand Rapids, MI: Baker, 1960), pp. 565–566.

t. Jesus said, "I saw Satan fall like lightning from heaven" (Luke 10:18). In Revelation 12:7–9 the Dragon, "the Devil and Satan," was defeated in the battle in heaven and thrown down to earth. Do these refer to the same event? If so, has it already taken place, or are the passages prophetic of what will take place in the end time?

u. In the Latin Vulgate "Day Star" is rendered "Lucifer," giving us this name for Satan.

v. R. B. Y. Scott, *Interpreter's Bible*, 12 vols. (New York and Nashville: Abingdon Press, 1951–1957) 5: 259, 261.

w. E. L. Allen, *Interpreter's Bible*, 6: 219–220.

x. On *sensus plenior* see W. S. LaSor, "Interpretation of Prophecy," *Baker's Dictionary of Practical Theology*, 128–135; "Prophecy, Inspiration, and *Sensus Plenior*," *Tyndale Bulletin* 29 (1978): 49–60.

ADDITIONAL READING

Aune, D. E. "Beelzebul." *ISBE* 1 (1979): 447.

Aune, D. E. "Demon, Demonology." *ISBE* 1 (1979): 919–923.

diabolos, *TDNT* 2: 71–81.

drakōn, *TDNT* 2: 281–283.

English, E. S. *A Companion to the New Scofield Reference Bible.* New York: Oxford University Press, 1972. Pp. 44–46.

Graebner, Theodore. *War in the Light of Prophecy.* St. Louis, MO: Concordia, 1941.

Gray, James M. *Satan and the Saint.* New York: Revell, 1909.

Langton, Edward. *Essentials of Demonology.* London: Epworth, 1949.

LaSor, William Sanford. "The *Sensus Plenior* and Biblical Interpretation." In *Scripture, Tradition, Interpretation; Essays Presented to Everett F. Harrison,* edited by W. W. Gasque and W. S. LaSor. Grand Rapids, MI: Eerdmans, 1978. Pp. 260–277.

Lindsey, Hal. *Satan Is Alive and Well on Planet Earth.* Grand Rapids, MI: Zondervan, 1972; New York: Bantam, 1974.

Lyons, Arthur. *The Second Coming: Satanism in America.* New York: Dodd, Mead, 1970.

ponēros, *TDNT* 6: 546–562.

satanas, *TDNT* 7: 151–163.

Sauer, E. *King of the Earth.* Grand Rapids, MI: Eerdmans, 1962. Pp. 60–71.

Sweet, L. M. "Satan." *ISBE* 4: 2694.

7. The Messianic Idea

The Problem

It may come as a shock to learn that the word "Messiah" does not occur in the Old Testament. This evokes the question, "Then if there is no Messiah in the Old Testament, where did the Jews get the idea?" Some scholars have attempted to trace it to the Zoroastrian Saoshyant, but this is both futile and unnecessary. The *idea* comes from the Old Testament. The *word*, as a technical term, developed in the Intertestamental Period. In the New Testament, the word "Christ"—which is simply a Greek translation of "Messiah"—took on further meaning. In this chapter I shall try to trace this development and show its relevance to Christian eschatology.*

The Hebrew word *māšîªḥ* is an adjective meaning "anointed," often used as a substantive meaning "(the) anointed (one)." Through Greek and Latin loan words it has given us the English word "messiah," from which we have derivatives such as "messianic" and "messianism." The Greek translation *christos* is an exact equivalent, an adjective meaning "anointed," often used as a substantive like the Hebrew word. It has come into English as "Christ" and given us words such as "christen," "Christian," and "Christmas."

The Kingdom and the King

The Israelite Demand for a King.   According to 1 Samuel 8, when Samuel the judge-prophet became old, "all the elders of Israel gathered together and came to" him, and said, " . . . now appoint for us a king to govern us like all nations."[1] Samuel resisted the idea, but God said, "Hearken to the voice of the people in all that they say to you; for they have not rejected you, but they have rejected

---

1. 1 Sam. 8:4,5.

me from being king over them."² Samuel was still reluctant to accede to the demand, and painted a picture of what it would be like to have a king,³ but finally he anointed Saul ben-Kish to be the first king of the Israelite monarchy.

Some Bible students tell us that it was not God's will for Israel to have a king. The nation was supposed to be a *theocracy*, that is, a nation ruled by God.ᵇ I find it hard to believe that an event of such lasting historical and theological significance "was not God's will," and I see it rather as a stage in the development of understanding among the people of God concerning his will. Just as the period of Egyptian bondage was a time of providential pedagogy, when tribes were learning what national existence entailed, so the period of the monarchy was an occasion to learn something about the purposes and problems of a kingdom. Certainly the promise to Abraham included the promise of kings,⁴ and while it is true that Abraham was to become "the father of a multitude of nations," it would be strange indeed if only the Israelite nation were excluded from the promise "kings shall come forth from you." Moreover, this promise was repeated to Jacob at Paddan-Aram⁵ in immediate connection with the land promise.⁶ Moses also foresaw the popular demand for a king and gave permission: "You may indeed set as king over you him whom the Lord your God will choose."⁷

The Ideal King. The rejection of Saul, the people's choice, and the selection of David, the Lord's choice,⁸ was likely intended as a revelation to the Israelites that the ultimate kingdom would be ruled by the king of God's own choosing. This idea is further developed in the account of David's desire to build a house for the Lord.⁹ God instructed Nathan to tell David: "When your days are fulfilled and you lie down with your fathers, I will raise up your son after you, who shall come forth from your body, and I will establish his kingdom. He shall build a house for my name, and I will establish the throne of his kingdom for ever."¹⁰

Obviously this prophecy was immediately relevant to Solomon, the son "who shall come forth from your [David's] body,"¹¹ but it had a far-reaching significance. The house that Solomon built was

---

2. i Sam. 8:7.   3. i Sam. 8:11–18.   4. Gen. 17:6.   5. Gen. 35:11.
6. Gen. 35:12.   7. Deut. 17:15.   8. i Sam. 15:16; 16:1ff.   9. 2 Sam. 7.
10. 2 Sam. 7:12–13.   11. 2 Sam. 7:12.

destroyed by the Babylonians, and the Davidic dynasty, humanly speaking, ended with Zedekiah.[c] The deeper meaning is demonstrated by the place occupied by the title "son of David,"[d] which was in use even in New Testament times,[12] and by the extension of the ideas of the "house of David"[13] and the "city of David."[14] "David" became an ideal king who would rule over God's people in the coming days[15] and a symbol of strength,[16] just as David became a measure of the piety of the kings of Judah. Thus it was said, for example, that Abijam's heart "was not wholly true to the Lord his God, as the heart of David his father";[17] while of Hezekiah it was said, "he did what was right in the eyes of the Lord, according to all that David his father had done."[18]

The Ideal Kingdom.   Alongside the concept of an ideal Davidic king developed the ideal of the kingdom. Amos foretold the raising up of the "falling booth of David"[19] and saw it as a time of agricultural plenty and permanence.[20] Isaiah foresaw a government of endless peace under the righteous and just rule of "the throne of David"[21] and pictured an idyllic age when "the wolf shall dwell with the lamb . . . and a little child shall lead them,"[22] when "they shall not hurt or destroy in all my holy mountain, for the earth shall be full of the knowledge of the Lord as the waters cover the sea."[23] Micah saw Bethlehem, the city of David's origin, as the place from which one shall come "who is to be ruler in Israel," who "shall stand and feed his flock in the strength of the Lord" and "they shall dwell secure."[24] Ezekiel also looked forward to a kingdom under "David" the "prince" when wild beasts would be banished, "so that they may dwell securely in the wilderness and sleep in the woods,"[25] when there would be plenteous produce,[26] and when the nations shall know "that they, the house of Israel, are my people."[27] Zechariah looked for the coming of a triumphant king,[28] whose dominion shall be "from sea to sea," at which time captives will be set free to return to their homes. "On that day the Lord their God will save them for they are the flock of his people; for like the jewels of a crown they

---

12. Matt. 20:30; 21:15.   13. Luke 1:69.   14. Luke 2:11.   15. Ezek. 34:23,24.   16. Zech. 12:8.   17. 1 Kings 15:3.   18. 2 Kings 18:3. 19. Amos 9:11, lit.   20. Amos 9:13–15.   21. Isa. 9:6,7.   22. Isa. 11:6.   23. Isa. 11:9.   24. Mic. 5:2–4 (MT 1–3).   25. Ezek. 34:25. 26. Ezek. 34:27,29.   27. Ezek. 34:30.   28. Zech. 9:9.

shall shine on his land."[29] Throughout the period of the prophets, preexilic to postexilic, this hope of an ideal kingdom was developing.

This kingdom was to be God's kingdom. Indeed, David recognized this as a fact from the beginning: "Thine is the kingdom, O Lord."[30] He sang, "For dominion belongs to the Lord, and he rules over the nations."[31] In a Psalm for the king's wedding, it was recognized that the throne was God for ever and ever.[32e] God was called "My God and King,"[33] and his kingdom was "an everlasting kingdom."[34] In his vision of the day of judgment, Isaiah said "for the Lord of hosts will reign on Mount Zion and in Jerusalem."[35] Daniel, in explaining the meaning of Nebuchadnezzar's dream, said, "In the days of those kings the God of heaven will set up a kingdom which shall never be destroyed."[36]

In a sense, then, the concept of theocracy was never entirely lost. The Lord had declared at Sinai, "You shall be to me a kingdom of priests and a holy nation."[37] In rejecting Saul God had shown that the prerogative of choosing the king was his alone. He gave his servants the prophets visions of a king and a kingdom that would be established on his principles of righteousness and justice. Later these ideas would develop into the concept of the Messianic Kingdom.

The Messianic Hope

Messianic Prophecy. In their desire to show that Jesus was the long-awaited king, the early Church—and some portions of the Church in later centuries—attempted to find "prophecies" that were "fulfilled" by Jesus.[f] This method violates the historical development of the idea, for first came the prophecies and later the fulfillment. A more reasonable approach is to ask first what the prophecies meant, that is, how they were understood, *at the time they were given,* and then to discover how later generations of the people of God came to understand them. Prophecy, I am convinced, is *not* "history written in advance," but rather it is revelation of truth from God that has immediate and continuing relevance to God's people until it attains its fullness. When it is filled full, it is fulfilled

---

29. Zech. 9:16.   30. 1 Chron. 29:11.   31. Ps. 22:28.   32. Ps. 45:6 (MT 7).   33. Ps. 145:1.   34. Ps. 145:13.   35. Isa. 24:23.   36. Dan. 2:44.   37. Exod. 19:6.

—this is the simple meaning of the word "fulfill," whether in English, Hebrew, or Greek.[g]

Since the word "Messiah" does not occur in the Old Testament,[h] there cannot be any passage which specifically refers to the Messiah. There are, however, many passages that foretell one or more of the following: the redemption to be accomplished by God, the one by whom or through whom that redemption is to be accomplished, the place where it is to be accomplished, and the results to the people of God and to the "nations." Such prophecies, often called "messianic," are more properly to be identified as "soteriological," "eschatological," or "teleological."[i]

The Coming Ruler.   In a number of passages, there are prophecies of a coming ruler who will rule his people Israel in righteousness. This ruler, as we have seen, is "the son of David," or simply "David." Perhaps as a result of the growing frustration of the people with kings, beginning with Solomon, who did not reign in righteousness and who could not maintain national or international peace, but who more and more led the people into sin, injustice, apostasy, and war, there developed a longing for the ideal king. Thus Hosea, foreseeing a time when there would be no king, said, "Afterward the children of Israel shall return and seek the Lord their God, and David their king."[38] Jeremiah said, "They shall serve the Lord their God and David their king, whom I will raise up for them."[39] And Ezekiel prophesied, "I, the Lord, will be their God, and my servant David shall be prince among them."[40]

David is not always named, but a term referring to him or his house is used as a surrogate. Isaiah spoke of a "shoot" or "rod" from the "stump of Jesse."[41] Jesse was David's father,[42] and the figure is that of a tree that has been cut down, leaving a stump out of which a shoot is to sprout.[43] Another term is "branch," used by Isaiah[44] and more clearly by Jeremiah: "Behold the days are coming, says the Lord, when I will raise up for David a righteous Branch, and he shall reign as king and deal wisely, and shall execute justice and righteousness in the land."[45] Zechariah made use of the same figure, but this occurs in passages that refer to Joshua the high

---

38. Hos. 3:4,5.   39. Jer. 30:9.   40. Ezek. 43:24; cf. 37:24.   41. Isa. 11:1.   42. Ruth 4:17.   43. Cf. Isa. 6:13.   44. Isa. 4:2.   45. Jer. 23:5; cf. 33:14,15.

priest,[46] which some scholars would emend to read Zerubbabel the governor. In any event, it seems clear that Zechariah had in mind prophecies of the coming ruler called "the Branch."

Another term used in these prophecies is "shepherd." Isaiah uses it,[47] but the messianic reference is not clear. Jeremiah uses the term with possible messianic reference, where just before speaking of "a righteous Branch," he quotes Yahweh as saying, "I will set shepherds over them who will care for them."[48] In another eschatological passage addressed to the "nations" he says, "He who scattered Israel will gather him, and will keep him as a shepherd keeps his flock."[49] But it is in Ezekiel that this term has its clearest messianic reference:

Behold, I, I myself will search for my sheep. . . . I myself will be the shepherd of my sheep. . . . And I will set up over them one shepherd, my servant David, and he shall feed them; he shall feed them and be their shepherd.[50]

The Messianic Kingdom. The coming king will reign from Jerusalem, which is often called "Zion," the name of that portion of Jerusalem most closely associated with David.[51j] The term "Zion" occurs frequently in passages that speak of the ideal future, particularly in Isaiah and in Psalms.[k] "I have set my king on Zion, my holy hill."[52] "O that deliverance for Israel would come from Zion! When God restores the fortunes of his people, Jacob will rejoice and Israel be glad."[53] "Those who trust in the Lord are like Mount Zion, which cannot be moved, but abides for ever."[54] The very familiar words of Isaiah and Micah say it perhaps best:

It shall come to pass in the latter days that the mountain of the house of the Lord shall be established as the highest of the mountains, and shall be raised above the hills, and all the nations shall flow to it, and many peoples shall come, and say:

"Come, let us go up to the mountain of the Lord,
    to the house of the God of Jacob;
that he may teach us his ways
    and that we may walk in his paths."

---

46. Zech. 3:8–10; 6:12,13. **47.** Isa. 40:11. **48.** Jer. 23:4. **49.** Jer. 31:10. **50.** Ezek. 34:11,15,23; see also 37:24,25. **51.** 2 Sam. 5:6–9. **52.** Psa. 2:6 (MT 7). **53.** Ps. 53:6. **54.** Ps. 125:1.

> For out of Zion shall go forth the law,
>   and the word of the Lord from Jerusalem.
> He shall judge between the nations,
>   and shall decide for many peoples;
> and they shall beat their swords into plowshares,
>   and their spears into pruning hooks;
> nation shall not lift up sword against nation,
>   neither shall they learn war any more.[55]

The covenant with Abraham included the promise of the land.[56] This promise was repeated many times and is included in the prophecies of the messianic age. Punishment for apostasy brought upon Israel exile from that land.[57] But God would restore the fortunes of his people and return them to that land. The most detailed prophecy on this subject is found in Ezekiel 36–39:

You shall dwell in the land which I gave to your fathers; and you shall be my people, and I will be your God.[58]

I will take the people of Israel from the nations among which they have gone, and will gather them from all sides, and bring them to their own land; and I will make them one nation in the land, upon the mountains of Israel; and one king shall be king over them all . . . and they shall be my people, and I will be their God. My servant David shall be king over them. . . . They shall dwell in the land where your fathers dwelt that I gave to my servant Jacob; they and their children and their children's children shall dwell there for ever; and David my servant shall be their prince for ever.[59]

Then they shall know that I am the Lord their God because I sent them into exile among the nations, and then gathered them into their own land. I will leave none of them remaining among the nations any more.[60]

The many elements of the ideal kingdom, some of which we have noted, belong to this messianic reign: national and personal safety, abundance of produce from the ground, justice for all and especially for the poor and the defenseless, peace among the nations, and the increased and universal knowledge of God's law.

---

55. Isa. 2:2–4; cf. Mic. 4:1–3.   **56.** Gen. 12:1; 15:7; 17:8, etc.   **57.** Cf. Deut. 28:36,64–67; Jer. 1:10; 18:7; 31:28.   **58.** Ezek. 36:28.   **59.** Ezek. 37: 21–25.   **60.** Ezek. 39:28.

The Messianic Claim of Jesus

One question must be squarely faced: Did Jesus claim to be the Messiah of the Jews, or was this idea developed by the Church at a later date? If Jesus, a Jew ministering to Jews, believed himself to be the Messiah, then we should assume that he accepted not only the Old Testament scriptures on the subject, but also much of the current Jewish interpretation of those scriptures. We should further assume that his followers, in accepting his claims, would have used the same scriptures as their authority and would have been largely guided in their understanding by Rabbinic interpretation and by whatever corrections Jesus had made to those interpretations. The New Testament will be our guide for this portion of our study—but we must continually bear in mind that the early Church did not yet have the New Testament; it was bound by the canonical scriptures of its day, the Old Testament.

The Jewish Concept of Messiah.   I refer here, of course, to the view held by Jews in the first century. The "Messiah" was the name that had been given to the coming Davidic king at some point in the Second Commonwealth. We first meet the term in its technical sense in the first century B.C. in Enoch[61] and Psalms of Solomon.[62] By the time of the Rabbinical writings, it was an accepted term, as it was in the New Testament. It meant simply the coming king, the son of David.[l] Judaism has never been monolithic, and there were other ideas besides those found in the Rabbinical writings. A Messiah ben Joseph is sometimes mentioned, who wages war against Gog and Magog and dies in the battle.[m] A Messiah ben Aaron, or priestly Messiah from the tribe of Levi, is mentioned in the Testament of the Twelve Patriarchs,[63] and also, according to one interpretation, in the Qumran documents.[n] In addition an apocalyptic "son of Man" is found in Book II (the Similitudes) of Enoch. But only the Davidic Messiah seems to have been accepted by the exponents of early Judaism—and also by Qumran, as I understand the texts.

Jesus' Messianic Claim.   On several occasions, Jesus was called "Christ" ("Messiah"), but his customary reply was "Tell no man."[64]

61. Enoch 48:10; 52:4.   **62.** Pss. of Sol. 17:36; 18:8.   **63.** T. Reuben 6; T. Levi 8,18; T. Dan 5.   **64.** Cf. Matt. 9:27–30; Luke 4:41.

This is understandable, for if Jesus had allowed a large popular following to call him "Messiah," he would have brought down on his head the mailed fist of the Romans before he had accomplished the training of the Twelve. However, when Peter made his confession at Caesarea-Philippi, "You are the Christ," Jesus accepted this statement and said that it was a revelation from God.[65] From that time he began to show the disciples the necessity of his death and resurrection.[66]

The "triumphal entry" seems to have been a deliberate act designed to present publicly his messianic claim, for he chose to act out Zechariah's prophecy, "Lo, your king comes to you; triumphant and victorious is he, humble and riding on an ass, on a colt the foal of an ass."[67] The action undoubtedly was understood by the crowds as messianic, and when the children repeated the cries, "Hosanna to the son of David!" the religious leaders rebuked Jesus; but he replied with a quotation of scripture, "Out of the mouths of babes and sucklings thou hast brought perfect praise."[68] It was also so understood by the chief priests and elders, who launched into an attack upon his words and works,[69] to which Jesus replied with two pointed parables,[70] the import of which was not lost on the leaders.[71]

The trial included questions about Jesus' messianic claim. "Are you the Christ, the Son of the Blessed?" the high priest asked. Jesus replied, "I am; and you will see the Son of man sitting at the right hand of Power, and coming with the clouds of heaven."[72] The high priest fully understood this as a messianic claim, tearing his mantle in the presence of what he considered to be "blasphemy."[73] Likewise, Pilate, who certainly must have gotten the idea from reports of the Jewish leaders, asked Jesus, "Are you the King of the Jews?"[74] Jesus' reply may seem at first glance to be evasive, but he did claim kingship, and Pilate so understood it[75] and put this claim as the official charge on the superscription on the cross.[76]

The Belief of the Early Church.   There can be no question that

---

65. Matt. 16:16,17.   **66.** Matt. 16:21.   **67.** Zech. 9:9; cf. Matt. 21:1–10. **68.** Matt. 21:15,16; Ps. 8:2.   **69.** Matt. 21:15,23.   **70.** Matt. 21:28–43. **71.** Matt. 21:45.   **72.** Mark 14:61,62.   **73.** Mark 14:63–65.   **74.** John 18:33.   **75.** John 18:37.   **76.** John 19:19.

the early Church looked upon Jesus as the Jewish Messiah. The birth stories⁰ include: the Davidic genealogy;[77] the visit of the Magi seeking the newborn "King of the Jews";[78] the angelic words to Mary, "the Lord God will give to him the throne of his father David, and he will reign over the house of Israel for ever,"[79] a hope echoed by Zechariah the father of John the Baptizer;[80] and the angelic announcement to the shepherds referred to the baby born in the "city of David" as "the Christ."[81] When they were sitting on the Mount of Olives, the disciples asked Jesus, "When will this be, and what will be the sign of your coming and of the close of the age?"[82] The question implies belief that he was the king who was to come at the end of the age, the time, according to Jewish teachings, when the messianic age was to begin. The disciples on the road to Emmaus, stunned by the crucifixion, told the one who had joined them (and whom they did not yet recognize as Jesus), "We had hoped that he was the one to redeem Israel."[83]

After the resurrection, the disciples asked the risen Jesus, "Lord, will you at this time restore the kingdom to Israel?"—again basing their question on their messianic hope.[84] On the day of Pentecost, Peter declared that the event was the fulfillment of Joel's prophecy[85] and further proclaimed, "Let all the house of Israel therefore know assuredly that God has made him both Lord and Christ."[86] Paul believed in the Davidic descent of Jesus[87] and connected the scriptures and the hopes of Israel with this Jesus.[88] He declared to the Jews at Rome that it was "because of the hope of Israel" that he was bound in chains[89] and spent a day trying to convince them that Jesus and his relationship to the kingdom of God were in accordance with the law and the prophets.[90]

The author of the epistle to the Hebrews, setting forth his faith that Jesus was the culmination of God's revelation,[91] quoted many "messianic" scriptures and repeatedly referred to Jesus as "Christ."[92] Because of the large place devoted to comparing Jesus

77. Cf. Matt. 1:17.   **78.** Matt. 2:2.   **79.** Luke 1:32,33.   **80.** Luke 1:68,69.   **81.** Luke 2:11.   **82.** Matt. 24:3.   **83.** Luke 24:21.   **84.** Acts 1:6.   **85.** Acts 2:16-21; cf. Joel 2:28-32 (MT 3:1-3).   **86.** Acts 2:36. **87.** Rom. 1:3.   **88.** Rom. 9-11.   **89.** Acts 28:20.   **90.** Acts 28:23. **91.** Heb. 1:1.   **92.** Heb. 3:3,6; 5:5; 8:6, etc.

with Aaron and with the high priest,[93] it is possible that the author was from those Jews who believed in a Messiah from Levi (or Aaron). It is also possible that the comparison with Moses[94] developed from the promise to Moses in Deuteronomy 18:18, "I will raise up for them a prophet like you."

It is in the book of Revelation that we find the fullest presentation of the messianic king and the events leading up to the messianic age. This book draws heavily on Ezekiel and Daniel, with many quotations from or allusions to Psalms, Isaiah, and other Prophets. There should be no question that it represents a Jewish viewpoint, although not necessarily the prevalent view (sometimes called "normative" Judaism). The book, however, is in the form of apocalyptic,[p] making interpretation difficult. Nevertheless there are portions of sufficient clarity that we can draw the following conclusions. The victor is "the Lion of the tribe of Judah, the Root of David,"[95] hence the Davidic Messiah. He has ransomed those "from every tribe and tongue and people and nation" and "made them a kingdom and priests to our God, and they shall reign on earth,"[96] fulfilling prophecies in Genesis[97] and Isaiah[98] and drawing on language of Exodus[99] and Psalms.[100] He comes from heaven, like the son of man of Daniel 7:13—a figure Jesus used of himself[101] although it was not part of the messianic figure of "normative" Judaism—to "smite the nations" and "rule them with a rod of iron,"[102] and his name was "King of kings and Lord of lords,"[103] as well as "the Word of God."[104] He reigns with his saints "a thousand years";[105] (note that the title "Christ" is used here). After that, Gog and Magog attempt the last battle, but they are destroyed by fire from heaven,[106] and then the final judgment takes place, and the "new heavens and new earth" are revealed.[107] This outline of events is basically in agreement with the Jewish belief that the days of the Messiah were to occupy a period of time[q] at the end of this age, prior to the age to come. That the Revelator has Jesus in mind throughout is clear from Revelation 1:5; 22:20.

---

93. Heb. 4:14–5:10; 6:20–10:25.   94. Heb. 3:1–4:10.   95. Rev. 5:5.
96. Rev. 5:9,10.   97. Gen. 49:4.   98. Isa. 61:1.   99. Exod. 19:6.
100. Ps. 33:3.   101. Mark 14:62.   102. Cf. Ps. 2:9.   103. Rev. 19:16.
104. Rev. 19:13.   105. Rev. 20:4.   106. Rev. 20:8,9.   107. Rev.
21:1.

Summary

The concept of the Messiah and the messianic age developed in the Intertestamental Period from teachings in the Old Testament, especially certain passages from the Prophets. The hope of One to come is clearly spelled out in the Old Testament, although the name "Messiah" is not used. Rather, he is called "David," "son of David," or a shoot (scion) from the stump of Jesse. The Jews of the Second Commonwealth developed these teachings into a messianic doctrine and gave the name Messiah (Greek, *Christos*) to this person. He was a human being, who would take the throne of David and bring in the glorious days foretold by the prophets. The tribes of Judah and Israel would again dwell in the land promised to their forefathers, enjoying the blessings of his reign. His rule would bring righteousness and peace to the world, and the nations would come to Jerusalem for instruction in the law of the Lord and to render gifts.

There were other teachings in the Old Testament that were taken up by Jesus and incorporated into the Christian doctrine of the Christ. He was the Son of man, to come on the clouds in glory, according to the prophecy of Daniel. He was the suffering Servant, who would give his life a ransom for many, after the prophecies in Isaiah 41–55, particularly 52:13–53:12. He was the lawgiver or prophet greater than Moses, the high priest greater than Aaron, the personification of wisdom greater than Solomon. He was the Son of God, whose reign was to be to the ends of the earth.[108]

To attempt to remove the "material" elements of the messianic age and leave only the "spiritual" is to cut the doctrine from its Old Testament roots and leave it as a structure more akin to Greek idealism. The judgment of J. Klausner is indeed valid: "In the belief in the Messiah of the people of Israel, *the political part goes arm in arm with the ethical part, and the nationalistic with the universalistic.* It is Christianity which has attempted to remove the political and nationalistic part which is there, and leave only the ethical and spiritual part."[r]

---

108. Ps. 2:7.

NOTES

a. The blanket statements in this paragraph require some support. I have dealt more fully with the subjects in the following: "The Messianic Idea in Qumran," *Studies and Essays in Honor of Abraham A. Neuman*, ed. M. Ben-Horin, et al. (Leiden: Brill, 1962), pp. 343–364; "The Messiah: An Evangelical Christian View," in *Evangelicals and Jews in Conversation on Scripture, Theology, and History*, ed. M. Tanenbaum, et al. (Grand Rapids, MI: Baker, 1978), pp. 76–95; "Zoroastrianism," *Baker's Dictionary of Theology* (Grand Rapids, MI: Baker, 1960), pp. 565–566; *The Dead Sea Scrolls and the Christian Faith*, pp. 94–99, 106, 151–163. For other treatments see J. Klausner, *The Messianic Idea in Israel* (London: Allen and Unwin, 1956); H. Ringgren, *The Messiah in the Old Testament* (London: SCM, 1956); E. O'Doherty, "The Organic Development of Messianic Revelation," *Catholic Biblical Quarterly* 19 (1957): 16–25; and J. Coppens, *L'attente du Messie* (Bruges: Desclée de Brouwer, 1954).

b. Cf. *SRB*, p. 976, n. 1; also the inserted title at 1 Samuel 8:7, p. 326. This view is moderated in *NSRB*, p. 329, n.1.

c. Jehoiachin is sometimes considered to have been the last legitimate king of Judah. It is true that Zerubbabel was also of the Davidic line, grandson of Jehoiachin (Ezra 3:2; Hag. 1:1; Matt. 1:12), but he was a "governor" under the Persian emperor and not a king. The Hasmoneans (Maccabees) were a priestly line, of the tribe of Levi, and their brief "kingdom" (162–63 B.C.) cannot be considered a continuation of the Davidic throne.

d. No other king is treated in similar fashion. There is no "son of Asa" or "son of Hezekiah" serving as an ideal. Only "the son of David" occupies this place.

e. The translation of this verse is complicated by the fact that it is quoted in Hebrews 1:8–9. However, it is possible to translate both the Hebrew and the Greek "Thy throne is God," and the context of Psalm 45 would seem to require this; see 45:1, "I address my verses to the king," and verse 9, "at your right hand stands the queen in gold of Ophir."

f. According to W. C. Kaiser, Jr., "there are some 456 Old Testament passages that refer to the Messiah or messianic times attested in 558 separate quotations from the Rabbinic writings"; see "Messianic Prophecies in the Old Testament," in C. E. Armerding and W. W. Gasque, eds., *Dreams, Visions, and Oracles*, p. 75, citing A. Edersheim, *The Life and Times of Jesus the Messiah* (New York: Herrick, n.d.), vol.2, Appendix 9, pp. 710–741. J. L. McKenzie, in *Myths and Realities* (Milwaukee, WI: Bruce, 1963), finds 75 allusions to Christ in the Old Testament (p. 233), and O. J. Nave, in *Nave's Topical Bible* (Lincoln, NE: Topical Bible Publishing, 1905), lists 62 Old Testament passages together with the New Testament passages in which the fulfillment is found (pp. 1009f.).

g. Hebrew *mālē'* means "be full, fill" (BDB, pp. 569–570), and the meaning of Greek *pleroō* is quite similar (A-G, pp. 676–678).

h. It is sometimes claimed that the word "Messiah" does occur in Daniel 9:25,26. However, the word in both instances is without the definite article, and the word order in verse 25 requires the reading, "an anointed one, a Prince." The adjective must stand *after* the word it modifies; see W. S. LaSor, *Handbook of Biblical Hebrew* (Grand Rapids, MI: Eerdmans, 1979), 2: §36.12.

i. See W. S. LaSor, *The Dead Sea Scrolls and the New Testament*, pp. 98–99, and the quotation from J. Coppens, *L'attente du Messie*.

j. In modern Jerusalem, Zion is the southwestern hill, where the "Tomb of David" is located. However, the correct original location is on the southeastern spur south of the Temple Mount. For evidence, cf. W. S. LaSor, "Jerusalem III.C.1.b," *ISBE* 2 (1982): 1006.

k. The word "Zion" occurs 154 times in the Old Testament, of which 38 occurrences are in Psalms and 47 in Isaiah. The word is sometimes used for all of Jerusalem; cf. Amos 6:7; Micah 3:10, and so forth.

l. Cf. Klausner, *The Messianic Idea*, pp. 7–25; G. Scholem, *The Messianic Idea in Judaism*, (New York: Schocken, 1971), pp. 4–17.

m. Cf. Klausner, *The Messianic Idea*, pp. 496–497; C. G. Montefiore and H. Loewe, *A Rabbinic Anthology*, reprinted (New York: Schocken, 1974), pp. 584–586.

n. But cf. W. S. LaSor, "The Messiahs of Aaron and Israel," *Vetus Testamentum* 6 (1956): 425–429; *The Dead Sea Scrolls and the New Testament*, pp. 100–102.

o. Whether we accept these as historical (I do) or as a product of the creative imagination of the early Church makes no difference on this point: this is what the early Church believed.

p. See G. E. Ladd, "Apocalyptic Literature," *ISBE* 1 (1979): 151–161; P. D. Hanson, "Apocalypse, Genre" and "Apocalypticism," *IDB* Supplementary Volume (1976): 28–34.

q. Sanhedrin 99a; cf. 4 Ezra 7:28; Klausner, *The Messianic Idea*, pp. 354f., 408–426; Montefiore and Loewe, *A Rabbinic Anthology*, pp. 598–599. The length of the messianic age in Rabbinic writings is uncertain, ranging from 40 years to 365,000 years; cf. G. F. Moore, *Judaism in the First Centuries of the Christian Era*, 2: 376 and n.6 thereto.

r. Klausner, *The Messianic Idea*, p. 10 (italics his). Klausner recognized that the first Christians, "the 'chiliasts,'" looked for Jesus the Messiah to return and set up the millennial kingdom, "filled with bodily and earthly pleasure, precisely as did the Jews."

ADDITIONAL READING

Bentzen, Aage. *King and Messiah*. London: Lutterworth, 1948.

Browne, L. E. *The Messianic Hope in its Historical Setting*. London: S.P.C.K., 1951.

Chafer, Lewis Sperry. *The Kingdom in History and Prophecy*. New York: Revell, 1915.

Delitzsch, Franz. *Messianische Weissagungen in geschichtliche Folge*. 2d ed. Berlin: Evangelisch Buch- und Traktat Gesellschaft, 1899; English translation, *Messianic Prophecies in Historical Succession* (from 1st German edition). New York: Scribner's, 1891.

Drummond, S. *The Jewish Messiah: A Critical History of the Messianic Ideas of the Jews from the Rise of the Maccabees to the Closing of the Talmud.* London: Longmans, Green, 1877.

Egnell, I. *Studies in Divine Kingship.* 2d ed. London: Basil Blackwell, 1967.

Frankfort, H. *Kingship and the Gods.* Chicago: University of Chicago Press, 1948.

Hooke, S. H. *The Labyrinth.* London: SPCK, 1935.

Hebert, A. G. *The Throne of David: A Study of the Fulfilment of the Old Testament in Jesus Christ and His Church.* London: Faber and Faber, 1941.

Heinisch, Paul. *Christ in Prophecy.* Translated by W. G. Heidt. Collegeville, MN: Liturgical Press, 1957.

Hengstenberg, E. W. *Christology of the Old Testament and a Commentary on the Messianic Predictions.* 1854. Reprinted Grand Rapids, MI: Kregel, 1956.

Holden, Richard, and Ridout, Samuel. *The Mystery; The Kingdom of Heaven.* Two works bound in one volume. New York: Loizeaux, n.d.

Huffman, J. A. *The Progressive Unfolding of the Messianic Hope.* New York: G. H. Doran, 1924.

Johnson, A. R. "The Role of the King in the Jerusalem Cultus." In *The Labyrinth,* edited by S. H. Hooke. London: SPCK, 1935. Pp. 135ff.

Lagrange, M. J. *Le messianisme chez les juifs.* Paris: Lecoffre, 1909.

Manson, W. *Jesus the Messiah.* Philadelphia: Westminster, 1946.

Kik, J. Marcellus. *An Eschatology of Victory.* Nutley, NJ: Presbyterian and Reformed, 1971.

Mowinckel, S. *He That Cometh.* New York: Abingdon, 1955.

Klausner, Joseph. *The Messianic Idea in Israel: From Its Beginning to the Completion of the Mishnah.* Translated by W. F. Stinespring. London: Allen and Unwin, 1956.

Lagrange, M.-J. *Le messianisme chez les juifs.* Paris: Lecoffre, 1909.

LaSor, William Sanford. "The Messiah: An Evangelical Christian View." In *Evangelicals and Jews in Conversation on Scripture, Theology, and History,* edited by M. H. Tanenbaum, M. R. Wilson, and A. J. Rudin. Grand Rapids, MI: Baker, 1978. pp. 76–95.

_____. "The Messiahs of Aaron and Israel." *Vetus Testamentum* 6 (1956): 425–429.

_____. "The Messianic Idea in Qumran." In *Studies and Essays in Honor of Abraham A. Neuman,* edited by M. Ben-Horin, B. D. Weinryb, and S. Zeitlin. Leiden: Brill, 1962. Pp. 343–364.

Manson, W. *Jesus the Messiah.* Philadelphia: Westminster, 1943.

McKenzie, J. L. "Royal Messianism." *Catholic Biblical Quarterly* 19 (1957): 25–52. Reprinted in *Myths and Realities.* Milwaukee: Bruce, 1963. Pp. 203–231.

"Messiah." *NDB.* Pp. 811–818.

Mowinckel, Sigmund. *He That Cometh.* Translated by G. W. Anderson. New York: Abingdon, 1955.

O'Doherty, E. "The Organic Development of Messianic Revelation." *Catholic Biblical Quarterly* 19 (1957): 16–25.

Reich, M. I. *The Messianic Hope of Israel.* Grand Rapids, MI: Eerdmans, 1940.
Ringgren, Helmer. *The Messiah in the Old Testament.* London: SCM, 1956.
Scholem, G. G. *The Messianic Idea in Judaism.* New York: Schocken, 1971.
Young, E. J. "The Immanuel Prophecy Isaiah 7:14–16." *Westminster Theological Journal* 15 (1952/53): 97–124; 16 (1953/54): 23–50.

8. The Second Coming
of Christ

The Problem

The expression "second coming" is not found in the New Testament. Yet belief in the "Second Coming of Christ" at the present time has reached almost a fever pitch. In the many books and articles that have appeared and are continuing to appear there is much truth, but—as must be the case with products of the limited human mind—there is also much error. The substance of the error is usually more sensational, hence more interesting and newsworthy. And when it is exposed and proven to be error, it is again newsworthy, and it also serves a satanic purpose of bringing ridicule on the Bible and on those who take it seriously. Witness a recent group in Arizona who followed a teacher who believed that the Second Coming would occur in June 1981.[a]

Interest in the coming of Christ is not a new phenomenon. In the years just before and after the birth of Jesus, there was widespread anticipation of the coming of the Messiah, and a number of persons claimed to be he. Even some Romans got caught up in this hope of a coming savior.[b] In the first century, hope in the return of Christ and fear that it had already taken place gave rise to questions that Paul sought to answer in the Thessalonian letters.[1] Around the year A.D. 1000, those who had accepted something akin to the Postmillennialist view (see Chapter 12) believed that the Millennium was drawing to a close and the Return was near. Other "prophetic" dates were 1260, 1560, 1844, 1934, and 1941—to which we might add the date 1984, which at this writing is still in the future.[c]

Yet it must be maintained that extreme views of enthusiasts and

---

1. Cf. 1 Thess. 4:13–5:11; 2 Thess. 2:1–11.

eccentrics of themselves do not invalidate truth in any department of human thought.[d] The doctrine of the Return of Christ, by whatever name it is called, is a scriptural doctrine and therefore to be accepted as authoritative by all who receive the Scriptures as the word of God. These Scriptures, I might add, include strong sanctions against date setting in any form.

The Universal Faith of the Church

To speak of "the universal faith of the Church" is, in the present age, somewhat presumptuous. However, there was a time when the Church formulated creedal statements of what it believed to be the authoritative teaching of Holy Scripture, and a comparison of these will sustain the position that belief in the Return of Jesus Christ at the end of the age was the faith of all Christians.

The Creedal Statements. The *Apostles' Creed* is possibly the earliest of the creeds and certainly the briefest. We reject, of course, the legend that the creed was composed by the twelve apostles, each of whom spontaneously recited a clause. More likely is the view that it was developed in Rome in the second century, then refined and rephrased in various parts of the Church.[e] After affirming the ascension of Jesus into heaven, it continues with the statement, "From whence he shall come to judge the quick and the dead." The *Nicene Creed,* which is sometimes called the "Nicene-Constantinopolitan Creed," comes from the Council of Constantinople (A.D. 381), probably an enlarged form of a creed adopted by the Council of Nicea (A.D. 325). It includes the statement "and shall come again in glory to judge the living and the dead."[f] The so-called *Athanasian Creed* reads, "Ascended into heaven, sat down at the right hand of the Father: to come from thence to judge the quick and the dead. At whose coming all men shall rise again with their bodies; and shall give account for their deeds (sections 39, 40). Historically, these three creeds (later, the "Athanasian" was removed from this category) have been recognized as universal creeds or symbols of the Church.[g]

In Protestantism, the Lutheran and Reformed branches likewise have clear statements concerning the Return of Christ. The *Augsburg Confession* states: "They [the Scriptures] also teach that Christ will appear at the end of the world for judgment, and that He will raise all the dead, and that He will give to the pious elect eternal life and perpetual joy, but condemn wicked men and devils, that they shall be tormented without end.[h]

The *Westminster Confession* contains no single clear statement of the doctrine, but the *Larger Catechism* states: "Christ is to be exalted in His coming again to judge the world, in that He, who was unjustly judged and condemned by wicked men, shall come again at the last day in great power, and in the full manifestation of His own glory and of His Father's, with all His holy angels, with a shout, with the voice of the archangel, and with the trumpet of God, to judge the world in righteousness" (Q. 36).

The New Testament.   Creedal statements, symbols, or confessions are not in themselves authoritative. They represent merely the expressions of the Church concerning what it believes to be taught in the canonical Scriptures. It is therefore more important to examine the biblical statements concerning the Return of Christ.

Almost every book in the New Testament contains some statement relative to the Return of Christ. The only exceptions are 2 and 3 John and Philemon, each of which consists of only one chapter. The epistles to Galatians and Ephesians do not contain explicit statements, but the doctrine is certainly implicit. Thus Galatians 5:5 reads: "For through the Spirit, by faith, we wait for the hope of righteousness." Ephesians contains the statements: "And do not grieve the Holy Spirit of God, in whom you were sealed for the day of redemption"[2] and "Be sure of this, that no immoral or impure man, or one who is covetous (that is, an idolater), has any inheritance in the kingdom of Christ and of God"[3] (where the word "inheritance" looks forward to something to be bestowed in the future). It would serve no important purpose to list here the references in the other twenty-two books, since these can be found in other places.[i] In fact, no work that I have consulted denies that the New Testament *teaches* that Jesus will return; the modern problem is one of *interpretation.*[j]

The Old Testament.   Since the first Christians were Jews who believed that the "Scriptures," that is, the Old Testament, were authoritative for faith, they combed these writings to justify their

---

2. Eph. 4:30.   3. Eph. 5:5.

faith in Jesus.[4] We, too, accept the Old Testament along with the New as the word of God. Now it is obvious that the "Second Coming of Christ" is not mentioned in the Old Testament, for the term "Christ" (or "Messiah") does not occur there. It is also beyond dispute that the Jews had come to look for a Messiah on the basis of their Scriptures. When Jesus had completed his earthly work, many believed that he was the Messiah.

But fulfillment of the Old Testament prophecies requires more than occurred in the first advent of Christ. The Davidic covenant[5] promised that the throne of David's son would be established for ever.[6] Isaiah also proclaimed this promise,[7] as did Jeremiah[8] and Ezekiel,[9] as well as Amos,[10] Micah,[11] and Zechariah.[12] But Jesus did not occupy the throne of David in Zion and was not called "king" except in jest.[13] As a result, his disciples looked forward to the fulfillment.[14] The same line of reasoning can be applied to other elements of the messianic promises: the establishment of Israel (both parts of the divided kingdom[15]); the fertility of the land; longevity of the people; righteousness and justice on earth; peace among the nations; the coming of the Gentile rulers to Jerusalem to learn the ways of Yahweh, and so forth.

Some indication that Jesus had the power to fulfill the promises was given during his ministry. For example, when disciples of John the Baptizer came and asked Jesus, "Are you he who is to come, or shall we look for another?"[16] Jesus performed a number of miracles[17] and then said, "Go and tell John what you have seen and heard: the blind receive their sight, the lame walk, lepers are cleansed, and the deaf hear, the dead are raised up, the poor have good news preached to them."[18] Jesus' acts on that occasion were reminiscent of Isaiah's prophecies[19] and therefore testified to his messianic office. In a similar manner, other mighty works done by Jesus, such as raising the dead, multiplying the loaves and fishes, and calming the storm, were foretastes of what could be expected when he established his kingdom and were therefore token fulfillments of

---

4. Cf. John 5:39; Acts 17:11.   **5.** 2 Sam. 7.   **6.** 2 Sam. 7:13,16; cf. Ps. 89:4,29,36.   **7.** Isa. 9:6,7.   **8.** Jer. 23:5,6.   **9.** Ezek. 34:12–15,23,24; 37: 24–28.   **10.** Amos 9:11.   **11.** Mic. 4:1,2; 5:2 (MT 1).   **12.** Zech. 9:9, 10.   **13.** John 19:3.   **14.** Acts 1:6.   **15.** Ezek. 37:19–22.   **16.** Luke 7:20.   **17.** Luke 7:21.   **18.** Luke 7:22.   **19.** Cf. Isa. 29:18,19; 35:5,6; 61:1.

prophecies. Above all, his own resurrection, as Paul recognized, was the sign of victory over the last enemy, death itself.[20] The Old Testament prophecies require another advent of the Messiah to complete the fulfillment of the promises. The disciples and the early Church believed this. We, too, should believe it.

The Terms Used

If the term "second coming" does not occur in the Bible,[k] what terms are used to refer to the Return of Christ? A study of this terminology will help us understand more of the doctrine itself.

"Coming." The usual term is "coming," particularly the participial form used as a noun, "the coming one."[l] (The expression "the coming one" is often disguised by translation.) The disciples of John the Baptizer asked, "Are you he who is to come (*ho erchomenos*)?"[21] The people said of Jesus, "This is indeed the prophet who is to come (*ho erchomenos*) into the world."[22] The author of Hebrews, quoting Isa. 26:20 (LXX), said, "For yet a little while, and the coming one shall come and shall not tarry."[23] And the Revelator wrote, "Grace to you and peace from him who is and who was and who is to come [lit. the coming one]."[24]

"The coming one," an Old Testament term, came to be used in the Intertestamental Period of the coming Son of Man. For example, in Psalm 118:26 (LXX 117:26) we read "Blessed be he who enters in the name of the Lord!" (LXX reads "the one coming in the name of the Lord"). In Habakkuk 2:3 (RSV), "If it seem slow, wait for it [the vision]; it will surely come, it will not delay"; the Septuagint renders the Hebrew "though he should tarry, wait for him, for the coming one shall come and he shall not delay." Daniel 7:13, which doubtless gave rise to expressions such as that found in Ascension of Isaiah 11:1, reads (RSV) "and behold, with the clouds of heaven, there came one like a son of man," but the Septuagint could be read "behold, with the clouds of heaven, like a coming son of man."[m]

"Parousia." The Greek word *parousia,* "advent," has been taken over into English, referring particularly to the Second Ad-

---

20. Cf. 1 Cor. 15:20–27.   **21.** Matt. 11:3; Luke 7:19f.   **22.** John 6:14. **23.** Heb. 10:37.   **24.** Rev. 1:4.

vent of Christ.° It can be used of the (first) advent of a person (of the coming of Titus;[25] of Christ's first advent[26]), of the presence of a person (of Paul's presence[27]), or of a future advent, usually with reference to Christ. The disciples asked Jesus, "What will be the sign of your coming (*parousia*) and of the close of the age?"[28] Paul wrote, "The coming (*parousia*) of the lawless one by the activity of Satan will be with all power. . . ."[29] James said, "Be patient, therefore, brethren, until the coming (*parousia*) of the Lord."[30] The context will usually make clear whether the "presence" is past, present, or future.

"*Epiphany.*"   The Greek word *epiphaneia*,[b] "appearing, appearance," has also been taken over into English, meaning "appearance," usually of a deity, or referring to the feast of Epiphany. It is used of Jesus' first appearance: "[God] now has manifested through the appearing (*epiphaneia*) of our Savior Christ Jesus."[31] It is also used of his second appearance: "I charge you in the presence of God and of Christ Jesus who is to judge the living and the dead, and by his appearing (*epiphaneia*) and his kingdom."[32] Note that Paul uses the word in both senses in the same letter, and that the context in each instance makes the meaning perfectly clear.

"*Revelation.*"   The Greek word *apokalypsis*,[q] "revelation, disclosure," has given us the English word "apocalypse." It is used of the Second Coming in 2 Thessalonians 1:7, "when the Lord Jesus is revealed from heaven with his mighty angels in flaming fire," literally "in the revelation (*apokalypsis*) of Jesus. . . ." Peter also uses the word: "so that the genuineness of your faith . . . may redound to praise and glory and honor at the revelation of Jesus Christ."[33] All three terms occur in a single sentence, the first in a verb form: "And then the lawless one will be revealed (*apokalyptein*), and the Lord Jesus will slay him with the breath of his mouth and destroy him by his appearing (*epiphaneia*) and his coming (*parousia*)," literally, "by the appearance of his coming."[34]

"*Be Seen,*" "*Appear.*"   The passive voice of the verb "to see," often translated "to appear" (= "to be seen") is also used of the

---

25. 2 Cor. 7:6,7.   **26.** 2 Pet. 1:16.   **27.** Phil. 1:12.   **28.** Matt. 24:3.
29. 2 Thess. 2:9.   **30.** James 5:7.   **31.** 2 Tim. 1:10.   **32.** 2 Tim. 4:1.
33. 1 Pet. 1:7; cf. 1:13.   **34.** 2 Thess. 2:8.

Second Advent of Jesus. Thus the statement, "so Christ, having been offered once to bear the sins of many, will appear [lit. be seen] a second time, not to deal with sin but to save those who are eagerly waiting for him."[35] The active form of the same verb is used, "will see," in the promise of his coming.[36]

Implications. From the words used, it would seem that Christ's "appearing" or "presence" (or advent) is looked upon as enduring, age-long, rather than cut into two pieces that are more or less discrete. In further studies we shall have to take this up in more depth. There is a sense in which the view that we are now living in the end time is true. There is also a sense in which it is not true, for there are many elements of the redemption that Christ accomplished that have not taken place, for which the whole creation groans and travails, and for which we wait.[37] But any system that suggests that, had the Jews accepted Jesus as Messiah the kingdom would have been immediately set up, does not take into account that the "advent" of Christ includes the entire redemptive process from the incarnation of the Son until the kingdom is delivered up to the Father.

Jesus' Teaching Concerning His Return

Some students of the Bible tend to place more significance on the "dominical teachings," or those portions of the New Testament that are given as the words of Jesus. This opens up a whole realm of thought into which we cannot enter here,[r] but we must indeed look at Jesus' teachings on the subject.

Development of the Teaching. Obviously Jesus could not give his disciples extensive teaching about his return until they were well indoctrinated in the necessity of his death and resurrection. There is no sense in saying "I will come again" to those who do not believe you are going away! The meaning of John 1:51, "you will see heaven opened, and the angels of God ascending and descending upon the Son of man," is not clear; it may refer to the end time. The choosing of the Twelve occurred about midway in Jesus' ministry, and it was followed by the Sermon on the Mount. It contains a passage that

---

35. Heb. 9:28.   **36.** Matt. 24:30; Mark 13:26; Luke 21:27.   **37.** Cf. Rom. 8:18–23.

seems to refer to the end time[38] (note "on that day"). The woes on Chorazin, Bethsaida, and Capernaum[39] link Jesus with the final judgment.

But clearer teachings of his relationship to the end of the age are found in the Parables of the Kingdom.[40] From this point on the teachings are more frequent and pointed.[41] After Peter's confession at Caesarea-Philippi[42] Jesus "began to show his disciples" the necessity of the death and resurrection,[43] and the account finally includes the statement, "For the Son of man is to come with his angels in the glory of his Father."[44] In the Perean Ministry[45] there are a number of teachings relevant to his presence at the end of the age. Luke 10:23,24 strongly suggests that his disciples were looking upon the fulfillment of the prophecies of the prophets. The judgment to come on his generation was based on its rejection of his words and works.[46] When Jesus said, "You also must be ready; for the Son of man is coming at an hour you do not expect,"[47] Peter asked, "Are you telling this parable for us or for all?" Jesus replied by speaking of a faithful and wise steward who is found doing his master's will "when he comes."[48] When he was warned that Herod sought to kill him, he expressed a lament over Jerusalem and added, "I tell you, you will not see me until you say, 'Blessed be he whom comes in the name of the Lord!'" He evaded the Pharisees' question about the coming of the Kingdom of God,[49] but he gave the disciples a clear teaching about his death, resurrection, and "the day when the Son of man is revealed."[50] The journey to Jerusalem[51] ended with the "triumphal entry," in deliberate fulfillment of Zechariah's prophecy.[52]

These teachings, taken by themselves, do not set forth a doctrine of "second coming." It would be possible to draw the conclusion that, except for the teachings concerning his death and resurrection, the end of the age was at hand. Judgment was about to be visited upon "this generation." But this is further clarified in the teachings of the last week before the Crucifixion.

---

38. Matt. 7:22,23.   **39.** Matt. 11:20–27; cf. 12:38–42.   **40.** Matt. 13, esp. vv. 37–42.   **41.** Cf. John 6:38–40.   **42.** Matt. 16:21.   **43.** Matt. 16:21.   **44.** Matt. 16:27.   **45.** Luke 9:51–18:34.   **46.** Luke 11:29–32. **47.** Luke 12:40.   **48.** Luke 12:43.   **49.** Luke 17:20,21.   **50.** Luke 17:22–30.   **51.** Luke 19:28; cf. 9:51.   **52.** Luke 19:29–38; cf. Zech. 9:9.

The Closing Teachings.   Jesus, after an exchange of words with the Pharisees and chief priests, said "the kingdom of God will be taken away from you and given to a nation producing the fruits of it."[53] "They perceived that he was speaking about them." This led to further exchanges, and Jesus put to them the question about the Messiah, the son of David.[54]

At last it was getting through to the disciples that Jesus could not immediately set up the kingdom, so they asked, "What will be the sign of your coming and of the close of the age?"[55] His reply is full of details.[56] The account of the Last Supper contains a promise of his coming,[57] and Paul wrote, "For as often as you eat this bread and drink the cup, you proclaim the Lord's death until he comes."[58] The risen Christ, replying to Peter's question about John, used the words, "until I come,"[59] which in context can only mean his return to earth.[5]

In the Fourth Gospel we find important teachings on the subject. That he was about to leave them is beyond question.[60] The disciples understood this.[61] There is some question, however, about the interpretation of his words. For example, when he said, "I will come again,"[62] was he talking about his return at the end of the age, or (as some interpreters hold) about coming for his own at their death? Again, when he said, "I will not leave you desolate; I will come to you,"[63] was he speaking of his return in glory, or of his coming in the Spirit, of which he had just spoken?[64] And when he said, "a little while, and you will see me no more; again a little while, and you will see me"[65]—a question that caused his disciples some difficulty of understanding—was he speaking about his return at the end of the age or his appearances after the resurrection?[66]

Once again we see that the "advent" of Jesus is a complex subject. It is the belief of the Church that Jesus is with us now. It is also the belief of the Church that he is coming again at the end of the age. Both items of faith are based on the Scripture. Both statements are true.

---

53. Matt. 21:43.   **54.** Matt. 22:41–45.   **55.** Matt. 24:3.   **56.** Cf. Matt. 24:30,42,44; 25:31.   **57.** Matt. 26:29; Luke 22:16.   **58.** 1 Cor. 11:26. **59.** John 21:22.   **60.** John 13:33; 14:25; 15:26; 16:5,16,28.   **61.** John 16:29.   **62.** John 14:3.   **63.** John 14:18.   **64.** John 14:16,17. **65.** John 16:16.   **66.** John 16:22.

The Manner of His Coming

From passages quoted and additional materials in the Bible it is possible to offer certain propositions concerning the manner of the Return of Christ. An objection is sometimes made that this is done by pasting together verses from various portions of the Bible, often without regard for context. The objection to a greater or lesser degree, depending on the work under consideration, is valid. On the other hand, there is practically no subject in the field of biblical theology for which there is a systematic treatment in the Scriptures. Biblical theology seeks to take biblical teachings and organize them into categories and subjects and ultimately into a system of theology. The doctrine of the Parousia has to be developed in this same way.

Public and Visible. The Return of Christ will be a public event. Jesus said, "they [all the tribes of earth] will see the Son of man coming on the clouds of heaven with power and great glory."[67] At the ascension, the men "in white robes" told the disciples, "This Jesus, who was taken up from you into heaven, will come in the same way as you saw him go into heaven."[68] Paul wrote, "The Lord himself will descend from heaven with a cry of command, with the archangel's call, and with the sound of the trumpet of God."[69] The Revelator declares, "Behold, he is coming with the clouds, and every eye will see him, every one who pierced him; and all the tribes of the earth will wail on account of him."[70]

To raise a question concerning the possibility of everyone seeing the Return, since on a global earth some are on opposite sides, some in daylight and others in darkness, is rather puerile, particularly in these days of television and space vehicles. Moreover, the common use of language, including that of the Bible, allows an expression such as "every eye" or "all the tribes" to be a generalization. The Return of Christ will be a public event, not private like the first advent in Bethlehem's stable or the ascension on the Mount of Olives. The whole world will know that he has returned.

In Great Power and Glory. Jesus said, "The Son of man is to come with his angels in the glory of his Father."[71] Again, he said:

---

67. Matt. 24:30. **68.** Acts 1:11. **69.** 1 Thess. 4:16. **70.** Rev. 1:7.
71. Matt. 16:27; cf. 24:30.

"When the Son of man comes in his glory, and all the angels with him, then he will sit on his glorious throne. Before him will be gathered all the nations."[72] And again: "For whoever is ashamed of me and of my words, of him will the Son of man be ashamed when he comes in his glory and the glory of the Father and of the holy angels."[73] Paul wrote: "But our commonwealth is in heaven, and from it we await a Savior, the Lord Jesus Christ, who will change our lowly body to be like his glorious body,"[74] and to Titus he included the words, "awaiting our blessed hope, the appearing of the glory of our great God and Savior Jesus Christ."[75]

The first advent was in great humility: he was born under circumstances which were even lower than those of the average "poor" family, tempted in all points as we are (yet without sin), despised and rejected of men, unjustly condemned to death on the cross, buried in a borrowed tomb. The Second Advent will be in great glory, fulfilling the vision of Daniel.[76]

Like a Thief in the Night.   The Second Advent will be sudden and unexpected, "like a thief."[77] Peter probably got this expression from Jesus, who said: "Watch therefore, for you do not know on what day your Lord is coming. But know this, that if the householder had known in what part of the night the thief was coming, he would have watched. . . . Therefore you also must be ready; for the Son of man is coming at an hour you do not expect."[78]

The time of his return has not been disclosed. "Watch therefore, for you know neither the day nor the hour."[79] "But of that day or that hour no one knows, not even the angels in heaven, nor the Son, but only the Father."[80] When the disciples asked the risen Jesus, "Lord, will you at this time restore the kingdom to Israel?" he replied, "It is not for you to know times or seasons which the Father has fixed by his own authority."[81] Paul gave the Thessalonian church similar advice: "But as to the times and the seasons, brethren, you have no need to have anything written to you. For you yourselves know well that the day of the Lord will come like a thief in the night."[82]

Preceded by Certain Signs.   In spite of the fact that the time of

---

72. Matt. 25:31.   73. Luke 9:26.   74. Phil. 3:20,21.   75. Tit. 2:13.
76. Dan. 7:13,14.   77. 2 Pet. 3:10.   78. Matt. 24:42-44.   79. Matt.
25:13.   80. Mark 13:32.   81. Acts 1:6,7.   82. 1 Thess. 5:1,2.

the Return is unknown, there are certain "signs of the times" that will precede the coming of Christ. Jesus named a number of them in the "Olivet Discourse":[83] "wars and rumors of wars,"[84] "famines and earthquakes,"[85] "tribulation,"[86] "Jerusalem will be trodden down by the Gentiles,"[87] "many will fall away,"[88] "false prophets will arise,"[89] "wickedness is multiplied,"[90] "and this gospel of the kingdom will be preached throughout the whole world, as a testimony to all nations; and then the end will come."[91] The following expressions in this passage seem to enlarge on some of the elements already mentioned: "great tribulation,"[92] and immediately after that, "the sun will be darkened, and the moon will not give its light, and the stars will fall from heaven, and the powers of the heavens will be shaken; then will appear the sign of the Son of man in heaven."[93]

Paul elaborates on the apostasy of the end of the age: "that day will not come, unless the rebellion comes first, and the man of lawlessness is revealed, the son of perdition";[94] "in the last days there will come times of stress."[95] So does Peter: "Scoffers will come in the last days with scoffing, following their own passions and saying, 'Where is the promise of his coming?' "[96] John also speaks of this apostasy: "Children, it is the last hour; and as you have heard that antichrist is coming, so now many antichrists have come; therefore we know that it is the last hour"[97] (he enlarges this theme later[98]). According to one system of interpretation, the book of Revelation gives many details of the period leading up to the Return of Christ.[99]

Soon. At the close of the book of Revelation, Jesus says, "Surely I am coming soon."[100] James said, "The coming of the Lord is at hand."[101] Peter likewise said, "The end of all things is at hand."[102] Because of this teaching, some have claimed that the "Second Coming" is really two advents: first "for his saints," which can occur at any moment, and second "with his saints," which takes place after the Great Tribulation. Others have suggested that the early Church

83. Matt. 24 and Mark 13.   84. Matt. 24:6.   85. Matt. 24:7.
86. Matt. 24:9.   87. Luke 21:24.   88. Matt. 24:10.   89. Matt. 24:11.
90. Matt. 24:12.   91. Matt. 24:14.   92. Matt. 24:21.   93. Matt.
24:29,30.   94. 2 Thess. 2:3.   95. 2 Tim. 3:1; cf. 2 Tim. 3:2–7.   96. 2
Pet. 3:3,4.   97. 1 John 2:18.   98. 1 John 2:19–28.   99. Rev. 4:1–19:11.
100. Rev. 22:20.   101. James 5:8.   102. 1 Pet. 4:7.

expected the Return to take place within that generation and they were greatly mistaken. Still others hold that the Greek word *tachy* means "quickly" rather than "soon," and that the passage is intended to teach that once the final process begins, it proceeds quickly to its conclusion.[1]

In a sense, the only scriptural position is one of tension between the "at-any-moment" hope and the practicality of long-range planning. To lose the hope of the imminent Return is to move toward the scoffer's question, "Where is the hope of his coming?" To set a date for the Return and sell out any investment in the future is to turn over whatever is left of a future for us and our loved ones to the satanic forces of this world. The attitude of the Thessalonian Christians was good: "to serve a living and true God, and to wait for his Son from heaven."[103]

Remaining Questions

Is the Coming of the Spirit the Second Coming of Christ?   Some have taught that the only Return of Christ to be expected took place when the Spirit was given. This is sometimes based on passages in John.[104] But at the Ascension, the promises of the Spirit and of the Return of Christ are placed side by side.[105] Peter ascribed the Pentecostal phenomena to the fulfillment of Joel's prophecy[106] and attributed it to Christ who was "exalted at the right hand of God."[107] It is true that Christ is with us always in this world. It is also true that he will come again to complete the work of redemption, as Paul clearly taught.[108]

Is the Death of the Believer the Second Coming of Christ?   It has also been taught that the Second Coming takes place when Jesus comes to take the believer from this life to the next. This is sometimes based on the words of Jesus: "And when I go and prepare a place for you, I will come again and will take you to myself, that where I am you may be also."[109] Paul, facing an uncertain future in prison, wrote the Philippian church: "For to me to live is Christ, and to die is gain. . . . My desire is to depart and be with Christ, for that is far better. But to remain in the flesh is more necessary on your

---

103. 1 Thess. 1:9,10.   **104.** E.g., John 14:16–18,25,26; 16:7–11. **105.** Acts 1:6–11.   **106.** Joel 2:15–21.   **107.** Joel 2:33.   **108.** Rom. 8:9–11,18–24.   **109.** John 14:3.

account."[110] But to the Thessalonians, stricken with grief because of the death of loved ones, he did not offer this comfort; rather he proclaimed the Return of Christ, stating, "the dead in Christ will rise first; then we who are alive, who are left, shall be caught up together with them in the clouds to meet the Lord in the air; and so we shall always be with the Lord. Therefore comfort one another with these words."[111]

Summary

Jesus Christ will return to this earth, in his glorious resurrection body and with great power, at the end of the present age. Associated with his Return, although the order and the time schedule are not certain, are the resurrection of the dead, the establishment of the kingdom, the last judgment, and the destruction of Satan. These subjects will be considered in the following chapters.

NOTES

a. The group known as "The Lighthouse Gospel Tract Foundation," led by Bill Maupin, was located in Tucson. He originally calculated that the Rapture would take place on June 28, 1981. Some members of the group quit their jobs and/or sold their houses. When that date passed, Maupin said he had miscalculated by forty days, and predicted that the Rapture would take place on August 7, 1981. The Return of Christ is to occur May 14, 1988. Maupin calculated his dates on the basis of Daniel's seventy "weeks," and the founding of the State of Israel on May 15, 1948. My information is from the *Arizona Republic* by courtesy of Richard Lessner.

b. See Tacitus *History* 5.13, Suetonius *Vespasian* 4, and especially Virgil *Eclogue* 4 4–54.

c. For a survey of various views see D. H. Kromminga, *The Millennium in the Church* (Grand Rapids, MI: Eerdmans, 1945), pp. 125–241. In my opinion, Kromminga has needlessly complicated his study by including under the term "Chiliasm" all sorts of eschatological systems.

d. See R. G. Clouse, "The Danger of Mistaken Hopes," in C. F. Armerding and W. W. Gasque, eds., *Dreams, Visions, and Oracles*, pp. 27–39.

e. See A. Harnack, "Apostles' Creed," *New Schaff-Herzog Encyclopedia of Religious Knowledge*, reprint ed. (Grand Rapids, MI: Baker, 1949; original ed. 1907), 1: 242.

f. See W. Walker, *A History of the Christian Church*, rev. ed. (New York: Scribner, 1959), pp. 118, 138.

g. Thus, for example, Article VIII of the "Thirty-nine Articles of Religion" reads, "The Nicene Creed, and that which is commonly called the Apos-

---

110. Phil. 1:21–24.   111. 1 Thess. 4:16–18.

tles' Creed, ought thoroughly to be received and believed: for they may be proved by most certain warrants of Holy Scripture." See also F. Kattenbusch, "Symbolics," *New Schaff-Herzog Encyclopedia of Religious Knowledge*, 11: 200; and A. S. Wood, "Creeds and Confessions," *ISBE* 1 (1979): 805–812.

h. The statement goes on to condemn "others who scatter Jewish opinions, to the effect that before the resurrection of the dead the pious will occupy the kingdom of the world"—which seems to be aimed at Chiliasts, but certainly from a distorted understanding of Millennialism.

i. See O. J. Nave, *Nave's Topical Bible*, (Lincoln, NE: Topical Bible Publishing, 1905), pp. 734–737. Nave has omitted any reference to Romans. The Second Coming is certainly implicit in Romans 8:17–25, 28–30, 35–39, and clearly taught in 2:16; 11:25–26; 13:11–14; 15:8–13.

j. Thus H. K. McArthur in "Parousia," *IDB* 3, says: "Clearly primitive Christianity was an eschatological faith" (p. 660) and "The theological reinterpretation of the parousia concept deserves mention by way of conclusion. There are three basic possibilities: the entire eschatological pattern, of which the Parousia is a segment, may be regarded as part of the eternal Word and hence accepted with comparative literalness; the eschatological pattern may be discarded on the grounds that it was the temporal garb in which the eternal gospel appeared; or the eschatological pattern may be translated into other terms" (p. 661).

k. Hebrews 9:28 does say, "Christ, having been offered once to bear the sins of many, will appear a second time. . . ."

l. Greek *erchomai, ho erchomenos*, see *TDNT* 2: 668–675. It should be noted that the Greek present participle, like the Hebrew, has a timeless, continuous aspect, so that "the coming one" can be present or future or both.

m. Cf. *TDNT* 2: 667 and n. 7 thereto.

n. Cf. *TDNT* 5: 858–871.

o. *Webster's New International Dictionary, Unabridged*, s.v.

p. Cf. *TDNT* 9: 7–10.

q. Cf. *TDNT* 3: 560–592.

r. For example, are the teachings of Jesus more inspired than the rest of Scripture? Since we do not have his exact words, assuming that he spoke Aramaic or Hebrew and recognizing that the gospels are written in Greek, can we claim a higher authority for his words? Since the "assured" Pauline epistles are almost certainly earlier than the gospels, are they not more authentic? And so on. I personally accept the inspiration of the Spirit as applying to every part of the Bible; I believe that Jesus is the final Word, and that his teachings must be given high priority, and at the same time I believe that the New Testament writers were so inspired that their writings are equally authoritative. I do not set one against the other, but attempt to use all parts as constituting the authority of the whole.

s. It might be pointed out that teachings concerning the Parousia are found in *all* of the earliest sources: in "M," "L," "Mk," and "Q," of the synoptic sources; in Acts 1–12; in the Thessalonian letters; and (if we accept the early date of James) in James. See *IDB* 3: 660.

t. *Tachy* can mean either "without delay" or "speedily," see A-G, p. 814.

ADDITIONAL READING

Anderson, Robert. *The Coming Prince.* 13th ed. London: Pickering and Inglis, n.d.

Bultmann, Rudolf. "New Testament and Mythology." In *Kerygma and Myth,* edited by H. Bartsch. New York: Harper & Row, 1953.

―――. *Jesus Christ and Mythology.* New York: Scribner, 1958.

Brown, Raymond E. "The Sensus Plenior of Sacred Scripture." S.T.D. dissertation, Baltimore, MD: St. Mary's University, 1955.

―――. "The History and Development of the Theory of a *Sensus Plenior.*" *Catholic Biblical Quarterly* 15 (1953): 141–162.

―――. "The *Sensus Plenior* in the Last Ten Years." *Catholic Biblical Quarterly* 25 (1963): 262–285.

Brown, W. Adams. "Parousia." *HDB* 3: 674–680.

Chafer, Lewis Sperry. "Dispensationalism." *Bibliotheca Sacra* 93 (Oct. 1936): 390–449.

Cooper, D. L. *Messiah.* Los Angeles: Biblical Research Society, 1939.

Coppens, J. *Le messianisme royal, ses origines, son développement, son accomplissement.* Paris: Editions du Cerf, 1968.

―――. *L'espérance messianique, ses origines et son développement.* Louvain: Publications Universitaires de Louvain, 1963.

―――. *L'attente du Messie.* Bruges: Desclée de Brouwer, 1958.

Cullmann, O. "Die Hoffnung der Kirche auf die Wiederkunft Christi." *Verhandlungen des schweizerischen reformierten Pfarrvereins* 83 (1943): 34ff. English translation. "The Return of Christ: The New Testament Hope," in *The Early Church,* edited by A. J. B. Higgins. London: SCM Press, 1956.

Darby, John Nelson. *Collected Writings.* Edited by William Kelley. London: G. Morrish, 1967.

―――. *Lectures on the Second Coming.* London: G. Morrish, 1909.

Darmsteegt, P. Gerard. *Foundations of the Seventh-day Adventist Message and Mission.* Grand Rapids, MI: Eerdmans, 1977.

Delitzsch, F. J. *Messianische Weissagungen in geschichtliche Folge.* 2d ed. Berlin: Evangelisch Buch- und Traktat Gesellschaft, 1899; English translation, *Messianic Prophecies in Historical Succession* (from 1st German edition). New York: Scribner's, 1891.

Dodd, C. H. *The Parables of the Kingdom.* London: Nisbet, 1948.

Douglas, Herbert E. *The End: The Unique Voice of Adventists About the Return of Jesus.* Mountain View, CA: Pacific Press, 1979.

Edersheim, Alfred. *The Life and Times of Jesus the Messiah.* 2 vols. New York: Herrick, n.d.

―――. *Prophecy and History in Relation to the Messiah.* 1880. Reprint. Grand Rapids, MI: Baker, 1955.

Ehlert, Arnold D. *A Bibliographic History of Dispensationalism.* Grand Rapids, MI: Baker, 1965.

Ellison, H. L. *The Centrality of the Messianic Idea for the Old Testament.* London: Tyndale, 1967.

Engnell, I. *Studies in Divine Kingship in the Ancient Near East.* 2d ed. London: Basil Blackwell, 1967.

Erdman, Charles R. *The Return of Christ.* New York: Doran, 1922.

————. *The Revelation of John.* Philadelphia: Westminster, 1936.

Erdman, William J. *The Return of Christ.* Germantown, PA: p.p., 1913.

————. *Notes on the Revelation.* New York: Revell, 1930.

Frankfort, H. *Kingship and the Gods.* Chicago: University of Chicago Press, 1948.

Grant, F. W. *The Mysteries of the Kingdom of Heaven.* New York: Loizeaux, n.d.

————. *The Revelation of Christ to His Servants.* New York: Loizeaux, n.d.

Gray, James M., ed. *The Coming and Kingdom of Christ.* Chicago: Bible Institute Colportage Association, 1914.

Haldeman, I. M. *The Coming of Christ.* Los Angeles: Bible House, 1906.

Haynes, Carlyle B. *Our Lord's Return.* Rev. ed. Nashville, TN: Southern Publishing, 1964.

Jeremias, Joachim. *Jesus' Promise to the Nations.* Naperville, IL: Allenson, 1958.

Johnson, A. R. "The Role of the King in the Jerusalem Cultus." In *The Labyrinth,* edited by S. H. Hooke. London: SPCK, 1935. Pp. 135ff.

Kümmel, W. G. *Promise and Fulfilment: The Eschatological Message of Jesus.* 2d Eng. ed. London: SCM, 1961.

Ladd, George E. *The Blessed Hope.* Grand Rapids, MI: Eerdmans, 1956.

LaSor, William Sanford. "The Last Word." *The Presbyterian* 111 (7 Aug. 1941): 6–7.

————. "He Is Coming." *Moody Monthly* 45 (Oct. 1944): 72, 113.

————. "Have the 'Times of the Gentiles' Been Fulfilled?" *Eternity* 18 (Aug. 1967): 32–34.

Lindsey, Hal. *There's A New World Coming.* Santa Ana, CA: Vision House, 1973; New York: Bantam, 1975.

Mackintosh, C. H. *Papers on the Lord's Coming.* Chicago: Bible Institute Colportage Association, n.d.

Manson, W. *Jesus the Messiah.* London: Philadelphia: Westminster, 1946.

Moltmann, Jurgen. "Theology as Eschatology." In *The Future of Hope: Theology as Eschatology,* edited by F. Herzog. New York: Herder and Herder, 1970.

Munhall, L. W. *The Lord's Return and Kindred Truth.* 8th ed. Philadelphia: Munhall, 1895.

Pache, René. *Le Retour de Jesus Christ.* n.p., n.d. Translated by W. S. LaSor. *The Return of Jesus Christ.* Chicago: Moody, 1955.

Payne, J. Barton. *The Imminent Appearing of Christ.* Grand Rapids, MI: Eerdmans, 1962.

Reese, Alexander. *The Approaching Advent of Christ.* London: Marshall, Morgan & Scott, n.d.

Riley, W. B. "The Last Days; the Last War and the Last King." In *Christ and*

Glory, edited by A. C. Gaebelein. New York: "Our Hope," n.d. (ca. 1919). Pp. 163–176.

Robinson, James A. T. *In The End, God*. New York: Harper & Row, 1968.

————. *Jesus and His Coming*. New York: Abingdon, 1957.

Schweitzer, Albert. *The Quest of the Historical Jesus*. New York: Macmillan, 1961.

Scofield, C. I. *Rightly Dividing the Word of Truth*. Oakland, CA: Western Book and Tract, n.d.

Silver, Jesse F. *The Lord's Return*. 7th ed. New York: Revell, 1914.

9. The Antichrist

The Problem

Who or what is the Antichrist? Is it a power or force that is opposed to the spirit of Christianity? It is a person who is opposed to God and/or to God's Anointed? Is this Antichrist in the world now, or is it/he to come in the end time?

Many variations of these questions could be and have been asked, and many answers have been given. For example, Protestants since Reformation days have often held that the pope in Rome is the Antichrist, or (a slight variation) that the Roman church is the Antichrist. Two objections have been raised to this interpretation: (1) the Antichrist must be a Jew[1]—obviously not true of the pope—and (2) the spirit of Antichrist denies the incarnation[2]—which the Roman church has never done. The theory that the Antichrist must be a Jew is, however, not without its opponents. The Antichrist has often been identified with the "beast which rose out of the earth,"[3] and he is identified by the number "666." Many attempts have been made to identify the Antichrist by this number, as we shall see.

There was a popular belief in the first century that "antichrist is coming."[4] Except for the few references to "antichrist(s)" in 1 and 2 John, the term does not occur elsewhere in the Bible, hence our problem is very complicated.

The Origin of the Idea

Beliar. In the Sibylline Oracles[5a] there is a prophecy that Beliar shall come as Antichrist and work wonders. In Ascension of Isaiah[6b] Beliar is presented as an angel of lawlessness, responsible for witchcraft, magic, divination, fornication, and the persecution of

1. Rev. 13:11.   2. 1 John 4:3; 2 John v. 7.   3. Rev. 13:11.   4. 1 John 2:18.   5. Sib. Or. 2:167.   6. Asc. Isa. 2:4.

the righteous. Paul refers to Beliar (or Belial) in 2 Corinthians 6:15. What do we know about Belial?

The term "Belial" comes from the Hebrew Old Testament, and appears in the Greek translation as "Beliar," so we can accept these terms as interchangeable. The Hebrew word seems to be composed of two words meaning "without worth" and "sons of Belial" is often translated as "base fellows."[c] However, it appears to be a proper noun in Job ("worthless one"[7]), Psalms ("a deadly thing"[8]), Nahum ("the wicked," followed by the pronoun "he"[9]), and possibly other passages. The Vulgate translated the word in 3 Kings (1 Kings) 21:13 as *viri diabolici* ("diabolical men").[d]

In the Intertestamental Period, the word developed into a technical term, as we have seen in the Sibylline Oracles and the Ascension of Isaiah, above. It also occurs in the Testaments of the Twelve Patriarchs,[e] 4 Ezra 11,12, and the Dead Sea Scrolls.[f]

The Beast.   Daniel had a vision of four beasts rising from the sea,[10] one of which was different in that it was "terrible and dreadful and exceedingly strong" and had ten horns.[11] Then there came up another horn, "a little one," that had eyes like a man's eyes and "a mouth speaking great things."[12] This beast was slain, and the heavenly son of man came on the clouds.[13] The beasts in Daniel's visions represent "four kings who shall arise out of the earth,"[14] whose dominion was to be taken away and the kingdom given to "the saints of the Most High."[15] Daniel, however, wanted to know more about the fourth beast and the ten horns and "the other horn."[16] "This horn made war with the saints, and prevailed over them, until the Ancient of Days came." In a further description, the horns are "ten kings" and the other horn is "a little one"[17] that "shall arise after them,"[18] who "speaks words against the Most High," and into whose hand shall be given the saints of the Most High "for a time, two times, and half a time."[19]

This prophecy was used by the Revelator, who saw "a beast rising out of the sea, with ten horns and seven heads,"[20] to whom

---

7. Job 34:18, RSV.   8. Ps. 41:8 (MT 9), RSV.   9. Nah. 1:15, RSV.
10. Dan. 7:3.   11. Dan. 7:7.   12. Dan. 7:8.   13. Dan. 7:11,12.
14. Dan. 7:17.   15. Dan. 7:12,18.   16. Dan. 7:19,20.   17. Dan. 7:8.
18. Dan. 7:24.   19. Dan. 7:25.   20. Rev. 13:1.

the "dragon" (i.e., Satan,[21] "had given his authority."[22] This beast, like the little horn in Daniel,[g] uttered "blasphemies against God," and made war on the saints and conquered them.[23] To complicate matters, however, the Revelator saw "another beast which rose out of the earth."[24] We shall study this passage later on in this chapter.

The He-Goat and the Little Horn.   Daniel also had a vision of a ram[25] that was destroyed by a he-goat "from the west."[26] When this he-goat was strong, "the great horn was broken, and instead of it there came up four conspicuous horns. . . . Out of one of them came forth a little horn."[27] This little horn grew great, "even to the host of heaven,"[28] so that the continual burnt offering was given over to it, and the sanctuary. This was to take place "for two thousand and three hundred evenings and mornings; then the sanctuary shall be restored to its rightful state."[29h]

The "he-goat" is usually interpreted to mean Alexander the Great,[30] the four "horns" his successors (the Diadochoi[31]), and the "little horn" Antiochus IV, who desecrated the temple in Jerusalem.[32i] There is difference of opinion over the interpretation of the "two thousand and three hundred evenings and mornings" (a very unusual expression in the Hebrew text), some holding that it refers to the evening and morning sacrifices, hence the equivalent of 1150 days, others holding that it stands for 2300 days; some believe the days are to be taken literally, others that the days represent years. More important is the use made of this passage in other parts of the Bible.

The "transgression that makes desolate"[33] is mentioned again in slightly different ways somewhat later in Daniel.[34] This expression is picked up and used by Jesus, perhaps best known in the words of the King James Version, "the abomination of desolation."[35] Therefore, even if Daniel intended this figure to apply at first to the time of Antiochus Epiphanes, his later use, particularly in 12:11, refers to "the time of the end,"[36] and the "vision of the

---

21. Rev. 12:9.   22. Rev. 13:4.   23. Rev. 13:5-8; cf. Dan. 7:25. 24. Rev. 13:11.   25. Dan. 8:3.   26. Dan. 8:5-8.   27. Dan. 8:8,9. 28. Dan. 8:10.   29. Dan. 8:11-14.   30. Cf. Dan. 8:21.   31. Cf. Dan. 8:22.   32. Dan. 8:23,24.   33. Dan. 8:13.   34. Dan. 9:17,26,27; 11:31; 12:11.   35. Matt. 24:15; Mark 13:14.   36. Dan. 12:4,9,13.

evenings and the mornings" "pertains to many days hence."[37] This is confirmed by the use Jesus made of the expression. Study of Daniel's development of the idea in chapter 11 supports an end-time interpretation. The profaning of the temple[38] is usually interpreted to refer to Antiochus Epiphanes, but attack by kings of the south and north (usually taken to refer to the Ptolemies and Seleucids) is "at the time of the end."[39] And it is "at that time" that Michael gets into the battle,[40] the great time of trouble takes place, and the resurrection of the dead occurs.[41]

New Testament Figures

False Christs.   Jesus mentioned "false Christs and false prophets" as one of the signs of the end.[42] The word "Antichrist" in Greek is composed of the preposition *anti*, "instead of, against," and the word *christos*. It can therefore mean either "in place of Christ" or "opposed to Christ,"[j] and can be applied to false Christs, whether they are actively opposed to Jesus or not. Jesus was possibly referring to a specific Antichrist when he said, "I have come in my Father's name, and you did not receive me; if another comes in his own name, him you will receive.[43k] The false Christs and false prophets will "show great signs and wonders, so as to lead astray, if possible, even the elect."[44]

The Man of Lawlessness.   Because the Thessalonian Christians were disturbed by a report that the day of the Lord had already come, Paul devoted a lengthy passage to the subject.[45] He said specifically, "that day will not come, unless the rebellion comes first, and the man of lawlessness is revealed, the son of perdition, who opposes and exalts himself against every so-called god or object of worship, so that he takes his seat in the temple of God, proclaiming himself to be God."[46]

The term "man of lawlessness" (KJV "man of sin")[l] does not occur elsewhere, but Paul's description of him leaves little doubt about his identity. His "coming" (*parousia*) is "by the activity of Satan" and is accompanied by power, pretended signs and won-

---

37. Dan. 8:26.   38. Dan. 11:31.   39. Dan. 11:40.   40. Dan. 12:1.
41. Dan. 12:2.   42. Matt. 24:24; cf. v. 5.   43. John 5:43.   44. Matt.
24:24.   45. 2 Thess. 2:1–12.   46. 2 Thess. 2:3,4.

ders, and wicked deception.[47] He is opposed to religious practices but takes his seat in the temple of God and proclaims himself to be God.[48] "The mystery of lawlessness" is already at work but is at present being held back by him "who now restrains it," and when this restrainer is removed, the lawless one will be revealed.[49m] "The Lord Jesus will slay him with the breath of his mouth and destroy him by his appearing and his coming."[50n]

The Antichrist.   We have already noted that the word "Antichrist" occurs only in the Johannine epistles. We should note also what John says about "Antichrist." There were already "many antichrists,"[51] which was a sign of "the last hour" or the end time. These many antichrists were members of the group to which John refers as "us," and the words "they went out from us" suggests that they were apostates from the Church. A characteristic of these antichrists was denial of the Father and the Son, and denial that Jesus is the Messiah.[52] John draws a clear-cut distinction between light and darkness, between those who love God and those who love the world, between truth and error, between the children of God and the children of the Devil. There are spirits who are of God and those who are not of God. The conflict between these two categories belongs to this age ("the world"), but the victory is God's, "for whatever is born of God overcomes the world."[53] Although the doctrine of Antichrist is not fully developed in these epistles, it is clear that John sees a cosmic struggle, an opposition to God and his people, that reaches its crisis in the end time.

The Beasts.   Doubtless drawing his imagery from Daniel, the Revelator saw "a beast rising out of the sea, with ten horns and seven heads, with ten diadems upon its horns and a blasphemous name upon its heads."[54] This beast got its power and throne and great authority from the "dragon," who is identified as "the Devil and Satan."[55] John also saw "another beast which rose out of the earth," which "had two horns like a lamb and it spoke like a dragon."[56] The second beast had the authority of the first beast and made the earth

---

47. 2 Thess. 2:9,10; cf. Matt. 24:24; Rev. 13:11–13.   **48.** 2 Thess. 2:4; cf. Dan. 11:36,37.   **49.** 2 Thess. 2:7,8.   **50.** 2 Thess. 2:8; cf. Isa. 11:4; Dan. 7:25–27. Rev. 19:11–21.   **51.** 1 John 2:18.   **52.** 1 John 2:22; cf. 4:3; 2 John v. 7.   **53.** 1 John 5:4.   **54.** Rev. 13:1.   **55.** Rev. 13:2; cf. 12:9. **56.** Rev. 13:11.

and its inhabitants worship the first beast.[57] Who or what are these two "beasts"? Is one the Antichrist, and if so, which one?

According to R. Pache, the beast from the sea is the Antichrist, and the second beast is the "false prophet."[o] On the other hand, H. A. Ironside identifies the beast from the earth as the Antichrist.[p] These two examples were selected as representative of the problem of identification, for both men are thoroughly biblical and devoutly believe in the premillennial (and pretribulation-rapture) advent of Christ.[q]

Part of the problem arises from the fact that there is no *certain* identification of the Antichrist given in the Bible. Pache, for example, compares "The Beast of Revelation"[58] item for item with "The Antichrist"—but he has first made a composite picture of the Antichrist, drawn from verses in 2 Thessalonians 2 and Daniel 7,9, and 11. In none of these passages does the word "Antichrist" occur. As we have already seen, the words "antichrist" and "antichrists" are found only in 1 and 2 John and represent a spirit of apostasy[59] rather than a specific person—although I believe that this spirit will finally be found in a personal Antichrist. Ironside believes that "the most complete description of Antichrist is found in Daniel 11:36–45." Again, there is no mention of the word "antichrist" in this passage.

A greater element in the problem is the nature of prophecy, particularly apocalyptic prophecy. Are we justified in attempting to make one-on-one identifications? If we were to apply this same methodology to the "messianic" prophecies in the Old Testament, being totally ignorant of how they were "fulfilled" in Jesus, we would doubtless arrive at much the same position that various Jewish sectarians reached: we would have a number of separate persons, such as (1) a son of David who is to be king, (2) a messianic person who has been "pierced,"[r] (3) a heavenly Son of Man who is to accomplish what the human messiahs cannot do, (4) possibly a priestly Messiah greater than Aaron,[60] (5) a prophet greater than Moses,[61] (6) a personified Wisdom greater than Solomon,[62] and (7) a Servant of the Lord who is to suffer and bear

---

57. Rev. 13:12. **58.** Rev. 13:1–10. **59.** John 2:22; 4:3. **60.** Cf. Heb 7:11. **61.** Cf. Deut. 18:18. **62.** Prov. 8.

the sins of "many." But because of the revelation of God in Jesus and in the New Testament, we believe that these various prophetic figures are intended to present various aspects of God's redemptive activity that were accomplished historically in one person, Jesus. It is just possible that the beast "rising out of the sea" and the beast "which rose out of the earth" are both portrayals of the ultimate development of the spirit of antichrist.[5]

At any rate, it seems clear that a political tyrant with satanic power and authority,[63] who blasphemes God and makes war on the saints,[64] is given worldwide power "for forty-two months.[65] It is also clear that freedom of religion is completely abolished, first by deception[66] and then by force.[67] Finally, there is totalitarian economic control in the hands of "the beast."[68] The "number of the beast" is "a human number," 666.[69]

Attempts to identify the beast by working from this number have been many. The earliest efforts tried to equate "lateinos" or "Neron Kaisar" with the Antichrist. Other "solutions" are Mohammed, the pope, Hitler, Mussolini, and more recently Kissinger. More reasonable at present—although when the Great Dictator appears the numerical significance may become more precise—is the suggestion that "666" is "a human number." In biblical symbolism, "6" or a multiple is often connected with the human being, just as "7" is with the divine. The number "666" may therefore represent the quintessence of humanism, the effort to take the place of God, striving to be a "7," but always falling short, 6 . . . 6 . . . 6.[1]

The Two Babylons.   The introduction of "Babylon" into a discussion of the Antichrist may require a word of explanation. If the revealed purpose of God is to establish a redeemed humankind occupying a redeemed earth under the messianic king, then the purpose of Satan might be described as its opposite: to establish a satanic society on an unredeemed earth under the Antichrist. The introduction of "Babylon" in the book of Revelation, it seems to me, is to portray this satanic sham. The last of the bowls of the wrath of God is poured out, "and God remembered great Babylon, to make her drain the cup of the fury of his wrath."[70]

---

63. Rev. 13:2.   **64.** Rev. 13:6,7.   **65.** Rev. 13:5.   **66.** Rev. 13:14.
67. Rev. 13:15.   **68.** Rev. 13:16,17.   **69.** Rev. 13:18.   **70.** Rev. 16:19.

There are two Babylons. In chapter 17 the Revelator portrays "Babylon the great, mother of harlots and of earth's abominations."[71] She is called "the great harlot who is seated upon many waters,"[72] and the waters are interpreted as "peoples and multitudes and nations and tongues."[73] The woman is seated on seven hills[74] and is defined as "the great city which has dominion over the kings of the earth."[75] Since early Christian centuries, this has been identified as Rome." The "scarlet beast" on which the woman was sitting[76] had "seven heads and ten horns";[77] the seven heads not only represented the seven hills[78] but also seven kings.[79] They reign with the beast "for one hour."[80] But the thrust of this chapter is mainly religious. The harlot represents one who has become faithless to her husband, a familiar Old Testament concept[81] depicting the apostasy of Israel from Yahweh. In her apostasy she persecuted God's people, hence is described as "drunk with the blood of the saints and the blood of the martyrs of Jesus."[82] The beast and the kings "will make war on the Lamb"[83] —referring to Jesus—and also turn against the harlot and destroy her.[84]

The second Babylon is a "great city."[85] She portrays commerce, for when she is destroyed "the merchants of the earth weep and mourn for her, since no one buys their cargo any more."[86] Once again we must not attempt to force one-on-one identifications. Pache, for example, identifies Babylon the harlot with "the apostate religious world," and "Babylon the Great" with "all of civilization without God." He bases this distinction partly on the fact that Babylon is called the prostitute, the impure woman, nine times in chapter 17 and not at all in chapter 18, where Babylon is rather "the great." But Babylon is introduced as "great Babylon."[87] The kings of the earth have committed fornication with her.[88] A voice from heaven calls "Come out of her, my people, lest you take part in her sins,"[89] suggesting that the Babylon of chapter 18 is some kind of ecclesiastical community. And when she has been laid waste, the words are spoken, "Rejoice over her, O heaven, O saints and

71. Rev. 17:5.   72. Rev. 17:1.   73. Rev. 17:15.   74. Rev. 17:9.
75. Rev. 17:18.   76. Rev. 17:3.   77. Rev. 17:7.   78. Rev. 17:9.
79. Rev. 17:10.   80. Rev. 17:13.   81. Hos. 2:1–13; Isa. 1:21; 23:17; Jer. 3:6,8,9.   82. Rev. 17:6.   83. Rev. 17:14.   84. Rev. 17:16.   85. Rev. 18:10.   86. Rev. 18:11.   87. Rev. 16:19.   88. Rev. 17:2; 18:3.
89. Rev. 18:4.

apostles and prophets, for God has given judgment for you against her!"[90]

The Revelator has given us a detailed picture of an apostate community, a "city," that has turned against God and his people and allied with the satanic world-system. This has brought "Babylon the harlot" great wealth and prestige with the world's kings and merchants. If John was thinking of the Roman Empire and its emperors who had made themselves gods, of Rome's persecutions of the people of the true God, certainly this does not exhaust the divine message. Nor is it satisfactory (to me, at least) to find the Roman church and the papacy to be the fulfillment of this prophecy. Any religious system that turns from faith in God to traffic with the world is "Babylon the harlot." But especially in the end time, in the time of the great apostasy, the religious establishment turns to the world, only to find out at last that the "beast" which she thought she controlled (she was "mounted" on it!) hated her and destroyed her.

Summary

Antichrist is a satanic spirit in the present world-system, which is opposed to God, to God's Anointed (or Christ), and to God's people. This antitheistic spirit pervades the political, economic, and finally even the religious systems of this age. The political sphere is ultimately designed to destroy the kingship of God, specifically the king who reigns from the Davidic throne on Zion.[91] But in the historical development of this power, it first corrupts government, and then destroys it, leaving anarchy in its place. In the religious realm, this spirit ultimately seeks to destroy God's redemptive work, specifically the work of his Son and the testimony of his people. In the historical development, this takes place first by deception, by confusing humanism and humanitarianism, by exalting the human being and saying that sin is a delusion and salvation is a human work.

But as the age draws to its close, Satan moves to embody this spirit of Antichrist in a person, the Antichrist, to whom he gives power and authority. Whether this Antichrist is a religious leader,

---

90. Rev. 18:20.   **91.** Cf. Ps. 2.

a political leader, or both, is of secondary significance. Perhaps he will be a Jew, deceiving Jews into believing that he is the Messiah —only to turn against them. Perhaps he will be the leader of a superecclesiastical system that embraces all religions. How Satan will work out the details should be of less concern to us than the fact that he works by deception—and he can deceive even the elect. We need to be on guard against every spirit of antichrist that appears, whether in ourselves or our community!

NOTES

a. See J. Moffatt, "Sibylline Oracles," *DAC* 2: 477–490; *The Apocrypha and Pseudepigrapha of the Old Testament*, ed. R. H. Charles 2: 368–406. The Oracles "grew" in size and content from pre-Christian times until about fourth century A.D.

b. See A. L. Davies, "Ascension of Isaiah," *DAC* 1: 99–102; M. Rist, "Isaiah, Ascension of," *IDB* 2: 744–746. In its final form this work dates from about fourth century A.D.

c. BDB, p. 116.

d. See T. H. Gaster, "Belial," *IDB* 1: 377.

e. Cf. T. Dan 5:10,11: "And there shall rise unto you from the tribe of Judah and of Levi the salvation of the Lord, and he shall make war against Beliar, and execute everlasting vengeance on our enemies, and the captivity shall he take from Beliar and turn disobedient hearts unto the Lord."

f. Belial is mentioned twelve times in 1QM, ten times in 1QH, six times in CD, and five times in 1QS. See Y. Yadin, *The Scroll of the Sons of Light against the Sons of Darkness*, trans. B. and Ch. Rabin (Oxford: Oxford University Press, 1962), pp. 232f.

g. There is another "little horn" in Daniel 8:9, which came forth from the "great horn" of the he-goat. According to one interpretation, this little-horn prophecy was fulfilled in Antiochus IV Epiphanes (175–164 B.C.) who set up the altar of Zeus in the temple (considered to be "the abomination that makes desolate" of Dan. 11:31). If so, there has to be a *sensus plenior* of an end-time fulfillment in the light of the words both of Daniel (vv. 35,40; 12:1–4) and of Jesus (Matt. 24:15).

h. This is a key passage for Seventh-Day Adventism. The "cleansing of the sanctuary" was first interpreted to mean the Return of Christ to the earth, later interpreted to mean the heavenly sanctuary. By their reckoning, the 2300 years began in the autumn of 457 B.C. and ended in A.D. 1844. "Christ then entered the most holy place of the heavenly sanctuary to perform the closing work of atonement preparatory to his coming." Cf. E. G. White, *The Great Controversy* (Mountain View, CA: Pacific Press, 1950 [1911 ed.]), pp. 409, 422.

i. However, according to Daniel 8:25 he rises up against the "Prince of princes," and is to be broken "by no human hands"—statements which hardly apply to Antiochus. Cf. also 12:4–13.

j. Cf. LSJ 2: 153, C.2,5.

k. NSRB identifies "another" in this verse with "the Beast," p. 1131, note y.

l. The "best" manuscripts read *anomias*, "lawlessness," but "good" manuscripts have the reading *hamartias*, "sin," which has the support of a number of the Fathers. Cf. Bible Societies' *Greek New Testament* on 2 Thessalonians 2:3, which gives the former reading a rating of "C," indicating "a considerable degree of doubt" about which reading is better.

m. There is disagreement over the interpretation of this "restrainer." Some believe that he is the Holy Spirit who will be withdrawn in the end time. Others, that it is the Church which will be raptured. Still others, that it is government (specifically the Roman emperor, see *New Bible Commentary Revised;* ed. D. Guthrie and J. A. Motyer [London: Inter-Varsity Press, 1970], p. 1163) that will be "withdrawn" by end-time anarchy. Without great conviction on the matter, I incline to see this restrainer as the orderly process of government (cf. Acts 17:6; Rom. 13:1–3).

n. For a very full treatment of this passage, see William Hendriksen, *Exposition of I and II Thessalonians (New Testament Commentary;* Grand Rapids, MT: Baker, 1955), pp. 168–186. See also G. Milligan, *St. Paul's Epistles to the Thessalonians*, pp. 95–105, note I, "The Biblical Doctrine of Antichrist," pp. 158–165, note J, "On the interpretation of 2 Thess. ii. 1–12," pp. 166–173.

o. R. Pache, *The Return of Jesus Christ*, pp. 207–209.

p. H. Ironside, *Lectures on the Book of Revelation*, pp. 241–243.

q. This problem can be seén by comparing SRB with NSRB. SRB (p. 1342, n.3) positively identifies the Antichrist with " 'the Beast out of the earth' of Rev. 13.11–17, and the 'false prophet' of Rev. 16.13; 19.20; 20.10." NSRB (p. 1365, n.3) takes a more cautious position, giving both options.

r. Cf. Zech. 12:10, Sukkoth 52a; A. Cohen, *Everyman's Talmud* (New York: Schocken, reprint, 1975), p. 348.

s. C. E. Mason, Jr., arrives at this same conclusion in *Prophetic Problems with Alternate Solutions*, p. 207: "The answer, then, to the perennial question, 'Which of the two beasts of Revelation 13 is the Antichrist?' is unequivocally: 'both!' "

t. This suggestion is attributed to both C. A. Briggs and G. Milligan by H. B. Swete, *The Apocalypse of St. John*, p. 173. Swete gives a detailed explanation of the methods of calculation, pp. 171–173. We should perhaps note that in some manuscripts the figure is given as "616."

u. This identification goes back at least to the time of Tertullian; see A. W. Fortune, "Babylon in the NT," *ISBE* 1 (1979); 391.

v. Pache, *The Return of Jesus Christ*, pp. 219, 238.

ADDITIONAL READING

Bousset, W. *Der Antichrist*. Göttingen: Vandenhoeck & Ruprecht, 1905.
James, M. R. "Man of Sin and Antichrist." *HDB* 3: 226–228.

Lambert, J. C. "Antichrist." *DAC* 1: 67–69.
Langton, Edward. *Essentials of Demonology*. London: Epworth, 1949.
Moffatt, J. "False Christs." *DCG* 1: 574–575.
Pink, Arthur W. *The Antichrist*. Swengel, PA: Bible Truth Depot, 1923.

10. The Great Tribulation

The Problem

In the current discussion there is frequent mention of "the Great Tribulation" or "the Tribulation." Is this a biblical doctrine? Is there a difference between the age-long tribulation that comes upon the people of God and this Great Tribulation? How long does this Great Tribulation last—seven years, three-and-a-half years, or is it an indefinite period? Does the Church go through the Tribulation? Is it only for Jews as punishment for rejecting Jesus?

These and many similar questions have been asked and are still being asked. It is obvious, since the questions persist, that the answers that have been given do not completely satisfy. I do not assume that my answers will be totally satisfactory, and this is not my purpose. In this study I want to examine some of the biblical evidence and some of the questions, in an attempt to throw a clearer light on the complex problem.[a] Is there a scriptural basis for the idea of the Great Tribulation? I believe there is.

The Scriptural Basis

The Teachings of Jesus. In the "Olivet Discourse"[1] Jesus had just foretold the destruction of the temple, and his disciples asked, "Tell us, when will this be, and what will be the sign of your coming and of the close of the age?"[2] In his reply he included this statement: "Then they will deliver you up to *tribulation*, and put you to death."[3] This is followed by predictions of apostasy, treachery, wickedness, false prophets, and the preaching of the gospel, "and then the end will come."[4] Then Jesus spoke of "the desolating sacrilege spoken of by the prophet Daniel" and warned "those who are in Judea" to flee, stating "for then there will be *great tribulation*

---

1. Matt. 24; Mark 13; Luke 21.   2. Matt. 24:3; cf. Mark 13:4; Luke 21:7.
3. Matt. 24:9.   4. Matt. 24:14.

such as has not been from the beginning of the world until now, no, and never will be."[5] False Christs and false prophets working great wonders are mentioned. He continued: "Immediately after the *tribulation of those days* the sun will be darkened, and the moon will not give its light, and the stars will fall from heaven, and the powers of the heavens will be shaken; then will appear the sign of the Son of man in heaven, and then all the tribes of the earth will mourn, and they will see the Son of man coming on the clouds of heaven with power and great glory."[6]

There are a number of problems in this passage. In the parallels to Matthew 24:9, Mark and Luke do not use the word "tribulation." Where Matthew has "great tribulation"[7] Mark uses the expression "such tribulation."[8] Luke says, "For great distress shall be upon the earth and wrath upon this people,"[9] and adds the statement, "Jerusalem shall be trodden down by the Gentiles until the times of the Gentiles are fulfilled."[10] Where Matthew uses the expression "immediately after the tribulation of those days,"[11] Mark has "in those days, after that tribulation."[12] Luke proceeds to the "signs in sun and moon and stars" without mentioning again the distress and wrath.[13]

More serious, for these textual matters really do not alter the main teaching of the "Olivet Discourse," is the sequence of events. In Matthew 24, for example, does the portion beginning with verse 15 pick up the idea of verse 9 and enlarge upon it? Or are these two stages of the events of the end time that are to be taken as in sequence? Again, does verse 29 refer back to the tribulation mentioned in verse 9 or to that in verse 21? Such questions should keep us from becoming overly dogmatic in the systems we set up.

According to some interpreters, the passage answers three separate questions: "When will this [the destruction of Jerusalem] be?"; "What will be the sign of your coming?"; and "[What will be the sign] of the close of the age?" But any attempt to divide the reply into three parts, each of which answers one of the questions, is unsatisfactory. If, for example, the "desolating sacrilege" of 24:15 refers to the Roman eagles at the time of the war of A.D. 68–70,

---

5. Matt. 24:21.   **6.** Matt. 24:29,30.   **7.** Matt. 24:21.   **8.** Mark 13:19.
9. Luke 21:23.   **10.** Luke 21:24.   **11.** Matt. 24:29.   **12.** Mark 13:24.
13. Luke 21:25.

then what are we to do with the statement concerning the preaching of the gospel "throughout the whole world" in the preceding
verse?[14] In my opinion, there can be no disputing the view that
Jesus is answering all three (or perhaps there are but two) parts of
the disciples' question. But, as is so often the case in the Old
Testament prophets, the near-at-hand and the distant, not to
mention intervening events, are blended.

This becomes even more evident when we study the portion
given in Matthew 24:32–35.[15] The fig tree is often taken as a
symbol of Israel, and the putting forth of its leaves is interpreted to
mean the beginning of the resurrection of the nation.[16] "When you
see all these things, you know that he is near, at the very gates,"
said Jesus.[17] Then he added these cryptic words: "Truly, I say to
you, this generation will not pass away till all these things take
place."[18] If "this generation" is taken literally, all of the predictions
were to take place within the life-span of those living at that time.
This would seem to be contrary to the reference to the worldwide
preaching of the gospel.[19] It is clearly denied by the statement that
follows: "But of that day and hour no one knows, not even the
angels of heaven, nor the Son, but the Father only."[20b]

But regardless of the sequence that is intended (or that we impose upon the passage), Jesus does mention a "great tribulation" in
connection with the end time events. His reference to the prophet
Daniel strongly suggests that he has drawn not only the reference
to "the desolating sacrilege" from Daniel[21] but also that of the
Great Tribulation.[22]

The Prophecy of Daniel.   The prophecy of Daniel, which is
apocalyptic, is admittedly difficult to interpret. Nevertheless, there
are passages of brilliant clarity, and the progression of the events can
be traced in general, even if there is disagreement over many of the
details.

Beginning with chapter 7 Daniel is presenting the events of the
end time.[c] In his vision he saw "four great beasts,"[23] which
represent "four kings" (or kingdoms, governmental systems) that
ultimately are replaced by a "son of man" to whom is given an

---

14. Matt. 24:14.   15. Mark 13:28–31; Luke 21:29–33.   16. Cf. Ezek. 37.
17. Matt. 24:33.   18. Matt. 24:34.   19. Matt. 24:14.   20. Matt. 24:
36.   21. Dan. 11:31.   22. Dan. 12:1.   23. Dan. 7:2.

everlasting dominion.[24] Daniel was particularly interested in the "fourth beast" and the "other horn" that made war with the saints[25] and was overcome by the Ancient of Days. That this was a series of visions pertaining to the end time is clearly stated.[26] It is also implied by the predictions that, whereas the four kingdoms will be destroyed, the kingdom that was delivered to the son of man will be everlasting.[27]

The time sequence is a problem. Daniel was convinced that Jeremiah's prophecy of seventy years[28] was about to be fulfilled and Jerusalem's desolation ended. Whether Daniel understood Gabriel's prophecy of "seventy weeks"[29] to be weeks of days (490 days) or weeks of years (490 years) should not distract us from our main purpose. Toward the end of this period a "desolator" comes "upon the wing of abominations."[30] This abominable person or thing is mentioned again.[31] In connection with this prophecy, the destruction of the city and the sanctuary are foretold, and desolations are decreed.[32]

Neither should we be distracted by the references to Persia and Greece[33] and what seem to be obvious references to the Ptolemies and the Seleucids (the "king of the south"[34] and "the king of the north"[35]). Daniel was interested in the horn that made war with the saints[36]—which is our present concern. There is some connection between this horn and the "king of bold countenance"[37] who causes "fearful destruction," who rises up against "the Prince of princes," and who is broken "by no human hand,"[38] and this person, or one of these persons, must be the "desolator" of 9:26–27.

As we trace the action in chapter 11, it is clear that the "contemptible person"[39] is engaged in warfare using forces that ultimately profane the temple and erect "the abomination that makes desolate."[40] This king sets himself above God, and in fury sets out to exterminate and destroy many.[41] "At that time shall arise Michael, the great prince who has charge of your people. And

---

24. Dan. 7:13,14,17,18.   25. Dan. 7:19–21.   26. Dan. 8:17,19,26; 10: 14; 12:4,9,13.   27. Dan. 7:14.   28. Dan. 9:2; cf. Jer. 25:11.   29. Dan. 9:24.   30. Dan. 9:29.   31. Dan. 11:31; 12:11.   32. Dan. 9:26. 33. Dan. 11:2.   34. Dan. 11:5.   35. Dan. 11:6.   36. Dan. 8:21. 37. Dan. 8:23.   38. Dan. 8:25.   39. Dan. 11:21.   40. Dan. 11:31. 41. Dan. 11:36–45.

there shall be a time of trouble, such as never has been since there was a nation till that time."[42]

This is the passage that Jesus quoted. From the context of Daniel we may draw a tentative conclusion that this "time of trouble" or "great tribulation" involves the people of God, "every one whose name shall be found written in the book."[43] "Your people"[44] must refer to the Jews, for Daniel was a Jew, and "the king" who magnifies himself above every god[45] and gives "no heed to the God of his fathers"[46e] is quite possibly also a Jew. The setting is clearly the Near East, and if the Ptolemies and Seleucids are intended (which seems most reasonable), then Palestine is the locale.[f]

The Prophecy of Jeremiah. Since Daniel has referred to Jeremiah, we may infer that he has drawn not only the concept of seventy years from Jeremiah, but also the concept of the "time of trouble." In a passage that has to do with the end time Jeremiah records the words of the Lord, the God of Israel: "Write in a book all the words that I have spoken to you.[47] The message has to do with the restoration of Judah and Israel to the land which God had given to their fathers. But instead of speaking of joy, the Lord says, "We have heard a cry of panic, of terror, and no peace. . . . Alas! that day is so great there is none like it; it is a time of distress for Jacob; yet he shall be saved out of it.[48g] The passage concludes with the promise of deliverance: "and strangers shall no more make servants of them. But they shall serve the Lord their God and David their king, whom I will raise up for them."[49]

The outline is clear: restoration of Judah and Israel to their land, a time of distress, *followed* by salvation and the advent of the messianic king. This is precisely the outline that we can trace in Daniel.[50h]

The Book of Revelation. Like the prophecy of Daniel, Revelation is a difficult book to interpret. Again, like Daniel, the progress in Revelation is clear—it moves from the churches in proconsular Asia to the New Jerusalem—and the main points of the process are clear. Difficulties usually arise because we become bogged down in details or entangled in a chronological system that we have imposed

---

42. Dan. 12:1.   **43.** Dan. 12:2.   **44.** Dan. 12:1.   **45.** Dan. 11:36.
46. Dan. 11:37.   **47.** Jer. 30:2.   **48.** Jer. 30:5,7.   **49.** Jer. 30:8,9.
50. Dan. 9:1; 12:1,2.

on the book. And again, like Daniel, there is a period of great trouble just before the triumphant conclusion.

The book of Revelation purports to be "the revelation of Jesus Christ" that he revealed by an angel to John.[51] The message, then, is to be received with the authority of Jesus Christ himself, and not as the fantasies of an old man. A number of scholars have pointed out a similarity between the outline of the "Olivet Discourse" (particularly as presented in Matthew 24) and that of Revelation: War,[52] famine,[53] pestilence,[54] martyrdom,[55] earthquake and signs in the heaven,[56] and the great day of wrath[57] follow a familiar pattern. The great tribulation is mentioned in 7:14.

At this point, however, there is scholarly confusion. Do the "seven trumpets" of chapters 8 and 9 continue the sequence of events, or do they return and elaborate the events described under the "seven seals"?[58i] Regardless of how we answer this question, we must not overlook two facts: (1) the seventh trumpet heralds the advent of the kingdom of Christ,[59] and (2) prior to this advent the "holy city" is trampled by the nations (Gentiles) "for forty-two months"[60] in a context of terrible suffering.[j]

Once again the question is raised whether the chapters that follow are sequential, or whether they enlarge upon points that have already been revealed. And again, for our present purpose, we may ignore this problem, noting simply that the beast who utters "haughty and blasphemous words" exercises his authority for forty-two months,[61] making war on the saints and conquering them. This is clearly related to Daniel,[62] and the time-period mentioned (forty-two months = three-and-one-half years) agrees with a common interpretation of that given in Daniel ("a time, two times, and half a time"[63] and "half of the week"[64] are both usually taken to mean three-and-a-half years).

The "seven plagues,"[65] or "seven bowls of the wrath of God"[66] bring to an end the wrath of God.[67] The promise "Lo, I am coming like a thief!" is inserted just after the mention of the "battle on the

---

51. Rev. 1:1.   **52.** Rev. 6:4.   **53.** Rev. 6:6.   **54.** Rev. 6:8,9.
55. Rev. 6:9.   **56.** Rev. 6:12,13.   **57.** Rev. 6:16.   **58.** Rev. 6:1.
59. Rev. 11:15.   **60.** Rev. 11:2.   **61.** Rev. 13:5.   **62.** Rev. 7:8,21.
63. Rev. 12:7.   **64.** Rev. 9:27.   **65.** Rev. 15:1.   **66.** Rev. 16:1.
67. Rev. 15:1.

great day of God the Almighty."[68] The destruction of the beast and the false prophet is accomplished by the one called "The Word of God"[69] and "King of kings and Lord of lords."[70]

The Nature and Purpose of the Tribulation

We have seen that there are at least three kinds of suffering. The same approach can be taken when we ask why there must be a Great Tribulation. In addition, the element of the satanic must be considered.

The Wrath of God.   The judgments portrayed in Revelation are called "the wrath of the Lamb"[71] and "the wrath of God."[72] We have recently come through a period in which it has not been popular to speak of justice, judgment, or anger. We have been fed a mixture of psychology, sociology, and theology that has emphasized self-expression and opposed any form of repression or restraint. There are some who believe we are now reaping a harvest of such sowing in widespread juvenile vandalism and adult terrorism.[k] Some of us are ready to believe once more in the wrath of God, for we ask, "What kind of a loving God would put up with this kind of behavior?"

God is a holy God. He has absolutely no place in himself or the world of his ultimate plan for any kind of idolatry, immorality, or unrighteousness. Those who practice such things must be punished completely and finally.[73] This is the clear teaching of Jesus.[74] Paul stresses it in his letters.[75] God is patient and longsuffering, but there is an end to that patience. The Flood was an early demonstration of this truth[76] and the Babylonian exile was a demonstration to Israel.[77] The Great Tribulation will be the final outpouring of God's wrath, and then the voice from the throne can say, "It is done!"[78]

The Refiner's Fire.   The prophets often spoke of a "remnant," those who would come through the judgment by God's mercy. Isaiah, perhaps the greatest proclaimer of the remnant, said, "Behold, I have refined you, but not like silver; I have tried you in the

---

68. Rev. 16:14,15.   **69.** Rev. 19:13.   **70.** Rev. 19:16.   **71.** Rev. 6:-16.   **72.** Rev. 15:1; 16:1; 19:15.   **73.** Cf. Rev. 21:8; 22.15.   **74.** Matt. 13:41,42,49,50.   **75.** Cf. Eph. 5:5,6.   **76.** Gen. 6:13.   **77.** Jer. 1:15,16; Ezek. 36:17–19.   **78.** Rev. 16:17.

furnace of affliction."[79] Zechariah, possibly with the Tribulation in mind,[80] said, "I will put this third into the fire, and refine them as one refines silver, and test them as gold is tested."[81] Malachi, speaking of the Lord's coming,[82] said, "For he is like a refiner's fire and like fullers' soap; he will sit as a refiner and purifier of silver. . . ."[83] Paul, with a slightly different metaphor, but still referring to "the Day," wrote, "each man's work will become manifest; for the Day will disclose it, because it will be revealed with fire, and the fire will test what sort of work each one has done. . . . If any man's work is burned up, he will suffer loss, though he himself will be saved, but only as through fire."[84]

This sanctifying work will result in the holiness that God desires. The people of God at last will be "without spot or wrinkle or any such thing."[85] The aged John wrote, "Beloved, we are God's children now; it does not yet appear what we shall be, but we know that when he appears we shall be like him, for we shall see him as he is."[86]

[Satan's Last Assault.   We greatly miss the point of the Tribulation if we see it simply as the result of an angry God who has lost patience with his children and is throwing all sorts of things at them. Let no one try to find support for child abuse in the Bible! The Great Tribulation is the backlash on this planet of Satan's last attempt to defeat God.]

Paul warned us about contending "against the spiritual hosts of wickedness in the heavenly places."[87] The Revelator introduces the portion of the book containing the bowls of wrath with the words: "Now war arose in heaven, Michael and his angels fighting against the dragon; and the dragon and his angels fought, but they were defeated and there was no longer any place for them in heaven. And the great dragon was thrown down, that ancient serpent, who is called the Devil and Satan, the deceiver of the whole world—he was thrown down to earth, and his angels were thrown down with him." John heard a loud voice in heaven, saying, ". . . woe to you, O earth and sea, for the devil has come down to you in great wrath, because he knows that his time is short!"[88]

---

79. Isa. 48:10.   80. Zech. 13:2.   81. Zech. 13:9.   82. Mal. 3:1.
83. Mal. 3:2,3.   84. 1 Cor. 3:13,15.   85. Eph. 5:27.   86. 1 John 3:2.
87. Eph. 6:12.   88. Rev. 12:7–12.

In the course of this struggle, Satan concentrates his efforts on the people of God. Daniel does not mention Satan, but his message conveys this truth. The "other horn" made war with the saints,[89] who were given into his hand "for a time, two times, and half a time."[90] The "little horn" has great power, and destroys "mighty men and the people of the saints"[91] for a limited time ("two thousand and three hundred evenings and mornings"[92]). Daniel also associated the angel Michael with this time of trouble.[93] Jesus used a different figure, but he taught that the Devil has sown weeds among the wheat (representing the Kingdom of God), and that the weeds will continue to grow until the harvest, at which time the angels will "gather out of his kingdom all causes of sin and all evildoers, and throw them into the furnace of fire."[94] Our study of the Antichrist gave us some details on this aspect of the Tribulation.

How Long Will the Tribulation Last?

The period of the Great Tribulation is calculated in various ways from the data given in Daniel and in Revelation. It is usually defined as lasting seven years, and more precisely as three-and-a-half years.[m]

Daniel's Seventy Weeks.   Many students refer to the seventy "weeks" of Daniel[95] in their efforts to set up some kind of schedule. This is particularly true of those following the Dispensational system. The discussions are voluminous[n] and confusing, and at this point we need not enter into the entire schedule. The "weeks" are divided into seven, sixty-two, and one, and this last "week" is further divided into halves. Daniel does not indicate that these heptads (groups of seven) are to be understood as years, and there is nothing in the Hebrew word to lead to this conclusion. However, there are other data that support this interpretation. For one, there is the reference to Jeremiah's prophecy of "seventy years"[96] in the immediate context, from which some would conclude that Gabriel has moved from this to the "seventy heptads [of years]" in his revelation to Daniel.[97]

89. Dan. 7:21.   90. Dan. 7:25.   91. Dan. 8:24.   92. Dan. 8:14.
93. Dan. 12:1.   94. Matt. 13:36-43.   95. Dan. 9:25-27.   96. Dan. 9:2.
97. Dan. 9:24.

Moreover, the period when the "other horn" has the saints of the Most High in his hand is defined as "a time, two times, and half a time."[98] Again, there is no indication that "time" is to be read as "year," but this is the common interpretation.[p] There are other figures in Daniel. "Two thousand and three hundred evenings and mornings,"[99] the period that the sanctuary and host are to be trampled under foot, is usually applied to the time of Antiochus Epiphanes. Efforts have been made, however, to read it as "2300 evening and morning sacrifices" or 1150 days, and make it approximate three-and-a-half years (actually about 3.2 years). In chapter 12 Daniel mentions 1,290 days and 1,335 days,[100] related in some way to the setting up of "the abomination that makes desolate." Again, these are read as approximating three-and-a-half years. While admitting that these figures may have significance that will become clear when the time comes, I prefer to take them as symbols of a short period of time.

The Figures in Revelation.   In Revelation 12, the dragon stood before a woman about to bear a child, in order to devour that child.[101] The child is described as "one who is to rule all the nations with a rod of iron,"[102] a reference to Psalm 2:9, usually understood to be a messianic prophecy. The child was "caught up to God and to his throne, and the woman fled into the wilderness" where she was taken care of by God "for one thousand two hundred and sixty days."[103] If this is a representation of the nation Israel, which produced the Messiah, and of the death, resurrection, and ascension of the Messiah, and of the Tribulation (1260 days = three-and-a-half years), it is certainly cryptic in the extreme. Nevertheless, where this passage is placed in the development of the book, it appears to have some such meaning.[r] Furthermore, the same period is defined in verse 14 as "a time, and times, and half a time," reminiscent of Daniel.[104]

The expression "one thousand two hundred and sixty days" is found in Revelation 11:5, where it is preceded by the equivalent "forty-two months,"[105] referring to the time during which the

---

98. Dan. 7:25.   99. Dan. 8:14.   100. Dan. 12:11,12.   101. Rev. 12: 4.   102. Rev. 12:5.   103. Rev. 12:6.   104. Dan. 7:25; 12:7. 105. Rev. 11:4.

nations (Gentiles) trample over the holy city.[106] Similarly, the expression "forty-two months" is given as the period during which the "beast" was allowed to exercise authority.[107] In the light of this evidence, expressed variously as half of the seventieth week, three-and-a-half times, forty-two months, and 1260 days, it seems reasonable to conclude that the Great Tribulation extends over a period of about three-and-a-half years.

Does the Church Go Through the Tribulation?

The Rapture.   In his description of the Second Advent, Paul wrote the Thessalonians," . . . then we who are alive, who are left, shall be caught up together with them in the clouds to meet the Lord in the air."[108] This "catching up" or "snatching away" is commonly called "the Rapture." Paul was once "caught up to the third heaven,"[109] and the woman's "child" whom the dragon sought to devour was "caught up to God."[110] There is no problem with the meaning of the word. At the Advent of Christ (whether this means a moment of time or a period) the dead in Christ will be raised, and those who are still alive will be caught up.

Pre- and Posttribulationists.   According to a widely held view, Christ comes for his Church *before* the Tribulation. This view is called the "pretribulation (Rapture)" or simply "pretrib" view and those who hold it are "Pretribulationists" or "Pretribs." An older view considers the Advent, with the resurrection and the Rapture, to take place at the *end* of the Tribulation and the beginning of the Millennium. This is the "Posttribulationist" position—although it was never known as such until Pretribulationism came into existence. There are some who believe that the Rapture takes place in the midst of the Tribulation, called "Midtribulationists."[s]

The majority of Dispensationalists, I believe, hold to the pretribulation-rapture view. The scriptural basis for the view, as some have admitted, is not strong.[t] The position is held more on a logical or theological basis. The church age is a "parenthesis," a mystery not revealed in the Old Testament, and is not considered in Daniel's

---

106. Cf. Isa. 63:18; Luke 21:24.   **107.** Rev. 13:5.   **108.** 1 Thess. 4:17.
109. 2 Cor. 12:2.   **110.** Rev. 12:5.

seventy "weeks." The "clock stopped running for Israel" when Jesus was rejected, and starts again when the Church is raptured. The Church is not mentioned after chapter 3 of Revelation, and the words "Come up hither" of 4:1 are taken to refer to the Rapture (actually, they are addressed to John). The Church is to be kept from "the hour of trial."[111] If the Return can take place at any moment, it obviously could not be preceded by a seven- (or three-and-a-half-) year tribulation. If Christ is coming "with his saints," he must first come "for his saints." These, and similar statements—not all of which are held by all Pretribulationists—sound rather convincing on the surface. The truth, however, is that they lack clear scriptural teaching.

God has never spared his people. The righteous have always been called upon to suffer. Our paradigms in Scripture are Job, the Suffering Servant of Isaiah, and Jesus. The Christian Church has no scriptural right to ask for special privileges for which our Lord did not ask. Paul, who rejoiced in his sufferings,[112] exhorted believers to continue in the faith, "saying that through many tribulations we must enter the kingdom of God."[113] "In the world you have tribulation," Jesus told his disciples; "but be of good cheer. I have overcome the world."[114] The wrath of God, which will be part of the end-time Tribulation, is not poured out on the people of God, "for God has not destined us for wrath, but to obtain salvation through our Lord Jesus Christ."[115]

Will the Church go through the Tribulation? Perhaps this is the wrong question to ask. Will the Church be preserved? Beyond doubt, yes! The "servants of our God"—whether this includes the Church in this passage must be decided on other grounds—are sealed. And when John asks who they are, he is told, "These are they who have come out of the great tribulation."[116] If the Church is called upon to pass through these deep waters, we can be sure that God will keep us. Those "who had not worshipped the beast or its image and had not received its mark on their foreheads or their hands" will rise and reign with Christ "a thousand years."[117]

---

111. Rev. 3:10.   112. Rom. 5:3; 2 Cor. 7:4.   113. Acts 14:22.
114. John 16:33.   115. 1 Thess. 5:9.   116. Rev. 7:14.   117. Rev. 20:4.

Summary

There will be tribulation throughout this satanic age. It will be more intense at times, but it will never be lacking. But the Scriptures teach that just prior to the end of the age there will be great tribulation such as never before. This will be Satan's last attempt to destroy the people of God by political, economic, and religious means, led by the Antichrist and other agents of Satan. At that time, the wrath of God will be poured out on all who serve Satan, who worship the Beast and his image, or accept his mark. In many instances, this wrath is the unloosing of cause-and-effect conditions in the world: "For men have shed the blood of saints and prophets, and thou hast given them blood to drink. It is their due!"[118]

The "saints," the servants of God, which includes those "out of every tribe of the sons of Israel" as well as an innumerable host "from every nation, from all tribes and people and tongues,"[119] will bear God's seal, and will enjoy the blessings of his presence evermore.[120]

NOTES

a. I say "some," although I am seeking to use all of the relevant scriptures vis-à-vis all of the major questions. But I know that there are certain systems that use many scriptures, some torn badly out of context, and out of deference to them I qualify my statement.

b. The suddenness of the second Advent is suggested in Matthew 24:40–44. The "delay" is suggested in the parable of the wicked servant (24:45–51) and that of the wise and foolish maidens (25:5).

c. The first six chapters also concern future events, but there does not seem to be a chronological sequence in those events such as appears to be present in chapters 7 through 12.

d. The RSV adds "of years," which is lacking in the original text.

e. The RSV reads "the gods of his fathers," but the Hebrew certainly can be read "the God of his fathers," which is how it is translated in the Vulgate. The LXX translates in the plural. Once again we need to resist an overly dogmatic attitude.

f. Since the vision applies to the end time (Dan. 12:4), the Ptolemies, Seleucids, and Kittim (11:30) must be understood as symbolic of nations or powers of the end time.

---

118. Rev. 16:6.   **119.** Rev. 7:4,9.   **120.** Rev. 7:15–17.

g. We can readily see how this could be applied by some interpreters to the modern State of Israel.

h. The messianic king is not mentioned here (or possibly elsewhere) in Daniel. However, the deliverance is final and the kingdom to be established is everlasting; see Daniel 7:12–14, 17–18. The savior is the one like a son of man (7:13), and Michael is also involved (12:1). The "messiah" in 9:25, 26, as we have seen is "a prince, an anointed one" or simply "an anointed one," in both expressions without the definite article.

i. According to one system, the trumpets parallel the seals, while another makes the six trumpets an elaboration of the seventh seal.

j. Adding to the difficulty of interpretation is the mention of "the beast that ascends from the bottomless pit" (11:7), which suggests to some the scene in Rev. 20:3, 7–10.

k. According to E. A. Wynne, "What Are the Courts Doing to Our Children?" *The Public Interest* (Summer 1981), "American courts have undercut the parental role of the schools." Children grow up without any idea of the place of authority in society. Cf. *Evangelical Newsletter* 8,26 (25 Dec. 1981):2.

l. It is not clear that John intends to give us a chronological schedule of events, hence I am not contending here that the casting out of Satan marks the beginning of the Tribulation. I would emphasize, however, the point—a scriptural truth, I believe—that the Tribulation is the result of satanic activity on a vast scale.

m. Cf. *NSRB*, p. 1359, n.1, where "tribulation" is used of the seven-year period, and "great tribulation" of the second half of this period.

n. For a lengthy (and tedious) discussion, see C. F. Keil, *Daniel*, Biblical Commentary on the Old Testament, ed. C. F. Keil and F. Delitzsch, trans. J. Martin (ca. 1850–1890; reprint ed., Grand Rapids, MI: Eerdmans, 1950), pp. 336–402. From another angle (and also tedious) is E. B. Pusey, *Daniel the Prophet* (London: Rivington's, 1864), pp. 162–231.

o. The word translated "two times" is morphologically a plural, but is read as a dual, cf. *BHS*, note b on 7:25. The same expression occurs (in Hebrew) in 12:7, where again the plural is used. At that time, neither Aramaic nor Hebrew commonly used the dual.

p. See BDB, p. 1105.

q. 1,290 days = 3.5 years of 365 days, but those who have tried to work out the 62 "weeks" to represent the actual time between the word to rebuild the city and the cutting off of the Messiah, insist that "years" in prophecy are always figured at 360 days. See H. A. Ironside, *Lectures on Daniel*, p. 166. On that basis, 1,290 days = 3.58 years. Other scholars, however, have attempted solutions using the solar year (365 days) or the lunar year (354 days).

r. Cf. H. A. Ironside, *Lectures on the Book of Revelation*, pp. 205–218. Ironside takes this to be the first half of the "week" prior to the Great Tribulation.

s. This distinction is somewhat blurred, owing to the fact that the "tribulation" is sometimes looked upon as the last seven-year period, and sometimes as the last half of that period. A "pretrib" may look for the Second Advent at the beginning of the Great Tribulation, i.e., the last three-and-a-half years, and therefore be considered a "midtribber." If you're confused, I have been for years, not knowing quite how to label myself.

t. J. Walvoord, *The Rapture Question* (Findley, OH: Dunham, 1957), p. 148, admitted that it was not explicitly taught in the Bible, but he deleted this statement in later editions of the book.

u. For arguments against the pretribulationist position, see G. E. Ladd, *The Blessed Hope*, pp. 71–129; O. T. Allis, *Prophecy and the Church* (Philadelphia: Presbyterian and Reformed, 1945), pp. 192–217; H. Lindsell, *The Gathering Storm* (Wheaton, IL: Tyndale, 1980), pp. 141–161.

ADDITIONAL READING

Allis, O. T. *Prophecy and the Church.* Philadelphia: Presbyterian and Reformed, 1945.

English, E. S. *Companion to the New Scofield Reference Bible.* New York: Oxford University Press, 1972, Pp. 136–147.

Gundry, Robert H. *The Church and the Tribulation.* Grand Rapids, MI: Zondervan, 1973.

Cohn, Joseph Hoffman. *Will the Church ESCAPE the Tribulation?* Findlay, OH: Fundamental Truth Publishers, n.d.

Ladd, George E. *Crucial Questions about the Kingdom of God.* Grand Rapids, MI: Eerdmans, 1952.

Scofield, C. I. *Will the Church Pass Through the Great Tribulation?* Philadelphia: Philadelphia School of the Bible, 1917.

Walvoord, John F. *The Rapture Question.* Findlay, OH: Dunham, 1957.

Wilson, W. H. *The Destiny of Russia and the Signs of the Times.* Chicago: p.p., 1914.

11. Armageddon

The Problem

"Armageddon" has become a much-used term, although it is perhaps no better understood by many who use it than "born again." We speak of "the battle of Armageddon." The dictionary gives as one definition of the word, "a great and decisive battle." Is the term biblical? What does the Bible say about it?

The word is indeed found in the Bible—once.[1] It is indeed connected with a battle: the "kings of the whole world" are to be assembled there by "demonic spirits" for battle "on the great day of God the Almighty."[2]

But around this single and brief notice, students of the end time have gathered other material, mostly biblical but some from non-biblical sources. In our study we must therefore consider also this other material. The description of the conflict led by Gog of the land of Magog,[3] which is mentioned in Revelation,[4] is certainly to be considered. Since "the great day of God" is mentioned in connection with Armageddon, we must also study what the Bible says about "the day of the Lord" and similar expressions. According to Ezekiel, the battle takes place after Israel has been restored to the land, so the significance of the establishment of the modern State of Israel and the Arab-Israeli conflict comes into our study.

From here the problems increase. "Gog" is connected with "Rosh," "Meshech," and "Tubal," and these are often identified with Russia, Moscow, and Tobolsk. Forces from beyond the Euphrates numbering two hundred million[5] are led by the "kings of the east,"[6] once thought by some to be Japan but now Red China.

---

1. Rev. 16:16.   2. Rev. 16:14.   3. Ezek. 38,39.   4. Rev. 20:8.
5. Rev. 9:16.   6. Rev. 16:12.

Kings from the north[7] and south[8] as well as "ships of Kittim," obviously from the west,[9] are included to round out the prophecy that "all the nations of the earth" shall come against Jerusalem.[10] Many suggestions have been made for the identities of these various rulers.

Where does scriptural exegesis end and fantasy begin? What does the Bible actually teach us concerning the great battle of the end time?

The Day of the Lord

Since Armageddon is mentioned only once, and the Day of the Lord, with which it is connected, is mentioned a number of times, perhaps this is the place to start our investigation. But we are at once confronted with various terms that are interpreted in different ways.

The Day of the Lord and the Day of Christ.   According to one school of interpretation, "the day of the Lord" begins with the Rapture of the Church and ends with the cleansing of heaven and earth.[a] It has to do with "judgment upon unbelieving Jews and Gentiles, and blessings on millennial saints."[b] "The day of our Lord Jesus Christ," on the other hand, "is the period of blessing for the Church beginning with the rapture."[c] This is an oversimplification that fits the biblical material only with much difficulty.

"The day of the Lord" ("the day of Yahweh") is mentioned in sixteen passages in the prophets.[11] By the time of Amos (perhaps the earliest of the prophets, ca. 760 B.C.) it was already a popular subject, thought to be a time of "light" when in reality it would be a time of darkness and judgment,[12] a day of wrath,[13] of justice and punishment[14] upon Israel[15] and upon the nations.[16] Only by twisting the Scriptures can this day be said to begin with the Rapture of the Church, for the term is used in Scripture for any day in which the Lord moves in judgment, not only against Israel, but

---

7. Dan. 11:15.   8. Dan. 11:14.   9. Dan. 11:10.   10. Zech. 12:3.
11. Amos 5:18–20; Joel 1:15; 2:1,11,31 (MT 3:4); 3:14 (MT 4:14); Isa. 2:13; 13:6,9; 22:5; 34:8; Jer. 46:10; Zeph. 1:7–8,14–18; Obad. 15; Ezek. 7:10; 13:5; 30:3; Zech. 14:1.   12. Amos 5:18–20.   13. Zeph. 1:14–16.   14. Ezek. 7:10.
15. Ezek. 13:5.   16. Isa. 13:6–13; 34:8; Jer. 46:10–12; Ezek. 30:3–5.

also against the nations. In particular it was related to the end time.[17]

"The day of Yahweh" cannot be completely separated from prophecies concerning "that day," "those days," "in the latter days," and "the days are coming." While it is true that the day of the Lord is a time of darkness and gloom, of judgment and wrath, it is also true that these same ideas are associated with "that day."[18] At the same time, the day or days that are "coming" are days of restoration, of salvation, of blessing for God's people. Many of the prophecies containing some reference to the "day" are messianic (using the term broadly), and therefore should have for Christians relevance to Christ and the Christian Church as well as to the Israelite people of God.

In the New Testament, the "day" (sometimes capitalized as "the Day" in RSV) can be a day of judgment,[19] of wrath,[20] or of resurrection and reward.[21] The Hebrew phrase *yôm Yāhwêh* ("day of Yahweh") was translated into Greek as *hē hēmera tou kuriou* ("the day of the Lord",[22]) and since the word *kurios*, "Lord," came to be applied as a title to Jesus in the New Testament, the expression "day of the Lord" was readily applied to the day of his Parousia.[23]

"That day" is particularly the end of God's patience with the satanic world-system, the outpouring of his wrath on all that offends his righeousness, and the beginning of the glorious days of the kingdom.[24] Thus it combines the two concepts as two sides of the same coin.[d]

Gog of the Land of Magog

Many of the details that are found in discussions of the battle of Armageddon are drawn from the Gog–Magog prophecy in Ezekiel.[25] It is therefore necessary to examine this prophecy in its context. Ezekiel has divided his prophecy by a number of date formulas.[e] One of these, coming immediately upon news of the fall of Jerusalem,[26] introduces a section that continues to the next date

17. Zech. 14:1–3.   18. Cf. Amos 8:3,9,11,13; Ezek. 38:14,18–23.
19. Matt. 7:22; 10:15; 2 Pet. 3:7.   20. Rom. 2:5.   21. John 6:39; Phil.
1:6,10.   22. Cf. Amos 5:18, Lxx.   23. 1 Thess. 5:2.   24. Cf. Ezek. 38:
14–21.   25. Ezek. 38,39.   26. Ezek. 33:21.

formula[27]—in other words, from 33:21 to 39:29. It is my judgment that this passage, by Ezekiel's own plan, constitutes the context of chapters 38 and 39, and therefore must be studied in its totality.

The Promise of the Land.   The people of Israel presumed that the land was theirs with no strings attached.[28] This was the same sinful attitude against which Jeremiah had prophesied.[29] The Lord, however, required his people to be an example before the nations, and in this they had failed. Therefore they would be taken from the land.[30] The responsibility for the people's sin was largely that of the "shepherds," a term usually applied to the kings, but here probably including all who were responsible for the common weal: kings, prophets, and priests.[31] Judgment would therefore be poured out on the shepherds,[32f] and God himself would be the shepherd, searching out his sheep and bringing them "back into their own land."[33] There is also judgment on the sheep.[34]

The prophecy concerning "David"[35] points to the consummation of the prophetic promises, and the paragraph that follows,[36] containing promises of peace and plenty, also suggests the messianic age. Chapter 35, the prophecy against Edom, can be looked upon as symbolic of the judgment to come upon the nations that have taken over the "inheritance of the house of Israel."[37] Chapter 36 resumes the prophecy of the land.[38] God made clear, however, that this was "for the sake of my holy name" and not because of any virtue of Israel.[39] In their own land they would be cleansed, given a new heart, and receive God's spirit,[40] and then walk according to his statutes.

The vision of the valley of dry bones[41] portrays the resurrection of the Israelite nation,[42] accompanied by the return to the land.[43] That a messianic ideal is intended we may infer from the following facts. Both the northern and southern kingdoms (Israel and Judah) are included[44] and are made "one stick," no longer two nations and two kingdoms,[45] but rather one nation under one king, namely

---

27. Ezek. 40:1.   28. Ezek. 33:24.   29. Jer. 14:13–15.   30. Ezek. 33: 25–29.   31. Ezek. 34:2–6.   32. Ezek. 34:10.   33. Ezek. 34:11–16. 34. Ezek. 34:20.   35. Ezek. 34:24.   36. Ezek. 34:25–31.   37. Ezek. 35: 15.   38. Ezek. 36:5–7.   39. Ezek. 36:20,21.   40. Ezek. 36:24–27. 41. Ezek. 37.   42. Ezek. 37:11.   43. Ezek. 37:12.   44. Ezek. 37:19. 45. Ezek. 37:22.

David, and in the land where their fathers dwelt.[46] God sets his
sanctuary in their midst and dwells with them.[47]

The Prophecy Against Gog. To establish chronological sequence on the basis of apocalyptic prophecy is questionable methodology. Since this prophecy[48] follows that of the restoration of Israel
under the Davidic king (or the Messiah), we might conclude that
the assault of Gog and his forces against God's people is to take place
at the end of the millennial age. In fact, this is where it is placed
in Revelation 20:7,8 and in Rabbinical writings.[g] However, most
Bible scholars interpret this prophecy to apply to the period
immediately before the Advent of the Messiah, therefore connected
with the battle of Armageddon.

Gog is described as "of the land of Magog"[49] and "chief prince of
Meshech and Tubal."[50h] The Hebrew for "chief prince" is $n^e \hat{s}\hat{i}$'
$r\hat{o}$'š, sometimes translated "prince of Rosh."[51i] Long before the rise
of the Soviet Union, some Bible interpreters were suggesting that
Rosh meant Russia and that Meshech and Tubal meant Moscow and
Tobolsk.[j] With the rise and spread of Communism, it has become
popular among students of the end-time prophecies to erect an
elaborate schedule that puts the spotlight on Gog and his allies who
come "out of the uttermost parts of the north"[52] against Israel.[k]

However, to remove a prophecy from its contemporary situation
and apply it only to a future "fulfillment" is not acceptable exegetical methodology. This prophecy had to be meaningful, first of all,
to the people to whom Ezekiel was speaking (or writing). In the
sixth century B.C., the names Gog, Magog, Meshech, Tubal, and
so forth had to have some relevance to the Judeans in exile. The
suggestion has therefore been made that "Gog" was Gyges of Lydia,
"Meshech" the Moschi (Greek moschoi, Akk. muški), "Tubal" the
tabâlu of Assyrian records, and so forth. This is entirely possible
and even probable, although there may be other identifications
that would fit that period, some as yet unknown.

At the same time we must remember that this part of Ezekiel
(and perhaps all of it) is apocalyptic, and one of the principles of
apocalyptic prophecy is to use names as symbols without intending

---

46. Ezek. 37:24,25.　47. Ezek. 37:26,27.　48. Ezek. 38.　49. Ezek.
38:2.　50. Ezek. 38:2,3, RSV.　51. Cf. LXX, NASB.　52. Ezek. 38:15.

dualistic?

historical accuracy. Thus "Babylon" in Relevation probably meant "Rome," and "Nebuchadnezzar" of Daniel 4 may have incorporated elements of Nabonidus. Ezekiel was talking about the end time.[53] If he used the names of fierce and feared enemies known to the Israelites of his day, he did not intend the prophecy to be fulfilled by them. The fulfillment lay in the future.

From the Gog–Magog prophecy we may derive support for a biblical doctrine of final punishment upon the enemies of God's people (cf. Chapter 14, below). In this present satanic age, the judgments of God upon nations (and upon individuals) often come in the form of cause-and-effect. Assyria was "the rod of my anger"[54] to punish the northern kingdom of Israel. When we study the historical situation, we find that Assyria's action against Israel was prompted by the advance of a coalition of small nations that included Israel against Judah[55] and Judah's appeal to Assyria for support of its vassal.[56] The Babylonians were subsequently used to punish the Assyrians for their cruelty; the Persians, the Babylonians; the Greeks, the Persians; the Romans, the Greeks—and so it goes. But if God punishes nations only in this manner, there can never be an end. There must always be an unjust nation to punish another. The prophecy of Gog-Magog breaks this cycle. God himself acts. He summons every kind of terror, pestilence, torrential rains and hail stones, fire and brimstone,[57] until nothing is left but corpses and their weapons.[58]

Other Old Testament Prophecies

Daniel 11–12. We have already looked at this portion of Daniel in the last chapter, and it contributes little specifically to the study of the battle of Armageddon. Interpreters differ over the handling of this material, some holding that it is a prophecy of the near future (i.e., the Ptolemies and Seleucids, second century B.C.), and others that it moves on to the end time (i.e., Antiochus Epiphanes to 11:35, then the Man of Sin from 11:36). For our purpose in the present study we should note that the passage continues into chapter 12, at least through 12:1. The wars of chapter 11 (or at

---

53. Ezek. 39:8.   54. Isa. 10:5.   55. Cf. Isa. 7:1.   56. Cf. 2 Kings 16:7.   57. Ezek. 38:21,22.   58. Ezek. 39:9,12.

least that of the latter part of the chapter) are ended by the intervention of Michael.[59] The details of the prophecy in Daniel are different than those in Ezekiel, but the principal message is the same: the final war is ended by God and his holy angels, not by human power.

Zechariah 12–14. Zechariah is also an apocalyptic prophecy.[1] We must therefore handle it as such and be aware of the problems of interpretation in such prophecies. The advent of the Messiah is foretold,[60] a prophecy which Jesus deliberately fulfilled in the "triumphal entry" on the first Palm Sunday.[61] However, this was not the complete fulfillment, for that is to take place when Messiah comes to set up his kingdom.[62] Some interpret the prophecy of the "idol shepherd"[63] to refer to the Beast of Revelation 19:20. Zechariah continues with a prophecy of the siege of Jerusalem,[64] an attack on the people of God that is ended by God himself.[65]

The term "Megiddon" (with final n) occurs in this context: "On that day the mourning in Jerusalem shall be as great as the mourning for Hadadrimmon in the plain of Megiddon.[66] The word "Armageddon" is supposed to have come into Greek from the Hebrew phrase *har mᵉgiddôn,* "mountain of Megiddon." The spelling of Megiddon is unusual and is found only in Zechariah 12:11 and in the hypothetical Hebrew behind "Armageddon"; elsewhere it is always "Megiddo" (without final n). The reference to "the mourning of Hadadrimmon" is generally taken to relate to the death of Josiah in the battle with Pharaoh Neco (609 B.C.), which occurred at Megiddo.[67] But the mourning for Josiah took place at Jerusalem,[68] and Hadadrimmon is not mentioned elsewhere in the Bible.[m] Attempts to locate Hadadrimmon in the plain of Jezreel (Esdraelon) near Megiddo are therefore not convincing. The possibility remains that "the valley of Megiddon" may not be the plain of Esdraelon near Megiddo, but somewhere in the vicinity of Jerusalem.

Chapter 14 of Zechariah takes up "a day of the Lord"[n] that is coming. In this prophecy, "all the nations" are gathered against

---

59. Dan. 12:1. **60.** Zech. 9:9. **61.** Matt. 21:1–9. **62.** Cf. Matt. 23:39; Zech. 9:10. **63.** Zech. 11:17. **64.** Zech. 12:2. **65.** Zech. 12:11. **66.** Zech. 12:11, RSV slightly altered. **67.** 2 Kings 23:29. **68.** 2 Kings 23:30.

Jerusalem for war.[69] "Then the Lord will go forth and fight against those nations as when he fights on a day of battle."[70] This is followed by the statement, "On that day his feet shall stand on the Mount of Olives,"[71] generally taken by Christian interpreters to refer to the Second Advent of Jesus. That it introduces the messianic age seems to be implied by the fact that the survivors of the nations go up annually to Jerusalem "to worship the King, the Lord of hosts."[72]

There are difficulties of interpretation, as a study of several commentaries will show, and great difficulties of chronological order. It seems best (to me, at least) not to try to force the prophecies in Zechariah 9–14 into a chronological system. Nevertheless there are significant facts that should not be overlooked. The nations go up against the Lord's people in Jerusalem.[73] The Lord protects his people[74] and defeats their enemies.[75] There is a fountain for cleansing[76] and idolatries cease.[77] There will be a great earthquake, rending the Mount of Olives.[78] Living waters will flow from Jerusalem.[79] The Lord will come with his holy ones,[80] and he will become king over all the earth.[81]

Joel 3:2–17.   Joel prophesies a judgment against the nations. "I will gather all nations, and will bring them down into the Valley of Jehoshaphat,° and will judge them there," says Yahweh, because of what they had done to "my people," Israel.[82] That this is to be an assembly for war is clear from the words, "Prepare war."[83] It is brought to an end by the Lord himself, for it is the "day of the Lord"[84] when there are signs in the heavens,[85] and the Lord "shall roar out of Zion" and "the heavens and the earth shall shake."[86] The Lord is the hope of his people. He is portrayed as "dwelling in Zion" and Jerusalem is "holy."[87] The location of the Valley of Jehosphaphat is uncertain ("Jehoshaphat" means "Yahweh has judged"—or "will judge," as a prophetic perfect—and may not even be a geographical name), but it has come to be associated with the Kidron valley, between Jerusalem and the Mount of Olives, in Jewish, Christian, and Moslem tradition. Some have attempted to locate it in the

---

69. Zech. 14:2.   70. Zech. 14:3.   71. Zech. 14:4.   72. Zech. 14:16.
73. Zech. 12:2; 14:2.   74. Zech. 12:8, but cf. 14:2.   75. Zech. 12:4,5; 14:3.   76. Zech. 13:1.   77. Zech. 13:2.   78. Zech. 14:4,5.   79. Zech. 14:8.   80. Zech. 14:5.   81. Zech. 14:9.   82. Joel 3:2 (MT 4:2).
83. Joel 3:9.   84. Joel 3:14.   85. Joel 3:15.   86. Joel 3:16.   87. Joel 3:17.

valley of Jezreel, to harmonize it with their interpretation of Armageddon.[p]

New Testament Teachings

Since Armageddon is mentioned only once in the New Testament (and in the entire Bible), is it possible for us to find other passages that refer to it?

The Teachings of Jesus. Jesus predicted that there would be "wars and rumors of wars."[88] He also spoke of the Great Tribulation,[89] false christs and false prophets,[90] and the coming of the Son of man.[91] He warned his disciples that when the "desolating sacrilege" was erected in the holy place, those who were in Judea were to flee to the mountains.[92] A cryptic reference to the sun, moon, and stars that includes the words, "the stars will fall from heaven, and the powers of the heavens will be shaken," has sometimes been interpreted to refer to the collapse of governments on earth, and has accordingly been associated with the great war of the day of the Lord. The words in Jesus' teaching may have been suggested by Joel's prophecy.[93] There is, however, no clear teaching concerning the battle of Armageddon in the eschatological discourses of Jesus.

The Teachings of Paul. Paul speaks of an end-time apostasy and the revealing of the "man of sin (or lawlessness)."[94] He refers to sufferings and tribulations for the people of God.[95] He has given us a graphic picture of the conflict with the "world rulers of this present darkness"[96] and of our need for spiritual armor.[97] He knew that in a day of "peace and security" there would be sudden destruction from which there will be no escape.[98] He connects the "apostasy" (RSV "rebellion") and the man of lawlessness with some "restraining one,"[99] and tells us that the removal of this restraint or restrainer will bring an outburst of activity which will end when the man of lawlessness is slain by the Lord Jesus at his coming.[100] But again, while these events can be fit into plans that we might construct concerning the events surrounding the battle of Armageddon,

---

88. Matt. 24:6.   **89.** Matt. 24:21.   **90.** Matt. 24:24.   **91.** Matt. 24:30.   **92.** Matt. 24:15.   **93.** Joel 3:15 (MT 4:15).   **94.** 2 Thess. 2:3.   **95.** 2 Thess. 1:5–8.   **96.** Eph. 6:12.   **97.** Eph. 6:11.   **98.** 1 Thess. 5:3.   **99.** 2 Thess. 2:3–7.   **100.** 2 Thess. 2:8.

there is in Paul's writings no clear teaching concerning Armageddon.

Other Scriptures.   The writer of Hebrews recalls the promise of God: "Yet once more I will shake not only the earth but also the heaven,"[101] and he calls upon his reader to "be grateful for receiving a kingdom that cannot be shaken."[102] He quotes a portion of Haggai,[103] the context of which speaks of shaking "all nations, so that the treasure of all nations shall come in, and I will fill this house with splendor."[104] The prophecy of Haggai has end-time relevance,[105] and this "shaking" could include the battle of Armageddon—but this is inference and not exegesis.[r]

Peter believed that "the end of all things is at hand,[106] and warned of a "fiery ordeal."[107] In his second letter, he speaks of false prophets[108] and of God's judgment, in which he "knows how to rescue the godly from trial."[109] He speaks of "fire" and "the day of judgment and destruction of ungodly men"[110] (note the insistence on fire[111]), and the new heavens and new earth. Interpreters differ on the exegesis of these passages, some referring this destruction by fire to the period after the Millennium, when Jesus will deliver up the kingdom to the Father and the age of the New Earth begins.[112]

Jude speaks of "the judgment of the great day"[113] and reminds his readers of the "scoffers" of the last days, "worldly people, devoid of the Spirit."[114] Quoting Enoch he says, "The Lord came with his holy myriads, to execute judgment on all."[115] It is possible to fit these details into a system of our making, but in itself this epistle does not give us details about Armageddon.

The Book of Revelation.   There remains, as we have already seen, but one reference to "Armageddon," namely Revelation 16:16. Attempts to locate this final battle in the valley of Jezreel (Esdraelon) near Megiddo rest on flimsy evidence as already mentioned.[s] There is no "mountain" of Megiddo; it was a "tell"[t] or mound, the remains of a succession of fortified cities that commanded the pass (Wadi ʿAra) between the valley of Jezreel and the

---

101. Heb. 12:26.   **102.** Heb. 12:28; cf. Ezek. 38:19,20.   **103.** Hag. 2:6.
104. Hag. 2:7; cf. 2:21,22.   **105.** Cf. Hag. 2:23.   **106.** 1 Pet. 4:7.
107. 1 Pet. 4:12.   **108.** 2 Pet. 2:1.   **109.** 1 Pet. 2:4–10.   **110.** 1 Pet.
3:7.   **111.** 1 Pet. 3:10–12.   **112.** Cf. 1 Cor. 15:24; Rev. 20:8–10; 21:1.
113. Jude v. 6.   **114.** Jude vv. 18,19.   **115.** Jude v. 14; cf. Enoch 1:9.

coastal highway. In other scriptures, the final battle is located near Jerusalem. The hordes associated with Gog will fall "upon the mountains of Israel,"[116] which usually means the region south of the valley of Jezreel (i.e., Ephraim or Samaria). The only reference to a valley is the Valley of Abarim "east of the sea,"[117] to be called the Valley of Hamon-gog ("the multitude of Gog"), because it will become the burial place for the corpses. There is no question that the valley of Jezreel has been the scene of bloody wars in the past, or that it would be a reasonable place for a great war in the future. The only question I raise is this: Is it the biblically defined scene of the battle of Armageddon?

Revelation furnishes other material pertinent to our study. "The sixth angel poured out his bowl [of the wrath of God] on the great river Euphrates, and its water was dried up, to prepare the way for the kings of the east."[118] There can be no doubt that this refers to the last effort of the "dragon," the "beast" and the "false prophet"[119] to assemble the nations of this satanic age for battle.[120] It is "the great day of God the Almighty,"[121] and the battle is ended by the actions of God: lightning, a great earthquake, and huge hailstones.

Is this the same event as that described in Revelation 19? There, heaven opens and a white horse is seen.[122] The rider is called "Faithful and True"—the very opposite of the "deceiver"[123] —and he judges and makes war in righteousness. He is known by the name "the Word of God."[124] The armies of heaven follow him,[125] and "from his mouth issues a sharp sword with which to smite the nations, and he will rule them with a rod of iron."[126] He is further called "King of kings and Lord of lords."[127] The scene does indeed seem to be the same, namely that of the last great battle in which the satanic "beast" and "false prophet" lead the "kings of the earth and their armies" against "him who sits upon the horse and his army."[128] The resulting carnage does resemble that of the war of Gog and his hordes.[129] We should note, however, that the battle

116. Ezek. 39:4.   117. Ezek. 39:11.   118. Rev. 16:12.   119. Rev. 16:13.   120. Rev.16:14.   121. Rev. 16:14.   122. Rev. 19:11. 123. Rev. 12:9.   124. Rev. 19:13.   125. Rev. 19:14.   126. Rev. 19:15. 127. Rev. 19:16.   128. Rev. 19:19.   129. Rev. 19:17,18; cf. Ezek. 39:4, 17–20.

which is led by Satan, who has deceived "the nations which are at the four corners of the earth," that is Gog and Magog,"[130] takes place *after* the "thousand years."[131] Once again we have scriptural evidence that should warn us against easy identifications and carefully constructed (but synthetic) time sequences.

Summary

Without attempting to assemble the various scriptural passages into a system, we are able to make the following statements:

There will be a final conflict between the forces of Satan and the people of God. This conflict will involve the nations of the world. The attack centers on Jerusalem, or at least that is its intended target. This conflict is ended by the direct intervention of God and his angels. The climax is the advent of the Son of man, the messianic king, and the establishment of his kingdom.

We can possibly go further, while still maintaining acceptable principles of exegesis and hermeneutics. Since the final conflict is mentioned in several places in the Bible, we may join the various passages to form a biblical doctrine of the last satanic war. In this doctrine we may include certain personages (studied in previous chapters) and the parts they play in the conflict. However, when we try to make more precise identifications by cross-reference of the various passages, we enter an area requiring great caution.[v] Since different names or different descriptions are used, it is precarious to identify the "Antichrist" as, for example, the leader of the western bloc which is headquartered at Rome, or to insist that Armageddon is the location of the battle portrayed in Ezekiel 38–39.

When we attempt to connect biblical prophecies with modern events, we enter the area requiring the greatest caution. It is attractive to see the demand for oil, perhaps including the desire of Russia to control the Persian Gulf, as the spark that ignites the conflagration—or the juxtaposition of Israel and the Arab nations, or more generally the growing anti-Jewish sentiment often erroneously called "anti-Semitism," or the tremendous wealth of the minerals in the Dead Sea, or any combination of these. But if we follow the scriptural teaching, we shall probably come to the con-

---

130. Rev. 20:7,8.   131. Rev. 20:7.

clusion that the essential cause of the conflict is the work of Satan in his opposition to God and God's people. How this is to work out in history, we are not explicitly told.

NOTES

a. NSRB, p. 1372, n.5.
b. NSRB, p. 1233, n.1.
c. Ibid.
d. For this reason I cannot accept the distinction between "the day of the Lord" and "the day of Christ." These two terms do indeed serve to bring out two aspects of the "day," but the distinction is supported less by careful exegesis than by a theological system. For further discussion see M. Rist, "Day of Christ," IDB 1: 783, E. Jenni, 'Day of the Lord," IDB 1: 784–785 (with bibliography).
e. That these are not later additions to the text of Ezekiel is strongly indicated by the fact that of the thirteen date formulas, all but two (or probably three) are in chronological order. A later editor would most likely have removed this inconsistency, making them all chronological.
f. The description, "on a day of clouds and thick darkness" (Ezek. 11:12), is reminiscent of prophecies of the Day of the Lord (cf. Joel 2:1,2). The Day of the Lord, in my opinion, must be taken as a day of judgment in any age, and a type of the final judgment.
g. Cf. G. F. Moore, Judaism in the First Centuries of the Christian Era, 2: 337, 344.
h. In Revelation 20:8, "Gog and Magog" is read by some as two persons (cf. Gen. 10:2). Magog is probably a gentilic, referring to the people of the land, in which case, Meshech, Tubal, Gomer (Ezek. 38:5), and Persia (= Madai?) are other Japetic peoples (cf. Gen. 10:2–5), and Cush and Put (Ezek. 38:5) are Hamitic peoples (cf. Gen. 10:6). The Japetic peoples occupied the region north of "the land," and the Hamitic peoples the region to the south.
i. As pointed in MT, n^{e}śî' is construct state, with rô'š as the governing noun. If we accept this pointing, the better translation is "prince of Rosh."
j. Cf. SRB, p. 883, n.1. J. A. Selbie, "Rosh," HDB 4: 314, published in 1902, says, "Gesenius actually thought of the Russians, but this is impossible." (His reasons need not concern us.) LXX Ros has also been taken to mean Russia; note C. F. Keil's objection to this in Commentary on Ezekiel, Biblical Commentary on the Old Testament, C. F. Keil and F. Delitzsch, trans. J. Martin (ca. 1850–1890; reprint ed. 1950), p. 160. BDB, p. 912, takes the word to be a gentilic, but leaves it "not identified."
k. For a detailed construction of the events, along with a map, see C. E. Mason, Jr., Prophetic Problems, pp. 177–203; the map is on p. 188. With Mason's work, which is not tied to a contemporary situation, cf. L. Sale-Harrison, The Coming Great Northern Confederacy (New York: Loizeaux, n.d. [ca. 1940]), which interpreted the prophecies to mean an alliance of Nazi Germany and Russia.

l. On the problems of authorship and date of Zechariah 9–14, see W. S. LaSor, D. A. Hubbard, and F. W. Bush, *Old Testament Survey*, chap. 37.

m. Other scholars, starting from the name that is compounded from the divine names "Hadad" and "Rimmon," connect this "mourning" with the weeping for Tammuz (see Ezek. 8:14). Cf. *IDB*, 2: 507; cf. also *NBD*, p. 497 and *ISBE* 2 (1929): 1314.

n. The Hebrew word order is significant, literally, "a day is coming for (or belonging to) Yahweh." According to a well-established rule, an indefinite noun cannot be expressed by annexation with a proper name, hence *mizmôr ľdāwîd* means "a Psalm of David," and *yôm bāʾ ľYHWH* means "a day of Yahweh is coming." See W. S. LaSor, *Handbook of Biblical Hebrew* (Grand Rapids, MI: Eerdmans, 1979), 2: §36.244.

o. See G. A. Barrois, "Jehoshaphat, Valley of," *IDB* 2: 816.

p. Cf. W. S. LaSor, "The Sanctity of the Mount of Olives," *Christian News from Israel* 13 (Dec. 1962): 16–23.

q. No mention is made here, or elsewhere that I have been able to find, that they were to flee to "the mountains and canyons of Petra," a view that is found in several works on prophecy; cf. H. Lindsey, *The Late Great Planet Earth* (Grand Rapids, MI: Zondervan, 1970; New York: Bantam, 1973), p. 142.

r. I do not derogate inference, if it is carefully controlled. There is a vital quality of Scripture ("quick and active") that requires us to draw inferences under the Spirit's illumination. But these should be indicated as such and not given as doctrines of the Bible.

s. Questioning the common "location" of Armageddon is not to be understood as a denial of the theory, but rather as an insistence that we walk into these interpretations with our eyes open.

t. A *tell*, archeologically speaking, is a hill that has been formed by successive layers of occupation, each atop the earlier layers, over hundreds or thousands of years. Megiddo is a large tell (but not the largest), standing about 70 feet (21.3 meters) high—hardly a high hill, much less a mountain.

u. Some writers have set up an elaborate schedule for this war, including the king of the north and his allies (Gog; cf. Ezek. 38:6; Jer. 1:14; Joel 2:20), the king of the south and his allies (Egypt, Libya, Ethiopia; cf. Dan. 11:42,43; Ezek. 38:5), the kings of the east (Japan or China or India [?]; cf. Dan. 11:44; Rev. 16:12), and the western bloc of the restored Roman Empire (Dan. 11:41–45, cf. 2:43,44). Cf. R. Pache, *The Return of Jesus Christ*, pp. 279–282; C. E. Mason, Jr., *Prophetic Problems*, pp. 187–189; H. Lindsey, *The Late Great Planet Earth*, pp. 142–145.

v. The works of H. Lindsey are particularly open to this criticism. On page after page he makes positive identifications of persons, places, and events, often citing a biblical reference which, in context, does not support his identification. For example, "The Roman force will establish common headquarters on Mount Moriah or the Temple area in Jerusalem," followed by a quotation of Daniel 11:45 (Amplified). (*The Late Great Planet*

Earth, p. 147.) Study of the passage quoted *in its context* will show that there are several problems here, as disagreement among the commentators readily indicates.

ADDITIONAL READING

Burton, Alfred H. *Russia's Destiny in the Light of Prophecy*. New York: Gospel Publishing, 1917.

Lindsey, Hal. *The 1980's: Countdown to Armageddon*. New York: Bantam, 1980.

Pache, René. *L'Au Delà*. Vennes sur Lausanne: Éditions Emmaüs, 1955.

Riley, W. B. "The Last Days; the Last War and the Last King." In *Christ and Glory*, edited by A. C. Gaebelein. New York: "Our Hope," n.d. (ca. 1919). Pp. 163–176.

Sale-Harrison, L. *The Resurrection of the Old Roman Empire*. 12th ed. New York: Loizeaux, n.d.

Walvoord, John F., and Walvoord, John E. *Armageddon*. Grand Rapids, MI: Zondervan, 1974.

Wilson, Dwight. *Armageddon Now!* Grand Rapids, MI: Baker, 1977.

12. The Millennium

The Problem

There is widespread teaching in certain Christian circles that there will be a "Millennium"—a thousand-year period during which the Kingdom of God is established on earth. Others say that the Kingdom of God is entirely a spiritual concept, and that the idea of an earthly kingdom is the product of a pre-Christian age.

Does the Bible teach there will be a millennial kingdom? If so, is it established by the Church militant in this age? Or is it to be established by Jesus Christ at his Return? What is the nature of this kingdom? Is it for the Jews who finally accept Jesus as Messiah at his coming? Will Jesus sit on the throne of David in Jerusalem? Will the temple be rebuilt and the bloody sacrifices reinstituted? Will there be physical changes on earth, so that the fields increase their productivity, carnivores become herbivores ("the lion shall eat straw like the ox"), and the human life-span is greatly lengthened?

There are many problems connected with the millennial concept, and a great number of books and articles have been written on parts or all of the subject. In this study I hope to take up the main idea and some of the more significant treatments of this idea —but after many years of study of the subject, I have both great confidence in the basic idea that there will be a millennium, and due humility in reaching conclusions on the satellite subjects.

Terms and Definitions

Millennium. The word "millennium"[a] comes from Latin *mille,* "thousand," and *annum,* "year." It therefore means, strictly speaking, "a thousand years," but the term has become generalized to mean an indefinite period of happiness and bliss in an indefinite future.

Millennial, Millennialism, Millennialist. The word "millennial" is an adjective meaning simply "pertaining to the Millennium," but in religious circles it often connotes sectarian or unstable doctrine. "Millennialism" is a system of doctrine that includes belief in the Millennium, and a "Millennialist" is an adherent of such doctrine.

Pre-, Post-, and Amillennialist. These terms are used with reference to the Second Coming. Belief that the Return of Christ will take place *before* the millennium is "Premillennialism," and its adherents are "Premillennialists."[b] The idea that the Church establishes the Kingdom of God on earth, which is to endure for a thousand years after which Christ will return, is "Postmillenialism" and its adherents are "Postmillennialists." Those who reject the idea of a millennial kingdom on earth, while still fervently believing in the Second Coming, are called "Amillennialists" and the system is "Amillennialism" ("a-" in this usage means "without").

Chiliasm and Dispensationalism. In older works, and sometimes with a pejorative sense in more recent works, the term "chiliasm" is used, and its adherents are called "chiliasts." The words come from the Greek *chilia* "thousand [years]," and should be used exactly the same as the words "premillennialism" and "premillennialist." No opprobrium should be attached to the word—nor to any of these terms, since the adherents of each system can be called "born-again, Bible-believing Christians."

Dispensationalism is a theological system that includes belief in the premillennial return of Christ.[c] It is therefore frequently taken to be a synonym for "Premillennialism"—which is only partly correct. All Dispensationalists are Premillennialists, but some (many?) Premillennialists are *not* Dispensationalists. Dispensationalists generally hold to belief in the pretribulation Rapture, and again the terms must be kept in clear categories.

The Biblical Basis

The charge is sometimes made that the entire millennial system is based on but six occurrences of the term "the thousand years" in one brief portion of a very obscure book, Revelation.[1] This is a distortion of truth. It is true that the only references to "the

---

1. Rev. 20:2–7.

thousand years" are in this passage in Revelation. It is also true that Revelation is a difficult book to interpret—but this is no reason to deny its authority. However, the millennial system (which I understand to mean the component parts of the doctrine) is built on the entire Bible, certainly beginning with the Davidic covenant,[2] or more likely with the covenant with Abraham.[3]

Hermeneutical Method.   The system of interpreting the Bible, particularly the prophetic passages, is the principal difference between those who believe in a Millennium and those who do not. There are many promises concerning the future time of peace and prosperity and righteousness. These promises, especially in the Old Testament, contain many elements that could be considered as "materialistic," such as the king and the throne in Jerusalem, the productivity of the vines and fig trees, the lion lying down with the lamb, and so on. Premillennialists are inclined to take such prophecies more or less *literally.*[d]

The Old Testament Teaching.   In our study of the messianic idea we saw something of the development of the concept of the ideal king and the ideal kingdom. This king, who later came to be called the "Messiah," was an essential element of the Davidic convenant,[4] a doctrine which was picked up and emphasized in the New Testament. The ideal kingdom is mentioned numerous times in the Prophets and Psalms, and we have examined some of the passages.

Prophecies of "the latter days" (and similar expressions, most of which have end-time or messianic-age relevance) include the regathering of the tribes of Israel and Judah to the land God had given to Abraham, Isaac, and Jacob. Some of the earlier prophecies might be interpreted to refer to the return of the exiles after the conquest of Babylonia by Persia,[5] but this disregards the meaning of the expressions "the days are coming," "in the latter days," and so on, all of which were understood by pre-Christian Jewish interpreters as well as by the early Christians as applying to the messianic age. That the return of the exiles is to be applied to a later return is underscored by the fact that the idea is found in

---

2. 2 Sam. 7:4–29.   **3.** Gen. 12:1–3; 17:1–8.   **4.** 2 Sam. 7:12,13.
5. E.g., Amos 9:14,15.

the postexilic prophet Zechariah.[6] The sequence of events in Ezekiel 34–37 also requires a restoration—or resurrection—of the tribes of Israel and Judah, that is, the once-divided kingdom, as part of the messianic age.[7c]

Jerusalem is to be the center of this ideal kingdom. God sets his king on Zion, his holy hill.[8] The Holy One of Israel is in Zion's midst.[9] Jerusalem will be rebuilt, never again to be uprooted or overthrown.[10] The temple will be rebuilt[11] in the city whose name shall be "The Lord is there."[12] This prophecy may be interpreted to imply a spiritual presence, but Ezekiel was obviously dealing with measurements and materials that have no relevance in a "spiritual temple." To Jerusalem the Gentiles come to worship the King,[13] bringing wealth and seeking to know the Lord the God of Israel.[14] From Jerusalem will go forth the Torah, the word of the Lord,[15] and "living waters"[16] will flow from Jerusalem eastward and westward, whether we interpret the expression to mean literal streams of water or spiritual life-giving streams.[17]

In these prophecies, there is sometimes no clear line between the king who is the "son of David" (i.e., of human descent) and the Lord. It is therefore possible to move from the physical or material to the spiritual while working from the same passage. Thus God and David are both portrayed as the shepherd over the people.[18] The king is addressed as "God,"[19] and his deeds and the requests addressed to him are remarkably similar to those that are commonly ascribed to God.[20f]

There will be worldwide *political* change. Daniel's prophecies, however difficult the book may be, are crystal clear on this point. The kingdoms portrayed by the parts of the statue (cf. Daniel's own interpretation[21]) will be smashed, and "the God of heaven will set up a kingdom which shall never be destroyed."[22] The "beasts" from the sea[23] are "four kings,"[24] but "their dominion was taken away"[25] and "the saints of the Most High shall . . . possess the

---

6. Zech. 12:6–9.   7. Ezek. 36:8–37:28.   8. Ps. 2:6.   9. Isa. 12:6.
10. Jer. 31:40.   11. Ezek. 40–48.   12. Ezek. 48:35.   13. Zech. 14:17.
14. Isa. 60:1–16.   15. Isa. 2:2–4; Mic. 4:1–3.   16. Zech. 14:8.   17. Cf.
Jer. 2:13; John 4:14.   18. Ezek. 34:15,23.   19. Ps. 45:6,7 (MT 7,8).
20. Ps. 72.   21. Dan. 2:36–43.   22. Dan. 2:44,45.   23. Dan. 7:3.
24. Dan. 7:17.   25. Dan. 7:12.

kingdom for ever, for ever and ever."[26] So far, these prophecies could be interpreted in a purely spiritual manner: the earthly, material kingdoms will be replaced by a heavenly, spiritual kingdom. But Daniel associates the events of the end time with Jerusalem,[27] the temple,[28] and the Jewish people.[29]

This idea of political change is found in other Prophets. Amos foresaw the raising up of "the booth of David" in order to possess "all the nations who are called by" the Lord's name.[30] Micah spoke of a coming "ruler in Israel" who "shall be great to the ends of the earth."[31] Isaiah prophesied of the "shoot from the stump of Jesse,"[32] who shall judge with righteousness and equity, who shall "smite the earth with the rod of his mouth"[33] —mentioning God's "holy mountain," an expression used of Jerusalem—so that "the earth shall be full of the knowledge of the Lord as the waters cover the sea."[34] In his prophecy of "the great day of the Lord,"[35] Zephaniah spoke of the destruction of the nations and said "the remnant of my people shall plunder them, and the survivors of my nation shall possess them."[36] The nations mentioned were indeed those in the immediate vicinity of Israel, but Zephaniah was certainly looking beyond the contemporary situation to the end time.[37] Ezekiel's prophecy of the resurrection of the nation does not end with Israel dwelling in the land under David the king,[38] but continues with the destruction of the nations that have gathered on "the mountains of Israel,"[39] and the establishing of the Lord's glory among the nations.[40]

There will also be *physical* changes in the end time. Isaiah's idyllic picture of the wolf and the lamb, the leopard and the kid, the child and the adder's den, is too well known to need repeating.[41] Ezekiel gives a similar picture: "I will make with them [the "sheep" under their "shepherd" David] a covenant of peace and banish wild beasts from the land, so that they may dwell securely in the wilderness and sleep in the woods."[42] Ezekiel goes on to say: "and the trees of the field shall yield their fruit, and the earth shall yield

---

26. Dan. 7:18.   27. Dan. 9:2,25.   28. Dan. 11:31; 12:11.   29. Dan. 10:14; 12:1.   30. Amos 9:11,12.   31. Mic. 5:2–4 (MT 1–3).   32. Isa. 11:1.   33. Isa. 11:4.   34. Isa. 11:9.   35. Zeph. 1:14.   36. Zeph. 2:9. 37. Cf. Zeph. 1:14; 3:8,9,14–20.   38. Ezek. 37:24,25.   39. Ezek. 38:8. 40. Ezek. 39:21.   41. Isa. 11:6–9.   42. Ezek. 34:25.

its increase. . . . And I will provide for them prosperous plantations."[43] Isaiah also speaks of this abundance: "He will give rain for the seed with which you sow the ground, and grain, the produce of the ground, which will be rich and plenteous. In that day your cattle will graze in large pastures. . . . And upon every lofty mountain and every high hill there will be brooks running with water. . . . Moreover the light of the moon will be as the light of the sun, and the light of the sun will be sevenfold . . . in the day when the Lord binds up the hurt of his people."[44] Human life-span will be lengthened: "No more shall there be in it an infant that lives but a few days, or an old man who does not fill out his days, for the child shall die a hundred years old . . . for like the days of a tree shall the days of my people be."[45g]

It is acceptable hermeneutic to take the language of such prophecies as poetic or figurative. Therefore we may interpret the passages to teach that the harmful and destructive elements, the causes of poverty and hunger, the frustrations of life,[46] and similar evils will be done away, without intending to teach that the lion's digestive system will be changed so that it will be able to eat straw like the ox.[47] But it is not acceptable, in my opinion, to remove these scenes from earth and try to make them apply only to incorporeal spirits floating on cloud nine. Jewish and early Christian students of Scripture may have fantasized them almost to ridiculous extremes, but modern spiritualizers have made them practically meaningless.

There will also be great *spiritual* changes. The survivors of Israel will be "holy"[48] (note the geographical details[49]), established in righteousness.[50] The nations will renounce war and turn to peace.[51] God will cleanse his people with "clean water"; he will give them a "new spirit," and replace the "heart of stone" with a "heart of flesh"[52] (again, note the geographical details[53]). God will make a "new covenant" with his people, putting his law within them, writing it on their hearts, so that all will know the Lord.[54] When he pours out his spirit on "all flesh," the means of revelation

---

43. Ezek. 34:27,29.   44. Isa. 30:23–26.   45. Isa. 65:20–22.   46. Cf. Isa. 65:22.   47. Isa. 65:25.   48. Isa. 4:2–4.   49. Isa. 4:5.   50. Isa. 54:14.   51. Mic. 4:3.   52. Ezek. 36:24,25.   53. Ezek. 36:28.   54. Jer. 31:31–34.

(dreams and visions) will be available to old and young alike, sons and daughters and even menservants and maidservants will have the prophetic spirit.[55] The inclusion of such prophecies should silence the objection that Millennialism is only crassly materialistic.

The New Testament Teaching.   It must be admitted at once that the emphasis in the New Testament is on the spiritual and ethical rather than on the material aspects of the kingdom. There were good reasons for this, and these must be taken into account in any study of the messianic kingdom.

For one thing, the Jews of Jesus' day were strongly influenced by a materialistic concept: freedom from Roman rule, the establishment of an independent kingdom, and material prosperity. This is understandable, and in mentioning it I intend no criticism of the emphasis. The Scriptures had taught them that they were a special people, precious in God's sight. Yet, for most of the preceding six hundred years they had been a conquered people, dominated by Assyrians, Babylonians, Persians, Seleucids, Ptolemies, and Romans. They had also been taught by the prophets to look for a coming deliverer, so it was in line with this background that many looked to Jesus to be that promised Messiah. They wanted to take him by force and make him king.[56] If Jesus had not played down the messianic concept, if he had not stressed that his kingdom was not of this world, if he had let the popular cry for deliverance alter the message he was proclaiming, there can be no doubt that he would have brought down on his people the wrath of Rome—as their leaders recognized.[57]

A second reason for stressing the ethical and spiritual was the religious attitude of the leadership of the people. The sins of the fathers were still present, and the Scribes had become slaves of their Tradition which had destroyed the true nature and purpose of the law.[58h] Selfishness, greed, injustice, and lack of care for the poor were strong. Even Hillel could find no place for the common man.[i] It was necessary for Jesus, as a true prophet, to condemn the sins and to call the people, especially the leaders, back to the law

---

55. Joel 2:28,29 (MT 31,2).   **56.** John 6:15.   **57.** John 11:48.
58. Cf. Matt. 15:1–6.

and the prophets. His stress on the spiritual implications was needed to counteract the absence of such emphasis among many of his contemporaries.

The most important reason for lack of emphasis on the material aspects of the messianic kingdom is the plan of salvation, which called for the sacrifice to take away the sins of the world,[59] for until sin is removed, a kingdom can only be a sinful continuation of the past. Nevertheless, the idea of the messianic kingdom on earth is not absent in the New Testament.

(1) Jesus is presented in the New Testament as king, indeed as the messianic king. While we Gentiles today may be able to spiritualize this concept, to the Jews of Jesus' day it had to carry with it the Old Testament prophetic symbols.[60] Satan's temptation, offering Jesus the kingdoms of the world, would have had no point if Jesus had not had this ultimate goal in mind.[61] The disciples were still looking for this messianic kingdom after the resurrection of Jesus, and he did not seek to correct their question.[62]

(2) Jesus stated clearly that he came to fulfill, not to abolish, the law and the prophets.[63] To his hearers, this certainly conveyed the material as well as the spiritual content of these scriptures. The Abrahamic promises are still in force,[64] and these included the possession of the land[65] to which the prophets so often referred in end-time prophecies. Peter spoke of "the times of refreshing" and said that Jesus must remain in heaven "until the time for establishing all that God spoke by the mouth of his holy prophets from of old."[66]

(3) Jesus was called "son of David,"[67] which to his contemporaries was a messianic title. He claimed to be the Messiah,[68] and when he was formally asked, "Are you the Messiah?"[69] and "So you are a king?"[70] his reply was "I am"[71] or "You say so."[72] This was not an evasive answer, as both the high priest and Pilate recognized.[73] While Peter did not refer to the risen Jesus as "king" he did ascribe to him the throne of David and kingly prerogatives.[74]

---

59. John 1:29; 3:3.   **60.** Cf. Luke 1:32,33; 2:4,10,11; Matt. 2:1–16; John 1:49; Matt. 3:2.   **61.** Matt. 4:8.   **62.** Acts 1:6.   **63.** Matt. 5:17,18.   **64.** Cf. Luke 1:54,55,68–75; Matt. 8:11; cf. also Rom. 9–11; Gal. 3:16–18.   **65.** Gen. 12:7; 15:18–21.   **66.** Acts 3:21.   **67.** Matt. 12:23.   **68.** John 4:25,26.   **69.** Mark 14:61.   **70.** John 18:38.   **71.** Mark 14:62.   **72.** Matt. 26:64; John 18:37.   **73.** Matt. 26:65,66.

At Thessalonica, the apostles must have conveyed the idea that Jesus is king.[75] But Jesus never reigned as king in his first advent. The fulfillment is portrayed in Revelation 19:11–16.

(4) Jesus performed, to a limited extent in space and time, works foretold of the messianic age.[76] Particularly noteworthy in this respect are his claim following the reading of a portion of Isaiah[77] and his reply to John the Baptizer.[78] The prophecies of messianic works require a much greater fulfillment in the messianic age to come,[79] and the "greater works" Jesus promised to his apostles[80] in no way complete the fulfillment. Jesus' power over the demonic[81] was likewise but a foretaste of his ultimate triumph over Satan.[82]

(5) Jerusalem was still the city of the great king,[83] to be trodden by the Gentiles "until the times of the Gentiles are fulfilled,"[84] still to be redeemed,[85] not to be replaced simply by a heavenly Jerusalem,[86] but even by one coming down to earth,[87] to which the kings of the earth bring their glory,[88] and in the light of which the nations walk.[89]

These and other passages that could be added have led me to believe that the concept of an earthly kingdom, during the period when Satan will be bound[90] and the saints will reign with Christ,[91] is a biblical doctrine. It is derived from the scriptures of the Old and New Testaments, and therefore should be accepted by those who accept the authority of the Bible. That it is not universally accepted in the Church may be due to several reasons. The doctrine has been made to look ridiculous by some of its interpreters, both in the ancient and in the modern Church, by pressing for a literalness that ignores the literary genres of the passages. Then, too, the stress on the spiritual and ethical elements of the kingdom, which is properly part of the messianic kingdom, has been de-emphasized or even ignored by many who are more interested in the future than in the present, more interested in "pie in the sky" than in bread on the poor woman's table.

---

74. Acts 2:30–36.   75. Acts 17:7.   76. Matt. 4:23–25; 8:14–17. 77. Luke 4:18–22.   78. Luke 7:20–22.   79. Cf. Rev. 21:3,4.   80. John 14:12.   81. Mark 1:23–26; Luke 4:33–37.   82. Rev. 20:2,3.   83. Matt. 5:35.   84. Luke 21:24.   85. Luke 2:38.   86. Heb. 12:22.   87. Rev. 21:2.   88. Rev. 21:26.   89. Rev. 21:24.   90. Rev. 20:2.   91. Rev. 20:5.

Development of the Dogma

There is a difference between *doctrine* and *dogma*. Doctrine, specifically biblical doctrine, is that which is taught in the Bible. Dogma is the systematization of doctrine by a church or a group and the presentation of this system as something to be received by the community. Thus far I have attempted to set forth biblical teachings that are basic for the doctrine of the millennial kingdom; now we must see what has been done with these teachings.

The Jewish Concept. Judaism is no more monolithic in its beliefs than is the Church. For each statement I might make, a qualifying or contradictory statement might be offered by another person. Nevertheless I believe the following is representative of the "classical" form of the doctrine. The Messiah, for which "Son of David" is an equivalent, will come and establish a kingdom on earth. This Messiah is a human being from the line of David, who will reign in Jerusalem. Before he comes, certain things are to take place. On the one hand, Israel is to repent, and this lack of repentance is delaying his coming.[j] At the same time, there is to be an outburst of wickedness, sometimes called "the birth pangs" of the Messiah. Elijah will come just before the Messiah. The messianic age will be a golden age, with political, physical, and spiritual changes. It will be of limited duration, the last part of "this age" and distinct from "the age to come."[k]

There is no question concerning the general interpretation of the ancient Jewish scholars. The messianic age is to take place on earth, with the messianic king located in Jerusalem. "Judaism," writes G. Scholem, "has always maintained a concept of redemption as an event which takes place publicly, on the stage of history and within the community."[l] J. Klausner states: "It is Christianity which has attempted to remove the political and nationalistic part which is there, and leave only the ethical and spiritual part."[m]

The Christian Interpretation. There can be no doubt that the early Christians held much the same viewpoint as the Jews on the matter of the Millennium. All scholars that I have consulted admit this—some ridiculing the idea, some trying to build support for a system that the evidence hardly provides, and some simply trying to handle the matter historically.[n] While Origen and others objected to some of the features of this early Chiliasm, it was Augustine who was largely responsible for developing the position that the Millennium is the present church age.° This concept has been claimed by both Postmillennialists and Amillennialists, depending somewhat on the support they find in Augustine for features of their systems.

A kind of Chiliasm can be traced through the Middle Ages and in modern times. Many of the Westminster divines and British authors of commentaries (notably in the Macmillan series) have been claimed by Premillennialists. It seems to me that this claim, while sometimes overdrawn, is basically valid: at least, there is little support for any kind of Postmillennialism.

Postmillennialism derived much of its support from emphasis on ethical teachings, reacting perhaps against the otherworldliness of many Premillennialists, and building on the basic optimism of the day—an optimism that was seriously shattered by World War II and subsequent developments. Amillennialism, which saw clearly that this church age is no age of glory, and doubtless tired of the date setting and the emotionalism that often replaced scholarly study in the Bible-conference movement, stresses the spiritual truths related to the Return of Christ.

Why Should There Be an Earthly Kingdom?

The Bible does not depend for its authority on the support of human reason. Yet, the biblical religion is reasonable, and the Creator of the human race gave us a rational as well as an emotional nature. To ask why there should be a Kingdom of God on earth is a reasonable question.

For God's Glory. The messianic kingdom on earth is a vindication of God's creation activity. God created this physical earth. God created Satan. God created Adam with a material as well as a spiritual nature. God permitted (or decreed) that Satan should tempt the human race and that the creation would come under bondage.[92] The triumph of God over the satanic dominion of this planet is necessary for the glory of God. If there were no messianic age, if God simply picked up the redeemed remnant and took them off to heaven, then we would have to conclude that God was unable to

---

92. Cf. Rom. 8:18–22.

complete what he began. If the human race, whether Israel or the Church or any other group, were to "bring in the kingdom," with no help or only minor help from God, then we would have to adopt a limited- or finite-God theology.

For the Sake of His Promises.   God promised Abraham and his heirs a kingdom here on earth. They were looking for that kingdom when Jesus was born and when he was about to be taken up to heaven. Many Jews and Christians believe that the scriptures cannot be broken. God has in the past kept his word. We believe that he will continue to do so.

Summary

The Bible teaches that there will be a millennial age of righteousness and peace, of justice and plenty, associated with the coming of the Messiah. This age completes the present, after which there is another age to come. It is my conviction that the messianic kingdom will be established on this earth by the Second Coming of Christ, and that it will last for a long period, given in Revelation as "a thousand years." There are other interpretations of the biblical data held by sincere Christians who are also looking for the Return of Christ, and while I may disagree with some of their interpretations I honor their love of Christ and their obedience to the word of God. We do now indeed "see through a glass darkly."

NOTES

a. "Millennium" is often incorrectly spelled with one *n*, perhaps due to confusion with "millenarian" which lacks the double *n*.

b. The longer terms "Millenarian," "Premillenarian," and so forth, are sometimes used in older writings, but are not in common use at the present time.

c. Dispensationalism (or one variety of it) is the system taught in the *Scofield Reference Bible* and with minor modifications in the *Revised Scofield Reference Bible*. For a history of the development of the system see G. E. Ladd, *The Blessed Hope*, pp. 35–60, 130–136; O. T. Allis, *Prophecy and the Church* (Philadelphia: Presbyterian and Reformed, 1945), pp. 1–54, 289–304; D. M. Beegle, *Prophecy and Prediction* (Ann Arbor, MI: Pryor Pettengill, 1978), pp. 157–182. These works are by authors who are not Dispensationalists and who differ considerably in their attitudes toward Dispensationalism. Ladd's work is the most irenic of the three. Cf. also C. C. Ryrie, *Dispensationalism Today* (Chicago: Moody, 1965).

d. This is a difficult word to define. Even "literalists" have enough sense to know that figures of speech, poetic language, symbolism, and the like, are not to be taken "literally," but are to be understood according to the intention of the author and the literary genres he used.

e. Ezekiel's prophecy is dated prior to the return under Zerubbabel, and it could be argued that he was looking forward to the return that took place in 538 B.C. Granted, for the sake of argument—but he was still giving a prophecy of the day when "David" would be king, when the everlasting kingdom would be established, and when *all* of Israel, not just the remnant of the tribe of Judah, would be restored to the land. We must interpret the meaning of his words by his intent. For other prophecies of the regathering to the land, cf. Isaiah 10:21-23; 11:11,12; 43:1-7; Jeremiah 31:10-14.

f. Jesus seized upon this point when he bluntly asked the Pharisees: "What do you think of the Messiah? Whose son is he?" When they correctly answered, "The son of David," Jesus put the second question: "How is it then that David, inspired by the Spirit, calls him Lord . . . ? If David thus calls him Lord, how is he his son?" (Matt. 22:41-45).

g. In a discussion of gerontology on the Merv Griffin show, 5 January 1982, Drs. Dirk Pearson and Saul Kent expressed the convictions that the human life-span will soon increase to a hundred years and that a thousand years is not unthinkable in the light of recent discoveries in this science.

h. Paul was involved in the same struggle with those who were legalists. This had led to a gross misunderstanding of both Paul and the Torah (Old Testament Law). The Law was never intended to save, and it was not a legal system. The Hebrew word *tôrāʰ* means "instruction." Salvation under the law was by the grace of God, not by works, as Paul and the author of Hebrews clearly point out.

i. "No ignorant man (*ʿam hā-āres*) is religious" (*Pirqe Abot* 2.5), quoted by G. F. Moore, *Judaism in the First Centuries of the Christian Era*, 2: 160. Cf. the words of the Pharisees in John 7:49, "But this crowd, who do not know the law, are accursed."

j. "R. Levi said: If the Israelites would but repent for one day, they would be redeemed, and the son of David would come straight away, as it says, 'Today, if ye would hear his voice' " (Canticles Rabbah v, §2, 2; see C. G. Montefiore and H. Loewe, *A Rabbinic Anthology* [New York: Schocken, 1974], p. 318).

k. While I have drawn this outline from many sources over many years, the basic elements can be found in J. Klausner, *The Messianic Idea in Israel*; G. F. Moore, *Judaism*, 2: 323-376, and C. G. Montefiore and H. Loewe, *Rabbinic Anthology*, pp. 580-608 and numerous references in the excellent index, pp. 773-853.

l. G. Scholem, *The Messianic Idea in Judaism* (New York: Schocken, 1971), p. 1.

m. Klausner, *The Messianic Idea*, p. 10. Klausner adds, "Yet the influence of Judaism on the first Christians was so strong, that the 'chiliasts' (those early Christians who believed that Jesus the Messiah would return, coming down to earth and setting up the millennial kingdom) pictured to themselves the Kingdom of Heaven filled with bodily and earthly pleasure, precisely as did the Jews."

n. W. H. Rutgers, *Premillennialism in America* (Goes, Holland: Oosterbaan & LeCointre, 1930), showing his bias by lumping together all sorts of heretical and less-than-orthodox sects with nondispensational as well as dispensational Premillennialists, admits grudgingly that the Fathers were "chiliastic," but only because they were anti-Gnostic (p. 58). For a more objective survey, cf. J. W. Montgomery, "The Millennium," in C. F. Armerding and W. W. Gasque, eds., *Dreams, Visions, and Oracles*, pp. 177–170 (condensed from the article on "Millennium" to appear in vol. 3 of the revised *ISBE*). Cf. also L. E. Froom, *The Prophetic Faith of Our Fathers*, 1: 458–459.

o. Augustine *City of God* 20.8.

ADDITIONAL READING

Prophetic Studies of the International Prophetic Conference. New York: Revell, 1886.

Bass, Clarence. *Background to Dispensationalism: Its Historical Genesis and Ecclesiastical Implication*. Grand Rapids, MI: Eerdmans, 1960.

Beet, Joseph Agar. *The Last Things*. New York: Methodist Book Concern, 1897.

Biederwolf, William E. *The Millennium Bible*. Chicago: Blessing, 1924.

Blackstone, W. E. *The Millennium*. New York: Revell, 1904.

Boettner, Loraine. *The Millennium*. Philadelphia: Presbyterian and Reformed, 1957.

Briggs, Charles A. "Origin and History of Premillennialism." *Lutheran Quarterly Review* 9 (1879): 207–245.

Brown, W. Adams. "Millennium." *HDB* 3: 370–373.

Cadbury, H. J. "Intimations of Immortality in the Thought of Jesus." In *Immortality and Resurrection*, edited by K. Stendahl. New York: Macmillan, 1975. Pp. 115–149.

Case, Shirley Jackson. *The Millennial Hope*. Chicago: University of Chicago Press, 1919.

Clarke, Adam. *Clarke's Commentary*. New York: Methodist Book Concern, n.d.

Cullmann, O. "Immortality of the Soul or Resurrection of the Dead?" In *Immortality and Resurrection*, edited by K. Stendahl. New York: Macmillan, 1975. Pp. 9–53.

English, E. S. *Companion to the New Scofield Reference Bible*. New York: Oxford University Press, 1972. Pp. 151–154.

Erickson, Millard J. *Contemporary Options in Eschatology*. Grand Rapids, MI: Baker, 1977.

Feinberg, Charles L. *Premillennialism or Amillennialism?* Grand Rapids, MI: Zondervan, 1936.

Fuller, Daniel P. "The Hermeneutics of Dispensationalism." Th.D. dissertation. Chicago: Northern Baptist Theological Seminary, 1957.

Kellogg, Samuel H. *Are Premillennialists Right?* New York: Revell, 1923.

Kik, J. Marcellus. *An Eschatology of Victory.* Nutley, NJ: Presbyterian and Reformed, 1971.

Kraus, C. Norman. *Dispensationalism in America: Its Rise and Development.* Richmond, VA: Knox, 1958.

Kromminga, D. H. *The Millennium in the Church: Studies in the History of Christian Chiliasm.* Grand Rapids, MI: Eerdmans, 1945.

Ladd, George E. *Crucial Questions about the Kingdom of God.* Grand Rapids, MI: Eerdmans, 1952.

————. *Jesus and the Kingdom.* New York: Harper & Row, 1964.

LaSor, William Sanford. "The Exegetical Basis of Premillennialism." Th. M. thesis, Princeton Theological Seminary, 1943.

Lindsey, Hal. *There's a New World Coming.* Santa Ana, CA: Vision House, 1973; New York: Bantam, 1975.

Mains, George P. *Premillennialism: Non-Scriptural, Non-Historic, Non-Scientific, Non-Philosophical.* New York: Abingdon, 1920.

Pink, Arthur W. *The Millennium.* Swengel, PA: Bible Truth Depot, n.d.

Rutgers, William H. *Premillennialism in America.* Goes, Holland: Oosterbaan and LeCointre, 1930.

Ryrie, C. C. *Dispensationalism Today.* Evanston, IL: Moody, 1973.

————. *The Basis of the Premillennial Faith.* Neptune, NJ: Loizeaux, 1954.

Snowden, James H. *The Coming of the Lord: Will It Be Premillennial?* New York: Macmillan, 1919.

Stendahl, Krister, ed. *Immortality and Resurrection.* New York: Macmillan, 1965.

Thielecke, H. "Life after Death." In *Evangelical Faith.* Translated by G. W. Bromiley. Grand Rapids, MI: Eerdmans, 1982. Vol. 3, chap. 32.

Walvoord, John F. *The Rapture Question.* Findlay, OH: Dunham, 1957.

West, Nathaniel. *The Thousand Years in Both Testaments.* Chicago and New York: Revell, 1889.

Wolfson, H. A. "Immortality and Resurrection in the Philosophy of the Church Fathers." In *Immortality and Resurrection,* edited by K. Stendahl. New York: Macmillan, 1975. Pp. 54–96.

Young, E. J. *The Messianic Prophecies of Daniel.* Grand Rapids, MI: Eerdmans, 1954.

13. The Resurrection

The Problem

An item of Christian faith expressed firmly in the New Testament and the early creeds of the Church is the resurrection of the dead. However, due to the impact of Greek philosophy, the study of oriental religions, and modern science, the word "resurrection" has undergone various alterations in meaning. We must first of all understand what the New Testament means by the word and insist that this be authoritative for discussion of the subject.

In addition, there are differences of interpretation, depending on the theological systems of the adherents, on questions such as the time of the resurrection (at the Rapture or at the beginning of the Millennium), and whether there is one resurrection (in connection with the Parousia and the final judgment) or two resurrections (that of the righteous before the Millennium, and that of the wicked after the Millennium).

There is also the matter of the intermediate state. What happens to those who die during this age while they await the resurrection? Their bodies decay, but what of their souls? Do they go to heaven at once, or to a temporary waiting room (Hades, Purgatory, Abraham's bosom), or do they sleep, with no conscious knowledge until awakened by the last trumpet?

What Is "Resurrection"?

Resurrection and Immortality. The words "resurrection" and "immortality" are sometimes interchanged, and the difference between these words is frequently blurred. Yet the dictionary makes a clear distinction. *Resurrection* refers primarily to that which has been dead and is brought to life. *Immortality* means "not subject to death." As we shall see, the resurrection body is no longer subject to death, therefore it is immortal. But the body that is buried was mortal, otherwise it would not have died. We believe that the human soul is immortal—not subject to death. This distinction is clearly preserved in the committal service of the Book of Common Prayer (The Order for the Burial of the Dead): "Forasmuch as it hath pleased Almighty God, in his wise providence, to take out this world the soul of our beloved brother, we therefore commit his body to the ground. . . ." The soul continues to exist "out of this world"; the body is committed to the ground or the sea. A shift in the meanings of the words can be seen in expressions such as, "He resurrected that old idea," and of one who has completed a work of art, "She has achieved immortality."

Words and Words. The Greek word for "immortal" was *athanatos* and for "immortality" *athanasia*, both from the word for "death" compounded with the prefix *a-*, "without," hence "death-less." In classical Greek, this belonged to the gods, but whether it also belonged to human beings was a matter of debate. R. Bultmann says that there is no Old Testament equivalent. The term is used of the eternal life of the righteous[1] and the *psychē* ("life principle, soul") is said to be deathless.[2] The word *athanatos* is not found in the New Testament, and *athanasia* occurs only twice: in 1 Corinthians 15:53 of those who have been resurrected or "changed" at the last trumpet, and in 1 Timothy 6:16 of the "blessed and only Sovereign."[a]

In another Greek word group *a-* is compounded with *phtheirō*, "without ruin," yielding *aphthartos*, "imperishable, incorruptible" and *aphtharsia*, "incorruptibility, immortality."[b] The words are used of God[3] and of the resurrection body.[4]

These words all approach from the negative, being compounded with *a-*, "without." Much more common in the New Testament is the positive word *zoē* "life,"[c] which is often found as the equivalent of "immortality," particularly in the expression "eternal life."

Words for "resurrection" are built from the words *egeirō*, "to awaken from sleep, rouse, raise up, erect" and *anistēmi*, "to raise, raise up, stand up." The former is used in the miracles of raising the dead, which are signs of the messianic age.[5] It is also used of

---

1. Wisd. 3:4; 4 Macc. 14:5. 2. 4 Macc. 14:6; 18:23. 3. Rom. 1:23; 1 Tim. 1:17. 4. 1 Cor. 15:42,50,52–54; cf. 2 Tim. 1:10. 5. Matt. 11:5; cf. John 11:24.

the resurrection of Jesus in such expressions as "whom God raised from the dead."[6] From the second are derived the words *anatasis* and *exanastasis*, "getting up, raising up, resurrection." Some idea of the spread of meaning can be seen in the use of *exanistēmi* in the question of the Sadducees to Jesus concerning the man who is required to "raise up children for his brother,"[7] where it refers not to raising the dead but to fathering unborn. In the New Testament, *anastasis* "resurrection" is used only of the resurrection of Jesus and that of the end time, usually joined to the phrase "of/from the dead."[d] The word *exanastasis*, which we shall study in more detail below, occurs only in Philippians 3:11.

From the words used, we can begin to get an idea of the meaning intended by the authors who used them. The basic idea in all cases is something like "raising up, setting up, getting up." A building can be set up or restored;[8] a king can be raised up;[9] a person can be lifted up[10] or get up[11] or awaken from sleep.[12] Therefore it is often necessary to add the words "from the dead" (*ek tou nekrou* or *ek nekrōn*) in order to make clear the reference to resurrection. In every case, "resurrection" is the *change* from one condition or state to another, and not merely the continuation that is implied by "immortality."

Development of the Idea

In the Old Testament. A number of scholars claim that the concept of resurrection is not found in the Old Testament until the exilic and postexilic periods. Some have attempted to trace it to Persian origins,[e] and the word "paradise" is of Persian origin[f] but is never used in connection with the dead in the Old Testament. The concept cannot be of Hellenistic origin, for to the Greeks resurrection was an impossibility.[g] Much more reasonable is the thesis of G. F. Moore: "the only logical way in which the Jews could conceive the fulfilment of God's promises to the righteous was that they should live again upon earth in the golden age to come and share in the salvation of Israel. The resurrection seems, indeed, so necessarily the consequence of the whole teaching of Scripture concerning the

---

6. Acts 3:15. **7.** Mark 12:19. **8.** John 2:19. **9.** Acts 13.22.
10. Acts 3:7. **11.** John 5:8. **12.** Rom. 13:11.

salvation of the righteous and their great reward that it is not strange that the Pharisees found it explicit or by intimation in all parts of their Bible."[h] Jesus put his finger on the kernel of truth when he said to the Sadducees, "He [the God of Abraham, Isaac, and Jacob] is not God of the dead, but of the living."[13]

Nevertheless, the doctrine developed slowly—or rather it was revealed more fully only when the ground had been prepared. To the Hebrews, the dead went to Sheol (translated as "Hades" and "Hell"), an underground place for both the righteous and the wicked.[14] There are differing statements in Psalms, representing various ideas (but not necessarily teaching a doctrine of Sheol):[i] "in death there is no remembrance of thee; in Sheol who can give thee praise?";[15] "the wicked shall depart to Sheol";[16] "thou dost not give me up to Sheol, or let thy godly one see the Pit."[17] If Samuel was "called up" from Sheol[18] then the "godly one" did indeed "see the Pit" and the Psalmist's faith was to be fulfilled in a future event, as Peter came to realize.[19]

Isaiah had some understanding of the doctrine: "Thy dead shall live, their bodies shall rise,"[20] as did Job: "I know that my Redeemer lives, and that in the end he will stand upon the earth. And after my skin has been destroyed, yet in my flesh I will see God."[21] The vision of the valley of dry bones[22] clearly has to do with the resurrection of the nation of Israel.[23] Nevertheless, the imagery used is based on the details of bodily resurrection. Bones that are "very dry" are covered with sinews, flesh, and skin, breath comes again, and the body comes to life.[24] Ezekiel necessarily had a concept of resurrection; moreover, the people to whom he addressed this prophecy must also have had some such idea for the prophecy to be meaningful. Daniel clearly speaks of a day of resurrection: "at that time [the time of trouble] your people shall be delivered, every one whose name shall be found written in the book. And many of those who sleep in the dust of the earth shall awake, some to everlasting life, and some to shame and everlasting contempt."[25]

In Deuterocanonical and Apocryphal Literature. In the Intertes-

---

13. Matt. 22:32.　14. 1 Sam. 28:14; Job 3:11–19.　15. Ps. 6:5 (MT 6).
16. Ps. 9:17 (MT 18).　17. Ps. 16:10.　18. 1 Sam. 28:12–14.
19. Acts 2:23–31.　20. Isa. 26:19.　21. Job 19:25,26, NIV.　22. Ezek. 37.　23. Ezek. 37:11.　24. Ezek. 37:2–6.　25. Dan. 12:1,2.

tamental Period, the idea of resurrection developed further. The mother who saw her seven sons die rather than give up their faith said, "Therefore the Creator of the world, who shaped the beginning of man and devised the origin of all things, will in his mercy give life and breath back to you again, since you now forget yourselves for the sake of his laws."[26] Enoch's view of the resurrection concerned only Israel:[k] "And in those days will the earth also give back those who are treasured up within it, and Sheol will give back that which it has received."[27]

In the New Testament. The doctrine of the resurrection is fully developed in the New Testament. Jesus took his stand with the Pharisees, as opposed to the Sadducees, on the subject of the resurrection.[28] His parable of Lazarus and the Rich Man made the point: "If they do not hear Moses and the prophets, neither will they be convinced if some one should rise from the dead."[29]

But it is with the resurrection of Jesus that the truth was fully revealed. His dead body was placed in the tomb. The tomb was found empty on the morning of the third day, and he was seen by many of his followers. For forty days he was with them; he ate with them;[30] they could touch him;[31] they recognized him;[32] and yet he was different, in that he appeared and disappeared,[33] entered through closed doors,[34] and was not always immediately recognized.[35] Finally, after he had spoken to them on the Mount of Olives, "he was lifted up, and a cloud took him out of their sight."[36]

Paul gives a lengthy discussion in 1 Corinthians 15. Contrary to a popular view, he was not trying to prove the resurrection of Jesus; that was an accepted fact by him and his readers. He was arguing *from that fact* that there will be a resurrection of the dead.[37] Since Christ was raised from the dead, how can we say that there is no resurrection? But indeed he has been raised, "the first fruits of those who have fallen asleep."[38]

It is important to read this entire passage very carefully. Some would say that Paul denies that it is a bodily resurrection, but

---

26. 2 Macc. 7:23; cf. 12:43,44.   **27.** Enoch 51:1.   **28.** Matt. 22:23–32.
29. Luke 16:31.   **30.** Luke 24:42,43.   **31.** John 20:27.   **32.** Matt. 28:9.
33. Luke 24:31.   **34.** John 20:26.   **35.** Luke 24:16; John 20:15.
36. Acts 1:9.   **37.** 1 Cor. 15:12–19.   **38.** 1 Cor. 15:20.

rather it is like a seed that has been sown that becomes something entirely different. There is indeed a difference between the resurrection body and the mortal body. "It [the body that died] is sown a physical body, it [the body that is resurrected] is raised a spiritual body."[39] But in both cases, it is a *body*. It is perishable; it must become imperishable. It is mortal; it must put on immortality. The first bears the image of "the man of dust"; the second bears the image of "the man of heaven." It is not flesh and blood, subject to disease and decay; it is a resurrection body like that which the risen Jesus has.[40]

This should remove concern with details that are purely physical. Will I go through eternity with poor eyesight, bad teeth, and other body defects? Will my friend have only one leg? Will that precious baby that was laid in the grave be a baby for all eternity? Will my mother be ninety-four and my father who predeceased her be only seventy-four; will my brother who was fourteen years older than I be my younger brother in heaven? These questions are all based on physical bodies. "Beloved, we are God's children now; it does not yet appear what we shall be, but we know that when he appears we shall be like him"![41]

Objections to the Doctrine

The objections to the doctrine of the resurrection of the body can be grouped into two categories: those that stem from idealism, and those that stem from materialism. Ultimately, the two can be considered as one basic objection: unbelief, for certainly no doctrine of Scripture is more clearly taught.

Matter Is Evil.   According to a system of thought that is probably more ancient than its Greek philosophers, material existence is evil and must be done away. The resurrection of the body would continue material existence, hence the doctrine must be rejected. "God is spirit," and if we are to be like him, we, too, must have only spiritual existence. The resurrection of Jesus was only the means by which he could demonstrate to his followers the truth of the continuity of life, and when he ascended into heaven, he cast aside the material body for it was no longer necessary.

---

39. 1 Cor. 15:44.   **40.** 1 Cor. 15:42–54.   **41.** 1 John 3:2.

We have dealt with this concept before. God created matter, and it was very good. We therefore reject the premise that it is evil and must be done away. Whether matter is eternal or not is another question, which we shall consider in a later chapter. As for Jesus casting aside his body after the ascension, we have the promise that he "will come in the same way as you saw him go into heaven."[42] If we subscribe to the doctrine of the messianic kingdom, we include in that doctrine the messianic king sitting on David's throne in Zion—details requiring material existence.

Matter Is Everything. According to "scientific" views, we live in a material universe and are the products of chance. We "live" in a material body, and when we "die" it is the end. The body decays, like that of other animals and vegetation. Our only immortality is in the influence we have made upon others and in the genes we transmit to our physical descendants.

Such a view is from the outset contrary to the teachings of Scripture and the teachings of Christ, and it fails to satisfy the longings of most human beings. To make such statements, I realize, is not to prove my point. It is simply the testimony of my faith. But in this day of subatomic science, when it is widely recognized that all matter consists of electrons, it is not incredible to believe that the God who brought such a universe into existence continues to have control of the elemental particles. Belief in the resurrection is belief in God's continued control of all things.

One Resurrection or Two?

The classical post-Reformation (and post-Augustinian) view might be stated somewhat as follows: at the end of this age, Christ returns, the dead are raised, the judgment takes place, and the curtain drops on this world.[m] The *Augsburg Confession* states of the Scriptures, "They also teach that Christ will appear at the end of the world for judgment, and that He will raise all the dead, and that He will give to the pious elect eternal life and perpetual joy, but condemn wicked men and devils, that they may be tormented without end." There is only one resurrection, which includes all the dead, the just and the unjust alike.

---

42. Acts 1:11.

The Basic Issue.   Premillennialists, however, point out that according to Revelation 20:4–15 the "first resurrection"[43] takes place before the "thousand years," whereas "the rest of the dead" will not "come to life again until the thousand years [are] ended."[44] It has been argued that this is the only place in the Bible where two resurrections are mentioned and that, since Revelation is an apocalyptic work, this is to be taken as some sort of symbolism and not the basis of a doctrine. Did not Jesus say, "the hour is coming when all who are in the tombs will hear his voice and come forth, those who have done good, to the resurrection of life, and those who have done evil, to the resurrection of judgment"?[45]

Those who hold to the two-resurrection theory reply that in the same context Jesus also said, "the hour is coming, and now is, when the dead will hear the voice of the Son of God, and those who hear will live."[46] This "hour" has already lasted for nearly 2000 years; why, then, could not the "hour" of the resurrection extend from the beginning to the end of the Millennium?

There is even a three-resurrection view, although it is not identified as such. According to this interpretation of Scripture, the first resurrection includes those who are raised when Christ returns for his Church prior to the Tribulation (the "Rapture") and those who were martyred during the Tribulation and who are raised at the end of that period.[n]

Some Pertinent Passages.   Truth is not arrived at by hurling scriptures at opponents, but by careful exegesis of the relevant passages. There are a number of such scriptures that demand our attention.

Some scriptures clearly teach that there will be a resurrection of the unjust as well as the just. "Many of those who sleep in the dust of the earth shall awake, some to everlasting life, and some to shame and everlasting contempt."[47] This appears to place the resurrection after the Tribulation.[48] We have already looked at John 5:28–29, which mentions "those who have done good" and "those who have done evil," and Revelation 20:5–13, where both groups are mentioned but in separate resurrections. The separation

---

43. Rev. 20:6.   44. Rev. 20:5.   45. John 5:28,29.   46. John 5:25.
47. Dan. 12:2.   48. Dan. 12:1.

of the evil from the righteous, but without any reference to resurrection, is found in some of the kingdom parables.[49] We may therefore state that the resurrection (however the components may be arranged) includes *all* human beings.

Some passages speak only of the resurrection of the elect. In his great presentation of the resurrection Paul says: "For as in Adam all die, so in Christ shall all be made alive. But each in his own order: Christ the first fruits, then at his coming those who belong to Christ. Then comes the end, when he delivers the kingdom to God the Father after destroying every rule and every authority and power."[50] There is no mention of the resurrection of the rest of the dead,° but two facts should be noted: (1) in Christ *all* are to be made alive, just as in Adam *all* die, suggesting that the unrighteous are included in resurrection; and (2) Christ must reign "until he has put all his enemies under his feet,"[51] these enemies ostensibly including "every rule and every power and authority" as well as "death."[52]

In his first letter to the Thessalonians Paul wrote: "For the Lord himself will descend from heaven with a cry of command, with the archangel's call, and with the sound of the trumpet of God. And the dead in Christ will rise first; then we who are alive, who are left, shall be caught up together with them in the clouds to meet the Lord in the air; and so we shall always be with the Lord."[53] No mention is made of the resurrection of the rest of the dead. Paul has not ignored them, however, for he speaks of those who are "of the night or of darkness,"[54] indicating that they are destined for wrath.[55]

The "Out-Resurrection." In Luke's account of the way Jesus met the question of the Sadducees, Jesus said "those who are accounted worthy to attain to that age and to the resurrection from the dead . . ."[56] The expression "the resurrection from the dead" (*tēs anastaseōs tēs ek nekrōn*) has been used in support of the idea of two resurrections. This has been placed alongside the statement of Paul in Philippians, "that if possible I may attain the resurrection from the dead" (*eis tēn exanastasin tēn ek nekrōn*). This is sometimes

---

49. Cf. Matt. 13:41–43,49,50; 25:31–46.   **50.** 1 Cor. 15:22–24.   **51.** 1 Cor. 15:27.   **52.** 1 Cor. 15:24,26.   **53.** 1 Thess. 4:16,17.   **54.** 1 Thess. 5:5.   **55.** 1 Thess. 5:9.   **56.** Luke 20:35.

translated as "the out-resurrection from the dead (ones)."[57] The inference is drawn that there are two resurrections, the first being a separation *out* from the remaining dead.

The question is valid whether such force can be attached to the word. *Exanastasis* occurs in the New Testament only in this passage. It does occur in extrabiblical passages, meaning "expulsion (trans.), rising [from bed] (intrans.)"[p] More profitable is the study of various expressions using the word *nekros*, "dead," such as "resurrection *of* the dead" (*tēs anastaseōs tōn nekrōn*[58]) and "resurrection *from* the dead" (. . . *ek* or *apo tou nekrou* or *tōn nekrōn*).

According to my count, the expressions "raise the dead" and "resurrection of the dead" occur fifteen times in the New Testament, in every instance except four having to do with the resurrection in general, and even these may be placed in the same category. John 5:21 ("for as the Father raises the dead") may refer to the general resurrection. Revelation 1:5 speaks of "the firstborn *of* the dead," referring to Jesus.[q] The remaining two passages are interesting, for the preposition *ex* "out of, from" precedes the words "resurrection of the dead."[59]

On the other hand, expressions using a partitive preposition occur forty-eight times (twice with *apo*; forty-six with *ek*), in every instance referring to a resurrection that is not general.[r] Usually the reference is to Jesus, but in a few instances the reference is to John the Baptizer (in the question whether John the Baptizer had been raised *from* the dead[60]), to Lazarus,[61] or figuratively used "as men who have been brought from death to life"[62]

Most instructive is Paul's use of the expressions in 1 Corinthians 15. Speaking of resurrection in general, he uses "resurrection of the dead," without the preposition.[63] Speaking of the resurrection of Jesus *from* the dead, he uses the preposition.[64] But in verse 12, the two are placed side by side: "Now if Christ is preached as raised *from* the dead (*ek nekrōn*), how can some of you say that there is no resurrection *of* the dead? (*anastasis nekrōn*)."

Philippians 3:11 is sometimes taken to be a *crux interpretum* (a

---

57. Phil. 3:11.   **58.** Matt. 22:31.   **59.** Acts 26:23, Rom. 1:4.
60. Mark 6:14 and parallel.   **61.** John 12:1,9,17.   **62.** Rom. 6:13.
63. 1 Cor. 15:21,42.   **64.** 1 Cor. 15:20.

critical point for interpretation), although in the light of the evidence just presented, I do not feel that it adds all that much to the argument. Paul says, "that if possible I may attain the resurrection from the dead," using the unusual phrase *eis tēn exanastasin tēn ek nekrōn*. A similar expression occurs in the words of Jesus: "The sons of this age marry and are given in marriage; but those who are accounted worthy to attain to that age and to the resurrection from the dead neither marry nor are given in marriage, for they cannot die any more, because they are equal to angels and are sons of God, being sons of the resurrection."[65] There is clearly a separation of the resurrected ones in these passages. Paul wishes to "attain" this resurrection—what point would this statement have if Paul were thinking only of a general resurrection? Jesus speaks of "those who are accounted worthy to attain" to this resurrection, stating that they "cannot die any more"[66] and calling them "sons of God"—certainly not true of those who are to be raised in the resurrection to condemnation.[s]

So, while I dislike the term "out-resurrection" and do not find strong support for the two-resurrection view in the word *exanastasis* in Philippians 3:11, I am convinced that the evidence in the rest of the New Testament teaches that there are two resurrections, the first of which is a partial resurrection (*ek*) of the dead, as described in Revelation 20:4–6.[t]

Between Death and Resurrection

The Christians at Thessalonica were concerned about those who had died ("those who are asleep,"[67]): would they miss the Second Coming? Paul said "the dead in Christ will rise first" at the Lord's coming. We all are concerned about our loved ones who have gone on before us: where are they? Do they know about us, hear us, pray for us? Or are they simply asleep?

The God of the Living.   The dead, according to the Old Testament, were in Sheol. They were gathered to their fathers. Were they conscious? Much has been made of the episode of Saul's visit to the Medium of Endor and the appearance of Samuel.[68] But we must keep

---

65. Luke 20:35,36.   **66.** Cf. Rev. 20:6.   **67.** 1 Thess. 4:13.   **68.** 1 Sam. 28:6–19.

in mind that the Old Testament vehemently prohibited such encounters with mediums (as Saul well knew[69]). This incident is the only one of its kind in the Bible, therefore hardly to be used as the basis for a doctrine. More important is the word of Jesus, concerning the God of Abraham, Isaac, and Jacob: "he is not God of the dead, but of the living; for all live to him."[70]

On the basis of Jesus' parable about the rich man and Lazarus, some teach that there were two parts in the abode of the dead: the place called "Abraham's bosom," and the part called "Hades," which was a place of torment, and between the two was a great gulf.[71] It is questionable whether Jesus intended to teach details of the intermediate state in this parable. Rather, he was speaking of difficulties that keep men from the kingdom of heaven, one of which was wealth,[72] and making the point that if the "five brothers"[73] did not listen to Moses and the prophets, they would not be convinced even by someone risen from the dead.[74u]

At the conclusion of his great chapter on the Heroes of Faith, the author of Hebrews makes this statement: "And all these, though well attested by their faith, did not receive what was promised, since God had foreseen something better for us, that apart from us they should not be made perfect."[75] Prior to the death and resurrection of Jesus there is no indication that the dead enjoyed immediate rewards and blessings, such as would be required if we interpret the Parable of Lazarus and the Rich Man in this manner. But Jesus, when he ascended on high, led captivity captive.[76] According to one interpretation, when he descended into Hades, he proclaimed the good news to "the spirits in prison."[77] There are many difficulties in the few passages on this subject, so we move on to clearer passages.

Present with the Lord.   Jesus told the thief on the cross, "Today you will be with me in Paradise."[78] Paul tells of an experience in which he was "caught up into Paradise" where he "heard things that cannot be told."[79] When it was not clear whether he would be released from prison or be put to death, he said: "For to me to live

---

69. 1 Sam. 28:9.   70. Luke 20:37,38.   71. Luke 16:22–26.   72. Cf. Luke 16:14.   73. Luke 16:28.   74. Luke 16:31.   75. Heb. 11:39,40. 76. Cf. Eph. 4:7–10.   77. 1 Pet. 3:18,19.   78. Luke 23:43.   79. 2 Cor. 12:3,4.

is Christ, and to die is gain. . . . My desire is to depart and be with Christ, for that is far better. But to remain in the flesh is more necessary on your account."⁸⁰ To the Corinthians he wrote: "For we know that if the earthly tent we live in is destroyed, we have a building from God, a house not made with hands, eternal in the heavens. . . . So we are always of good courage; we know that while we are at home in the body we are away from the Lord, for we walk by faith, not by sight. We are of good courage, and we would rather be away from the body and at home with the Lord."⁸¹

It is my belief, based on the small amount of revelation that God has given us on the subject, that those who die in the Lord go immediately into his presence. This is not the final resurrection, and the blessed dead are still awaiting the sound of the trumpet, when the earth and the seas shall give up the dead, when the dead in Christ shall rise, eternal souls and glorified bodies united in the new person, and so shall we be ever with the Lord.

Summary

The Scriptures teach that the body will be raised and the person (body and soul) will live again. All the dead will be raised, some to bliss and others to torment. The resurrection is connected with the Return of Christ, and it would seem that the "dead in Christ" rise first, to reign with him during the Millennial Kingdom, while the rest of the dead are not raised until the end of that period and then only for judgment.

NOTES

a. *TDNT* 3: 24.
b. *TDNT* 9: 103–105.
c. *TDNT* 2: 861–872. Since this article is by Bultmann, there is a tendency to stress his concept of authenticity.
d. A-G, pp. 59–60.
e. See T. H. Gaster, "Resurrection," *IDB* 4:40.
f. Hebrew *pardēs* from Zend *pairi-daeza*, "enclosure, park."
g. Cf. *Iliad* 24.551, and other citations in *TDNT* 1: 369.
h. G. F. Moore, *Judaism in the First Centuries of the Christian Era*, 2: 313f. The author of Hebrews attributes this same reasoning to Abraham, who,

---

80. Phil. 1:21–24.   81. 2 Cor. 5:1–8.

believing that the promise was to be fulfilled through Isaac, had to believe
also that God was able to raise men from the dead (Heb. 11:17–19).

i. Psalms are often in the category of Wisdom Literature and represent human observations. Therefore we should not accept some of the statements
as the basis of doctrine—a fact that is quite evident when we look at a
work such as Ecclesiastes.

j. The passage in Job is difficult; the RSV translates "then without my flesh
I shall see God." At question is the force of the preposition *min*, "apart
from, without." But, since Job is looking forward to a time when his
Redeemer "will stand upon the earth," he is more likely thinking of some
kind of bodily resurrection for himself.

k. "No Jewish book except IV Ezra teaches indubitably the doctrine of a
general resurrection; and this may be due to Christian influence"—R. H.
Charles, *The Book of Enoch* (Oxford: Clarendon, 1893), p. 139, note on
LI.1.

l. Jesus' words to the Sadducees might be introduced at this point: "in the
resurrection they neither marry nor are given in marriage, but are like
angels in heaven" (Matt. 22:30). I do not believe this is intended to void
earthly marriages, or destroy relationships that have become most dear in
this life. Rather, it removes the thrust of the Sadducees' problem by stressing the spiritual life of the resurrection body, as contrasted with the physical life of this earthly body.

m. The statement of Charles Hodge is representative: "The common doctrine
of the Church . . . , is that the conversion of the world, the restoration of
the Jews, and the destruction of Antichrist are to precede the second
coming of Christ, which event will be attended by the general resurrection
of the dead, the final judgment, the end of the world, and the consummation of the Church"—*Systematic Theology* (New York: Scribner, Armstrong, 1874), 3: 861.

n. Cf. H. A. Ironside, *Lectures on the Book of Revelation*, p. 337. Cf. also
NSRB, p. 1250, n.2 (cont. from p. 1249).

o. According to one interpretation *to telos* in verse 24 refers to the rest of the
dead and not the end of the world. A. Oepke states that this view "has
gradually gained acceptance" (*TDNT* 1: 371, n.13).

p. LSJ 1: 584.

q. Cf. Colossians 1:18, where Paul uses "the first-born from (*ek*) the dead."

r. Mark 12:25 appears to refer to a general resurrection, but in the parallel
passage (Luke 20:35) the partitive preposition *ek* is used.

s. G. Vos, dealing with the passage in Philippians, states: "If taking it at its
full meaning should have to be done at the cost of embracing the pre-
millennarian [sic] scheme, we should not over-dogmatically shrink from
the issue. Still, with all openness of mind, we cannot bring ourselves to
the conclusion that such is the absolutely necessary exegesis"—*Pauline
Eschatology*, pp. 256–257. In my opinion, his exegesis has been forced by
his strong amillennial a priori.

t. The objection is sometimes raised that those who take part in the first
resurrection are only those who had been martyred for not worshiping the

beast (cf. Rev. 20:4). But John also saw seated on the thrones "those to whom judgment was committed," an expression reminiscent of 1 Corinthians 6:2,3.

u. For an excellent discussion, cf. G. E. Ladd, *The Last Things* (Grand Rapids, MI: Eerdmans, 1978), pp. 33, 34. For an interesting study from an unusual approach cf. E. L. Martin, "The Real Meaning of Lazarus and the Rich Man," *The Foundation Commentator* 8,6 (Pasadena CA; August 1981): 1–5.

ADDITIONAL READING

Barth, K. *The Resurrection of the Dead.* Translated by H. J. Stenning. London: Hodder & Stoughton, 1933.

Cullmann, O. *Immortality of the Soul or Resurrection of the Dead?* London: Epworth, 1958.

———. *The Earliest Christian Confessions.* Translated by J. K. S. Reid. London: Lutterworth, 1949.

Dahl, M. E. *Resurrection of the Body.* Naperville, IL: Allenson, 1962.

Denton, D. R. "Hope in the Pauline Corpus." Th.D. dissertation, Fuller Theological Seminary, 1971.

Evans, C. F. *Resurrection and the New Testament.* London: SCM, 1970.

Fuller, D. P. *Easter Faith and History.* Grand Rapids, MI: Eerdmans, 1975.

Grossouw, W. "L'espérance dans le Nouveau Testament." *Revue Biblique* 61 (1954): 508–532.

Harris, M. J. *Raised Immortal.* Atlanta: John Knox, 1982.

Longenecker, R. N., and Tenney, M. C., eds. *New Dimensions in New Testament Study.* Grand Rapids, MI: Zondervan, 1974.

Nickelsburg, G. W. E. *Resurrection, Immortality, and Eternal Life in Intertestamental Judaism.* Cambridge, MA: Harvard University Press, 1972.

Niebuhr, R. R. *Resurrection and Historical Reason.* New York: Scribner's, 1957.

Salmond, S. D. F. *The Christian Doctrine of Immortality.* 4th ed. Edinburgh: T. & T. Clark, 1907.

Schep, J. A. *The Nature of the Resurrection Body.* Grand Rapids, MI: Eerdmans, 1964.

Smedes, L. B. *All Things Made New.* Grand Rapids, MI: Eerdmans, 1970.

Tenney, M. C. *The Reality of the Resurrection.* New York: Harper & Row, 1963.

Westcott, B. F. *The Gospel of the Resurrection.* 4th ed. London: Macmillan, 1879.

14. The Judgment

The Problem

It is the common belief of the Church that there will be a final judgment.[a] To modern men and women this raises a number of questions.

Can a God of love be a judge?[b] How can he send some of his children to hell, to be tormented day and night forever? Didn't Jesus come into the world to save us from that?[1] As for the Christian, doesn't the Bible teach that we shall never come into judgment?[2]

How many judgments are there? Some say one; others, four, five, or seven. Some writers speak of a constant process of judgment—doesn't this make a final judgment unnecessary?

There are a number of words that are used—"judgment," "justice," "retribution," "wrath," "condemnation," "vengeance," "anger," "chastisement." What do these words mean, and how are they used in the Bible? Can we say that certain attitudes (such as anger and vengeance) are wrong in human beings, but right in God?

Obviously the study of judgment could fill a book,[c] but I intend simply to deal with some of the principal themes of the subject.

Judgment and Government

Judgment is a necessary part of righteous government. The failure of modern governments to apply firm standards of judgment has led on the one hand to a rising crime rate at the local level and widespread terrorism on the national and international scene, and on the other hand to an outcry against the judicial system. When a rapist murders his victim because he figures he can get a lower sentence for murder than for rape, something has gone terribly wrong!

---

1. John 3:16,17.   **2.** John 5:24; Rom. 8:1.

God Is a Righteous God. The God of the Bible has revealed himself to be righteous, insisting on righteousness as the basis of his eternal kingdom. This is not always obvious in the present age, for God does not always apply the demands of justice at once, but he has reserved final judgment to the last day. The observation of Augustine is worthy of note: "If open punishment were now inflicted for every sin, it would be supposed that nothing would be reserved till the last judgment. Again, if God now did not openly punish any sin, it would be presumed that there was no divine providence."[d] We might amend that observation to state that if divine punishment were meted out at once for every sin, none of us would be left alive.

God's Righteous Acts. The Bible clearly teaches both God's mercy and his justice. The principle of judgment was demonstrated at the very beginning, after the Fall, when God banished Adam and Eve from the Garden and barred access to the tree of life.[3] If God had not so acted, and if the human race had gained eternal life in its fallen state, then the Kingdom of God would eternally have been under the dominion of sin. God, as always, "showed good judgment."

Likewise, the punishment visited upon Cain for the murder of his brother[4c] was a judgment from God. The antediluvian world was destroyed by God because of widespread and deep-rooted wickedness.[5] The pharaoh who oppressed the Hebrews suffered a judgment of God, a judgment that resulted in part from the hardness of Pharaoh's heart, and in part from the idolatry of the Egyptians.[6]

But most important, the judgment of God was visited upon his chosen people, at various times and in various ways. There was a succession of "oppressions" in the days of the judges[7] that were demonstrations of God's displeasure with Israelite idolatry. There was the destruction of Israel, the Northern Kingdom, by the Assyrians.[8] Finally, there was the destruction of Jerusalem by the Babylonians.[9] The sin of Judah, the Southern Kingdom, was the worse because the judgment on Israel should have served as a warning.[10]

---

3. Gen. 3:23,24. **4.** Gen. 4:10–12. **5.** Gen. 6:7,11–13. **6.** Exod. 8:32; 12:12. **7.** Judg. 3:7,8,12, etc. **8.** 2 Kings 17:6,7. **9.** Jer. 1:13–16. **10.** Cf. Ezek. 23, esp. 23:11.

Judgment and Righteousness.   It is of primary importance to note that the judgments of God upon his people are based upon his demand for righteousness. The words of Amos state it succinctly: "You only have I known of all the families of earth; therefore I will punish you for all your iniquities."[11f] Isaiah's words expand this basic idea.[12] Jeremiah relates the coming judgment to the original covenant.[13] Throughout the messages of the prophets we hear demand for righteousness, obedience to the Lord's commands, justice in humans' deal_ ith each other.[14]

The sin of idolatry, of turning away from Yahweh to serve other gods, is in itself heinous, but we miss the point if we fail to see that turning away from the Lord includes turning away from the principles of righteousness that are integral with the covenant relationship. Paul, in directing his words to the Jew,[15] was concerned not only with the Jew,[16] but with the witness to the rest of the world that comes from the behavior of those who claim to be God's people.[17] The words of Jacob (Israel) to his sons might well be addressed to everyone who claims to belong to Israel but who does not apply the principles of God's righteous demands: "You have troubled me by causing me to stink among the dwellers of the land, the Canaanites and the Perizzites."[18]

Coming to Grips with Terms

Since we in our modern society are addicted to using words loosely and often incorrectly, it is important to know more precisely the meanings of certain words that are used in connection with judgment.

Judgment.   When we refer to a person's "judgment" we usually mean his or her ability to discern good from bad, profitable from unprofitable, and so on. When we refer to God's "judgment" we often think only of the cosmic axe that falls on the neck of humankind at the end of the world. Judgment is the act of deciding, the place of the decision, and the execution of the decision. All of these meanings are found in the Hebrew word *mišpāṭ*. The Greek word *krinō* and its derivatives and compounds have this basic meaning.[g]

---

11. Amos 3:2.   12. Isa. 1:2–26.   13. Jer. 11:2–12.   14. Cf. Isa. 1:16,17; Amos 2:6,7; Jer. 35:8–22.   15. Rom. 2:17–24.   16. Cf. Rom. 2:9–11.   17. Rom. 2:24.   18. Gen. 34:30, lit.

The judgment of God, ultimately, is his decision whether a being or a condition should be finally terminated or made eternal.

Justice.   The word "justice" today often connotes segregation or white supremacy and is in widespread disfavor. In the Bible, however, it is usually the equivalent of "righteousness."[h] Righteousness could be defined simply as "rightness, rectitude." Of course, if this rightness is to be determined by sinful human beings, it will be deficient, but biblical righteousness is defined by the nature of God and is one of his communicable attributes. He requires that his people be righteous as he is righteous. In New Testament doctrine, "justification" is first of all the forensic declaration that we are considered to be righteous on the basis of Christ's righteousness,[19] and then by God's sanctifying work that we are finally made over in his image.[20]

Anger, Wrath.   "Anger" in the Bible, when used with reference to God, is the expression of his nature to unrighteousness, holiness manifesting itself against deliberate sin.[i] When it culminates in action, it is called "wrath." In human beings, anger and wrath are often selfish and vindictive, but we must not transfer these passions when speaking of the wrath of God. Since God is one, all of his attributes must be consonant with his person. Wrath and love are both expressions of his being.[j] The "patience" of God is an expression of his unwillingness that anyone should perish, and the holding in abeyance of his wrath to give man an opportunity to repent.[21k]

Vengeance; Retribution.   To most of us, "vengeance" is "getting even" with someone, and "retributive" justice is "an eye for an eye." In the Bible, vengeance belongs to God,[22] and the underlying idea is "the restoration of wholeness, integrity, to the community, by God and man."[l] Retribution is the return to every person of his or her due, whether reward or punishment.[23] Once we have understood the awful holiness of God, we are amazed at his grace, for we deserve to be punished for our disobedience, but God's return is in response to our faith, not our works.

Chastisement.   Chastening or chastisement, as the Hebrew

---

19. Rom. 5:1,7–10.   **20.** Rom. 8:3,4; 12:1,2.   **21.** Isa. 48:9; 2 Pet. 3:9.
22. Rom. 12:19.   **23.** Cf. 2 Thess. 1:5–8; Gal. 6:7,8.

mûsār and the Greek *paideia* indicate, is related to discipline or instruction. It includes corrective punishment[24] and instructive discipline.[25] It is an expression of the grace of God toward his people, and is part of the process of redemption or salvation.[m]

Condemnation. In a sense, this is the last stage in the process of God's judgment in response to stubborn refusal to repent, to accept his gracious offer, and to obey his word. This is indicated by the Greek word that is sometimes used, *katakrinō*, literally "decision against," to which we might add other compounds with *kata-*. In the Old Testament the word *rāšaʿ*, "wicked, criminal, guilty of crime" is used to express condemnation ("guilty of death"[26] means "found guilty, condemned to death"). The one who puts his faith in God for salvation will never come into condemnation.[27m]

Is Judgment an Act or a Process?

Judgment As a Process. In line with modern-day thinking is the view that there will be no final judgment; sins bring their own judgment in this life. Quoting John 12:48 ("the word that I have spoken will be his judge on the last day"), J. W. Bowman says: "This is a poetic way of saying that men judge themselves by their attitude toward Jesus and that their estimate of themselves will pass current at face value in God's eternal order."[o] There is a sense in which this is true.

God the Judge is also God the Creator. Natural laws were built into the universe by him, and among these laws is the relationship of effect to cause (denied by some modern scientists, who use the principle even while denying it). Paul expressed it in the words, "whatever a man sows, that he will also reap."[28] Psychologists seek to find the cause of the client's psychoneurosis. We have seen in previous studies that God uses sinful nations to punish other sinful nations. If we were to remove the theological element from this observation, we would simply say that nations bring on themselves, by their own greed and injustices, the animosity of other nations which often leads to war. So, whether at the personal or the national level, we must recognize that there is a constant judgment

---

24. Heb. 12:6–8.   25. 2 Tim. 3:16.   26. Num. 35:31, RSV.
27. John 3:17,18; 5:24; Rom. 8:1,33,34.   28. Gal. 6:7.

of attitudes and actions, and if we believe that God is the Judge of all the earth, we can see him judging by such means.

It is perhaps in this sense that the people of God are called upon to judge themselves. Thus Paul, speaking of an "unworthy manner" of behavior at the Lord's Supper and of illness and death that follows, wrote: "But if we judged ourselves truly, we should not be judged."[29] Likewise, we are to judge one another in a helpful way.[30] The objection will doubtless be made, "But we are told that we shouldn't judge." This is but a partial quotation of the Lord's words. The entire quotation contains the statements: "Judge not, that you be not judged. For with the judgment you pronounce you will be judged."[31] The application of this principle within the Church is set forth in Matthew 18:15–17, and is applied repeatedly by Paul in his first letter to the Corinthians.[32] The absence of discipline in the modern Church doubtless contributes to the worldliness of the Church.

Judgment As an Act. Unless we completely reject biblical authority we must admit that the Bible teaches that God does act in judgment. This was true at several points in the past, as we have already noted, and it will take place in the final judgment.[33] The "Day of the Lord" is a day of judgment, sometimes referring to God's acts that have already taken place, but most completely fulfilled in the Last Judgment.[34] It is this Last Assize that removes from the universe "all things that offend,"[35] and inaugurates the perfect Kingdom. We must now consider the biblical basis of this doctrine.

The Biblical Doctrine of the Last Judgment

In the Old Testament. In previous chapters we have seen how the prophets foretold an end to those who oppose God and the people of God. There is no need to repeat this material here. The difficulty in sorting out references to the Last Judgment lies in the characteristic of Old Testament prophecy, namely the phenomenon sometimes called "prophetic perspective" or "compenetration," which is the blending of the near and the distant. Some prophecies are fulfilled in part in the first advent and in part in the second

---

29. 1 Cor. 11:31.   **30.** Gal. 6:1,2.   **31.** Matt. 7:1,2.   **32.** 1 Cor. 5,6, etc.   **33.** Acts 17:31.   **34.** Rev. 20:11–15.   **35.** Matt. 13:41,42.

advent of Christ, a feature that may call forth the charge that we are manipulating the text to fit our theological suppositions.[p]

The Teachings of Jesus.   Jesus claimed that judgment had been delivered to him. "The Father judges no one, but has given all judgment to the Son."[36] He "has given him authority to execute judgment, because he is the Son of man."[37] Jesus claimed that his judgment was just "because I seek not my own will but the will of him who sent me."[38]

He pronounced woes on cities in which he had done mighty works, saying, "It shall be more tolerable on the day of judgment for Tyre and Sidon than for you."[39] Lest we miss the point, Jesus is claiming the right to pronounce judgment. A similar claim lies behind his statements about "this generation" and Jonah and the "queen of the South."[40]

In the Parables of the Kingdom, Jesus not only told the Parable of the Wheat and the Weeds, but explained its meaning. He included these statements: "The harvest is the close of the age," "so will it be at the close of the age," and "the Son of man will send his angels, and they will gather out of his kingdom all causes of sin and all evildoers, and throw them into the furnace of fire."[41] He made a similar statement, but without the personal claim of authority, in the Parable of the Fishing Net.[42] The import of the Parable of the Vineyard likewise has to do with a final judgment.[43]

The claims, explicit and implicit, in the "Olivet Discourse" leave no doubt that Jesus looked for a final judgment and believed that he would be active in that event. When "the tribes of the earth" see the Son of man "coming on the clouds of heaven with power and great glory; he will send out his angels with a loud trumpet call, and they will gather his elect from the four winds, from one end of heaven to the other."[44] The coming of the Son of man is likened to the judgment in the days of Noah.[45] The Parable of the Talents[46] culminates in a final judgment[47] and is immediately followed by the scene of the Son of man and his holy angels conducting the judgment of the nations.[48] The basis of this

---

36. John 5:22.   **37.** John 5:27.   **38.** John 5:30.   **39.** Matt. 11:22; cf. Luke 10:13,14.   **40.** Matt. 12:38–42.   **41.** Matt. 13:39–42.   **42.** Matt. 13:49,50.   **43.** Matt. 21:33–41.   **44.** Matt. 24:30,31.   **45.** Matt. 24:36–39.   **46.** Matt. 25:14–30.   **47.** Matt. 25:30.   **48.** Matt. 25:31–46.

judgment is the presence or absence of deeds of righteousness, but these are connected with the Son of man himself.[49]

The Teachings of Paul. The apostle Paul does not give an extended treatment of the Last Judgment, such as he has given for the bodily resurrection, but there can be little doubt that he held to the doctrine with no less conviction. In his address to the Areopagus, he spoke of "a day on which he [God] will judge the world in righteousness by a man whom he has appointed"[50] (the "man" is Jesus, as indicated by the reference to the resurrection in the same verse). Speaking about the Return of Christ, Paul went on to state that "God has not destined us for wrath, but to obtain salvation through our Lord Jesus Christ."[51] The final judgment was certainly in his mind when spoke about the Lord Jesus being "revealed from heaven with his mighty angels in flaming fire," mentioning also the "punishment of eternal destruction and exclusion from the presence of God."[52] He spoke of "the judgment seat of God" in his letter to the Romans,[53] and the "judgment seat of Christ" in his second letter to the Corinthians.[54] Judgment underlies the statement concerning the end in 1 Corinthians 15:24–28, as it does in the distinction between the "works of the flesh" and the "fruits of the Spirit" in the Galatian letter.[55] References to "the day of our Lord Jesus Christ,"[56] "the day of redemption,"[57] and "that Day"[58] imply the Last Judgment, as does the mention of the "wrath of God" that is coming.[59]

Other Epistles. The statement in Hebrews, "It is appointed for men to die once, and after that comes judgment,"[60] could be taken to mean that judgment immediately follows personal death, and does not refer to a final judgment, but the following verse would appear to join it with the Second Coming of Christ.[61] The following chapter deals with the same subject.[62]

In his comments on the injustices of the rich James refers to "the last days" and "the coming of the Lord."[63] The passage reminds us somewhat of the prophet Amos and underscores the connection

---

49. Matt. 25:40,45. **50.** Acts 17:31. **51.** 1 Thess. 5:9. **52.** 2 Thess. 1:7–10. **53.** Rom. 14:10. **54.** 2 Cor. 5:10. **55.** Gal. 5:19–24. **56.** 1 Cor. 1:8; cf. Phil. 1:10. **57.** Eph. 5:6. **58.** 2 Tim. 1:12; 4:1,8. **59.** Col. 3:6. **60.** Heb. 9:27. **61.** Heb. 9:28. **62.** Heb. 10:26–31. **63.** James 5:3,7.

between "salvation" and righteous living. "Behold, the judge is standing at the doors."[64]

Peter's word, "It is better to suffer for doing right, if that should be God's will, than for doing wrong."[65] in its context, implies a final judgment.[66] The idea is set forth more strongly in the statement, "For the time has come for judgment to begin with the household of God; and if it begins with us, what will be the end of those who do not obey the gospel of God?"[67] In his second epistle Peter clearly refers to "the day of judgment."[68]

Jude refers to "the judgment of the great day"[69] and quotes Enoch: "Behold, the Lord came with his holy myriads, to execute all the ungodly of all their deeds of ungodliness which they have committed in such an ungodly way."[70] From the context it should be clear that Jude has a future judgment in mind.[71]

The Book of Revelation.   The One who has "the keys of Death and Hades"[72] begins by sending messages to the seven churches, in each of which judgment is an essential part. In fact, the figures that are chosen[73] are connected with the One who comes to judge in the closing chapters of the book. Since the entire book, by whatever system we interpret it (preterist, historicist, or futurist), is moving to the climax in chapter 20 where judgment is the dominant theme, and this in turn leads into a presentation of the New Heavens and the New Earth, we may properly say that the entire book teaches the Last Judgment.

How Many Judgments Are There?   The classical answer to this question is "one—the Last Judgment." Over against this simplistic view, we find other answers, ranging to as many as seven. C. L. Feinberg says that Premillennialists "find four eschatological judgments: that of believers, that of Israel, that of the nations, and that of the Great White Throne."[q] C. I. Scofield lists five: sins of believers (at the Cross), self in believers (daily), works of believers (at the Rapture), the "Nations" (at the Revelation), and the wicked dead (at the Great White Throne).[r] The *New Scofield Reference Bible* distinguishes seven judgments: "(1) the judgment of the be-

---

64. James 5:9.   **65.** 1 Pet. 3:17.   **66.** 1 Pet. 3:18,22.   **67.** 1 Pet. 4:17.
68. 2 Pet. 2:4–10, esp. v. 9; 3:8–10.   **69.** Jude v. 6.   **70.** Jude vv. 14,15;
cf. Enoch 1:9.   **71.** Jude v. 18.   **72.** Rev. 1:18.   **73.** Rev. 2:12,18; 3:7,
14.

liever's sins in the cross of Christ;[74] ... (2) the believer's self-judgment;[75] ... (3) the judgment of the believer's works;[76] ... (4) the judgment of the individual Gentiles at the return of Christ to the earth;[77] ... (5) the judgment of Israel at the return of Christ to the earth;[78] ... (6) the judgment of the angels after the 1000 years;[79] ... and here,[80] ... the judgment of the wicked dead with which the history of the present earth ends."[5]

There can be no question that God's judgment is a complex matter, as we have already seen in the discussion of judgment as an act or a process. However, attempts to divide the judgment into fine compartments and to assign approximate times for each judgment is, in my opinion, reading more into Scripture than is required by the biblical texts. If we view the end of the age as having already come upon us with the first advent of Christ, and as culminating in the Second Coming, we can simply say that judgment has already come into this world,[81] that it continues through this age,[82] and that it reaches its final stage with the Return. If we further subscribe to belief in the Millennium, we can extend this judgmental process to include the beginning of the Millennium and the end, with the judgment of the "beast" and the "false prophet" taking place at the time when Satan is thrown into "the pit"[83] and the final judgment taking place when the thousand years are ended.[84] The judgment of "the dead, great and small"—which I understand to refer to the "great white throne," or the final judgment—takes place at that time.[85]

The Basis of Judgment.   The confusion over "faith" and "works" has had its effects on the people of God in every generation, and perhaps never more so that at present. The simplistic view that we are "saved by grace through faith"[86] fails to take into account the many biblical teachings that connect faith and works. James said it ("faith apart from works is barren"[87]) and Martin Luther objected strongly. But what of the words of Jesus? "Not every one who says to me, 'Lord, Lord,' shall enter the kingdom of heaven, but he who

---

74. John 12:31.   75. 1 Cor. 11:31.   76. 2 Cor. 5:10.   77. Matt. 25:
32.   78. Ezek. 20:37.   79. Jude v. 6.   80. Rev. 20:14.   81. John 9:
39; 12:31; 16:11.   82. Heb. 12:7; 1 Cor. 11:31,32.   83. Rev. 19:19,20;
20:2,3.   84. Rev. 20:5,7–10.   85. Rev. 20:11–15.   86. Cf. Eph. 2:8.
87. James 2:20.

does the will of my Father who is in heaven."[88] "Why do you call me 'Lord, Lord,' and not *do* what I tell you?"[89] "You call me Teacher and Lord; and you are right, for so I am. . . . If you know these things, blessed are you if you *do* them."[90] "Every branch of mine that bears no fruit, he [the Father] takes away, and every branch that does bear fruit he prunes, that it may *bear more fruit.*"[91] "If you *keep my commandments,* you will abide in my love, just as I have kept my Father's commandments and abide in his love."[92u]

We are, indeed, saved by the grace of God. The Last Judgment will be based on "the books" and "the book of life."[93] The books, as I understand the passage, contain the record of what the dead have done in their lifetimes.[94] The book of life will then consulted. This is based on the grace of God and the atoning death of his Son Jesus Christ. No one is saved by what is written in the other books. "All were judged by what they had done"[95] "and if any one's name was not found written in the book of life, he was thrown into the lake of fire."[96] Only those "who are written in the Lamb's book of life" will enter the Holy City.[97]

Some Burning Questions

Is There a Hell?   In the Old Testament, the word š^e'ôl, "Sheol," occurs sixty-five times, translated "grave, pit, hell, underworld," and so forth. It is sometimes used to express "death" or "dead," without any indication of place, state, or condition. This Jacob said, "I shall go down to Sheol to my Son [Joseph], mourning."[98] In other passages it is portrayed as a place of darkness,[99] of sorrows,[100] of no knowledge of God.[101] In the Intertestamental Period, the idea of two divisions is found, one for the righteous and the other for the wicked,[102] which may have originated from the biblical teaching that God will deliver the righteous[103] and from other words, such as 'ăbaddôn, "destruction,"[104] and šaḥat, "pit,"[105] which are used in connection with the wicked. The

---

88. Matt. 7:21.   **89.** Luke 6:46.   **90.** John 13:13–17.   **91.** John 15:2.
92. John 15:10.   **93.** Rev. 20:12.   **94.** Rev. 20:12.   **95.** Rev. 20:13.
96. Rev. 20:15.   **97.** Rev. 21:27.   **98.** Gen. 37:35.   **99.** Job 17:13.
100. Ps. 18:4–6 (MT 5–7).   **101.** Ps. 6:5 (MT 6).   **102.** Enoch 22:1–14.
103. Ps. 16:10; 30:3 (MT 4); 49:15 (MT 16).   **104.** Prov. 15:11.   **105.** Ps. 88:3,4 (MT 4–5).

two divisions in the place of the dead are reflected in the Parable of Lazarus and the Rich Man.[106] In Rabbinic literature, *Ge-Hinnom*, "Gehenna, the Valley of Hinnom," is the place to which the wicked go, and *Gan-Eden*, "The Garden of Eden, Paradise," is the place for the righteous.[v]

In the New Testament, two words are used: *hadēs*, "Hades, hell," and *geenna*, "Gehenna, hell." The former is the classical Greek word, and the latter obviously comes from the Hebrew *gê' hinnôm*.[w]

The English word "hell" originally meant an enclosed or concealed place. The idea of burning fire, eternal suffering, damnation, and related concepts came to be associated with the word from biblical passages and popular development. The valley of Hinnom to the south of Jerusalem was the place where trash and dead bodies of beasts and criminals were burned. The word *geenna* is used eleven times in the Synoptics and once in James, usually on the lips of Jesus, and described as a place of fire[107] or destruction of body and soul.[108] The word *hadēs* occurs ten times, usually conveying the idea of the place of the dead. Only once is it used specifically of a place of torment, in the Parable of Lazarus and the Rich Man.[109] In Revelation, it occurs always in the expression "Death and Hades."[110] Jesus has the key of Death and Hades.[111] Death and Hades are finally to be cast into the lake of fire.[112x]

What Is the Lake of Fire?   The term "lake of fire" occurs only in the closing chapters of Revelation.[113] It "burns with fire and brimstone"[114] and is called the "second death."[115] It is specifically the place into which the "beast" and the "false prophet" are cast[116] prior to the thousand years, and Satan,[117] Death and Hades,[118] and those whose names are not written in the book of life[119] after the thousand years and the final judgment.

The suggestion that the Dead Sea is the location of the lake of fire has been made, based partly on Genesis 19:24 and Enoch 67:4ff.[y] Other scholars have tried to connect the idea with the

---

106. Luke 16:19–31.   107. Matt. 5:22; 18:9; Mark 9:43.   108. Matt. 10:28.   109. Luke 16:23.   110. Rev. 1:18; 6:8; 20:13,14.   111. Rev. 1:18.   112. Rev. 20:13,14.   113. Rev. 19:20; 20:10,14,15; 21:8.   114. Rev. 19:20; 20:10; 21:8.   115. Rev. 20:14; 21:8; cf. 2:11.   116. Rev. 19:20.   117. Rev. 20:10.   118. Rev. 20:14.   119. Rev. 20:15; cf. 21:8.

Zoroastrian "stream of fire," but this is purifying, whereas the lake of fire in the New Testament is punitive forever.[120]

Does Hell Last For Ever?   Students of the Bible are divided over this question. The words of Jesus appear to teach that hell is a place of eternal suffering: "the eternal fire,"[121] "unquenchable fire"[122] "where their worm does not die, and the fire is not quenched,"[123] "there men will weep and gnash their teeth,"[124] "eternal punishment."[125] It has been suggested that "eternal" in these passages simply means "age-long." The reply has been made that the same word defines "life"[126] so that "eternal life" would then also be simply age-long.

On the other hand, God at last makes "all things new."[127] The first heaven and the first earth will pass away.[128] The lake of fire is "the second death,"[129] and this implies cessation of existence. Vos, however, contends that the scriptural passages teach an undesirable state of existence and not a cessation of existence.[2] In the absence of unanimity among scholars I would prefer to leave the question where, I believe, the Bible leaves it. It is not God's will that any should be condemned. The sacrifice of Christ is sufficient to atone for all the sins of all men. God asks nothing more than our trust in his saving grace and our desire to walk in his ways. For those who reject, and for Satan and his agents, there are threats of terrible punishment. And whatever the nature of this punishment, which cannot be described on the basis of our experiences in this world except in terms of fire, weeping, and gnashing of teeth, there is no reason why we should spend time and emotions worrying about it, for Christ came into the world to save us from it. Trust him!

Summary

The Bible clearly teaches that God is a judge, who has demonstrated his judicial nature in the past, who continually judges men and nations, and who has appointed a day when there will be a final judgment. Today is the day of grace, when God gives us an opportunity to repent and be saved. The final judgment ends this forebearance of God. After that there is a fixity of human nature

---

120. Rev. 20:10.   121. Matt. 18:8.   122. Mark 9:44.   123. Mark 9:48.   124. Matt. 13:42,50.   125. Matt. 25:46.   126. Matt. 25:46.   127. Rev. 21:5.   128. Rev. 21:1.   129. Rev. 20:14; 21:8.

described in the awful words: "Let the evildoer still do evil, and the filthy still be filthy, and the righteous still do right, and the holy still be holy."[130] Between the two there is a great fixed gulf, and we should not want it any other way. We have had enough evil in the present age. We long and pray "Thy kingdom come! Thy will be done on earth as it is in heaven!"

NOTES

a. On the idea of "common belief" see Chapter 8, above. The creedal statements quoted there join the Return of Christ and the Last Judgment. Belief in the final judgment was also a cardinal belief of the rabbis of early Judaism, cf. A. Cohen, *Everyman's Talmud* (New York: Schocken, 1975), p. 370.

b. The question is at least as old as Marcion; cf. *TDNT* 5: 425.

c. Cf. L. Morris, *The Biblical Doctrine of Judgment* (Grand Rapids, MI: Eerdmans, 1960); J. P. Martin, *The Last Judgment in Protestant Theology from Orthodoxy to Ritschl* (Grand Rapids, MI: Eerdmans, 1963).

d. *Augustine De Civitate Dei* 1.8, quoted by J. Calvin *Institutes* 1.5.10.

e. It is important to note that the word in Genesis 4:13, translated "punishment" in the RSV, is *'āwôn*, which means both "iniquity, guilt" and "punishment of iniquity"; see BDB, p. 730. There is good support for the view that iniquity and punishment are interrelated.

f. The verb "to know" should be studied carefully. It indicates an intimate relationship, not merely head-knowledge, and involves the covenant relationship between Yahweh and his people.

g. The cognates *krima* and *krisis* are used for the act of judging and the result of the action, or the judgment, with some overlapping; cf. *TDNT* 3: 941f. V. Herntrich points out that *krinō* means not so much to reach a decision as to restore the legal relationship; *TDNT* 3: 923. This approaches the basic idea of Heb. *šālôm*, "Shalom," generally translated "peace," but meaning "completeness, integrity, wholeness."

h. Hebrew *ṣedeq, ṣ'dāqā* (BDB, pp. 841f.), Greek *dikaiosunē* (*TDNT* 2: 192–210).

i. Cf. W. Evans, "wrath," *ISBE* 5: 3113.

j. See *TDNT* 5: 382–447; W. Eichrodt, *Theology of the Old Testament* 1: 259–269. Eichrodt makes the point: "*Yahweh's anger has nothing of the Satanic about it; it remains simply the manifestation of the displeasure of God's unsearchable greatness, and as such is far above human conception*" (p. 261, italics his). Cf. also Eichrodt, *Theology of the Old Testament*, 2: 423–443.

k. Cf. *TDNT* 4: 374–387; R. V. G. Tasker, *The Biblical Doctrine of the Wrath of God* (London, Tyndale, 1951).

l. W. J. Harrelson, "Vengeance," *IDB* 4: 748; cf. R. H. Swartzback, "A

---

130. Rev. 22:11.

Biblical Study of the Word 'Vengeance,'" *Interpretation* 6 (1952): 451–457; A. M'Caig, "Retribution," *ISBE* 4: 2570–2572.

m. For a fine study, cf. D. E. Aune, "Chastening, Chastisement," *ISBE* 1 (1979): 637–638.

n. Paul uses *katakrima* in Romans; John uses *krinein*. But it is obvious (to me, at least) that John is speaking of condemnation rather than judgment in this passage, for Jesus *did* come into the world to judge (John 5:22; 9:39). Exegesis of the text requires more than word study; grappling with the author's intention is also necessary.

o. *IDB* 2: 139 (c.)

p. I can only reply to this charge by saying that I find this methodology self-consistent, and that any other attempt to deal with the prophecies of the end time reduces them to meaningless or contradictory human guesses without divine revelation of what God intends to do.

q. C. L. Feinberg, *Premillennialism or Amillennialism?* (Grand Rapids, MI: Zondervan, 1936), p. 239.

r. C. I. Scofield, *Rightly Dividing the Word of Truth* (New York: Revell, 1917), pp. 28–32.

s. *NSRB*, p. 1375, n.1. I have omitted the word *"note"* which occurs after each reference, since it would only be confusing here. In NSRB it is intended to refer the reader to the notes on each of the judgments.

t. "Fruit-bearing" is often taken to mean winning converts. But the biblical concept is expressed in Galations 5:22, 23. We are to be "witnesses"; the Holy Spirit does the converting.

u. Those who follow an extreme form of Dispensationalism will object, saying that the Gospels do not belong to the Church age. I simply reply, Read Paul's epistles. He, too, connected the behavior of believers with their faith. Not by works but by faith—but not by faith without works, for faith works!

v. Cf. A. Cohen, *Everyman's Talmud*, pp. 379–389, and references to the Talmud.

w. A third word, *tartaroō*, occurs in 2 Peter 2:4, meaning "to consign to Tartarus," (RSV, "cast them into hell"). It is used with reference to the angels that sinned. In classical Greek *tartaros* is a term for "the nether world," cf. LSJ 2: 1759.

x. Cf. S. D. F. Salmond, "Hell," *HDB* 2: 343–346; "Hades," 274–276.

y. Cf. G. Vos, "Lake of Fire," *ISBE* 3 (1929): 1822. More recently E. L. Martin has revived this theory in great detail in "The Lake of Fire—Where Is It Located?" *Exposition* (Pasadena CA: Foundation for Biblical Research, 1981). I found the article interesting and thought-provoking, but not convincing. Incidentally, Dr. Martin's foundation is not connected in any way with my foundation of a similar name.

z. G. Vos, "Eschatology of the New Testament," *ISBE* 2 (1929): 990f.

ADDITIONAL READING

English, E. S. *Companion to the New Scofield Reference Bible.* New York: Oxford University Press, 1972. Pp. 149–151, 154.

Martin, James P. *The Last Judgment in Protestant Theology from Orthodoxy to Ritschl.* Grand Rapids, MI: Eerdmans, 1963.

Morris, Leon. *The Biblical Doctrine of Judgment.* Grand Rapids, MI: Eerdmans, 1960.

Tasker, R. V. G. *The Biblical Doctrine of the Wrath of God.* London: Tyndale, 1951.

15. The New Heavens and the New Earth

The Problem

The Bible speaks of "a new heaven and a new earth." What does this mean? Is God going to destroy the present universe and replace it with another? Or is all matter going to be ended, with only spiritual or nonmaterial existence continuing? Or does the expression perhaps mean simply that the present character of the age is to be changed, either by divine or by human action, to give us an ideal world?

Various answers to these questions have been given. Philosophers of the Idealist school generally hold that matter is evil or unreal or temporary. Humanists (or Humanitarianists)ᵃ are convinced that a new earth can be achieved only by human efforts, often rejecting any notion of divine activity or even divine existence.

What does the Bible teach? We should be aware, at the very outset of our study, that if the Bible is a divine revelation (as I believe it is), and if it tells us of eons either before or after this historical age, it can only speak in language of this space-time age. We must not press for literal or photographic details, for human eyes have not seen, no ears heard, that which lies beyond our earthly experience.

The Biblical Basis of the Doctrine

Specific References.　　Isaiah was the first to mention the concept: "For behold, I create new heavens and a new earth; and the former things shall not be remembered."[1] The context goes on to include the statement "I create Jerusalem a rejoicing"[2] and mentions "my

---

1. Isa. 65:17.　　2. Isa. 65:18.

people."[3] However, the passage also speaks of "the child" that "shall die a hundred years old," and "the sinner" that shall "be accursed,"[4] of building houses, and planting vineyards,[5] of child-bearing,[6] and of the wolf and the lamb feeding together.[7] In other words, the new earth that Isaiah portrays here is very much like the present earth, except that weeping, distress, frustrations, and hurting and destroying are removed. Isaiah mentions "the new heaven and the new earth" again in the following chapter,[8] comparing the permanence of the people to the permanence of the new creation. Again, his picture is drawn in this-world terms, for he tells us that "they shall go forth and look on the dead bodies of the men that have rebelled against me; for their worm shall not die, their fire shall not be quenched, and they shall be an abhorrence to all flesh."[9b]

Peter mentions "new heavens and a new earth"[10] in a context where he is speaking of the coming of the day of the Lord and the dissolution of the heavens.[11] He had previously mentioned that "the heavens and earth that now exist have been stored up for fire, being kept until the days of judgment and destruction of ungodly men."[12c] Peter seems to have been influenced by Isaiah's words, "All the host of heaven shall rot away, and the skies roll up like a scroll,"[13] which are found in a prophecy against Edom. Isaiah also said, "for the heavens will vanish like smoke, and the earth will wear out like a garment,"[14] in a passage where the Lord is stressing that his salvation will be for ever, and his deliverance never-ending.

Perhaps the best-known passage is in Revelation: "Then I saw a new heaven and a new earth; for the first heaven and the first earth had passed away, and the sea was no more."[15] The Revelator had previously spoken of the great white throne and him who sat upon it; "from his presence earth and sky fled away, and no place was found for them."[16] Earlier in his work, John described a great earthquake, when "the sun became black as sackcloth, the full moon became like blood, and the stars of the sky fell to the earth as the fig tree sheds its winter fruit when shaken by a gale; the sky vanished like a scroll that is rolled up, and every mountain and

---

3. Isa. 65:19.   4. Isa. 65:20.   5. Isa. 65:21.   6. Isa. 65:23.   7. Isa. 65:25.   8. Isa. 66:22.   9. Isa. 66:24.   10. 2 Pet. 3:13.   11. 2 Pet. 3:10,12.   12. 2 Pet. 3:7.   13. Isa. 34:4.   14. Isa. 51:6; cf. Heb. 1:11. 15. Rev. 21:1.   16. Rev. 20:11.

island was removed from its place."[17] Part of this figure comes from Joel[18] and was quoted by Peter on Pentecost.[19]

Inferential References. There are other passages in Scripture that mention the end of the present world, inferring that something else continues afterward. The Psalmist sang:

> Of old thou didst lay the foundation of the earth,
>   and the heavens are the work of thy hands.
> They will perish, but thou dost endure;
>   they will all wear out like a garment.[20]

Job used the expression, "till the heavens are no more."[21] Jesus included similar statements: "till heaven and earth pass away"[22] and "Heaven and earth will pass away."[23] However, we must be cautious in using such expressions to build doctrines, for the intent in each case is not to teach the end of heaven and earth, but rather to teach the permanence of death (in the case of Job's quotation) or of the words of the law or of Jesus (in Jesus' quotations).[d] It is reasonable to assume that, since the words of Jesus will endure even after heaven and earth pass away, there must something beyond that event, some reason for them to endure.

The Created World.   We have seen in previous studies that the material universe was created by God[24] and that he was pleased with his work.[25] We should therefore reject any system of thought that is built on the premise that matter is evil. It is the *use* to which matter is put, or the satanic perversion of material beings and things, that is evil. The human being was created in God's image[26] and was "good" until the Fall. The redemptive work of God will result in a new person—not a different kind of creature without material existence, but a being with a resurrection body, fit for life in the new heavens and new earth.

The Psalms contain many expressions of praise to God for his creation, and one Psalmist even ventured the observation they were established "for ever and ever."[27] In his "bitterness" of soul, Job would have asked God, "Does it seem good to thee to oppress,

---

17. Rev. 6:12–14.   18. Cf. Joel 2:10,30–31 (MT 2:10; 3:3–4).   19. Acts 2:17–21.   20. Ps. 102:25,26 (MT 26,27); cf. Heb. 1:10,11.   21. Job 14:12. 22. Matt. 5:18.   23. Job 24:35.   24. Cf. Gen. 1:1.   25. Gen. 1:31. 26. Gen. 1:26,27.   27. Ps. 148:6.

to despise the work of thy hands . . . ?"[28] Even in the face of "the designs of the wicked," Job thought he saw a creation that required God's own concern. In fact, the Bible is filled with statements about God's works of creation.[e]

The Redeemed Creation. In our study of the effects of satanic power on this world, we learned that even the physical world has suffered and must be redeemed. Paul treats this subject at some length in his letter to the Romans.

For the creation waits with eager longing for the revealing of the sons of God; for the creation was subjected to futility, not of its own will but by the will of him who subjected it in hope; because the creation itself will be set free from its bondage to decay and obtain the glorious liberty of the children of God. We know that the whole creation has been groaning in travail together until now; and not only the creation, but we ourselves, who have the first fruits of the Spirit, groan inwardly as we wait for adoption as sons, the redemption of our bodies.[29]

Biblical Description of the New Creation

The Meaning of "Heaven." The Revelator says, "I saw a new heaven and a new earth, for the first heaven and the first earth had passed away."[30] This raises the question of whether the entire universe is to be destroyed and replaced by another. It is my opinion that much of the language in the Bible is phenomenological, that is, things are described as they appear to us in our earthbound experience. Thus, the creation story in Genesis begins with the words, "In the beginning, when God created the heavens and the earth," moves at once to consider the "earth," and from the point of view of earth proceeds to describe the "firmament" which was called "Heaven."[31] The sun, moon, and stars were placed "in the firmament of the heavens."[32] Even their relative sizes are described from this earthly viewpoint.[f]

"Heaven" is also the dwelling place of God, the angels, and other heavenly beings and the place to which Satan had access.[33] It seems to me that this is to be distinguished from the material portions of the universe. Solomon recognized this when he said, in

28. Job 10:3.   29. Rom. 8:19–23.   30. Rev. 21:1.   31. Gen. 1:1,2 (lit.),8.   32. Gen. 1:15.   33. 1 Kings 8:30.

his dedicatory prayer, "Behold, heaven and the highest heaven cannot contain thee; how much less this house which I have built!"[34g] The heaven which is God's dwelling place is beyond the stars.[35h] It is "the heaven of heavens" (an idiom meaning the greatest or highest of heavens,[36] "eternity,"[37] God's "throne"[38]).

The destruction of the heaven and the creation of a new heaven must be interpreted against these biblical statements. Obviously, God's throne is not to be destroyed (cf. where "heaven" flees from before God's throne[39]). Nor is it likely that the distant stars, which are not identified in any way with the sinful nature of this earth, are to be destroyed, although there are passages that describe stars as falling from heaven.[40i] Since Satan has had access to heaven and has led some kind of war in heaven,[41] it is possible to understand the destruction of heaven and the creation of a new heaven to mean that the satanic influences have been removed.[42j] It is also possible to take the biblical passages to mean that the "firmament"—the solar system of which our earth is a part, including our sun, moon, and the planets and their satellites—will be destroyed and replaced by new "heavens." This destruction, if the passages are so interpreted, would be by fire.[43] But this view, I believe, demands great humility on the part of the interpreters, rather than confident dogmatism.

The New Earth.   There is more biblical material concerning the earth than concerning the heavens. We are still faced, however, with difficulties of interpretation. The "new earth" described in Revelation[44] follows the account of the thousand years, the final judgment, and the destruction of Satan, Death, and Hades. Therefore interpreters commonly understand chapters 21 and 22 of Revelation to refer to the age to come.[k]

In the Prophets there are, as we have seen in our study of the Millennium, several descriptions of the changes that are to take place in the "latter days." But these are expressed in material terms: productivity of the fields, domestication of the wild animals, longevity, and so forth. Interpreters have therefore either "spiritualized" such prophecies or have taken them as descriptions of the

---

34. 1 Kings 8:27.   **35.** Cf. Job 22:12–14.   **36.** Cf. 2 Chron. 2:6 (MT 5).
37. Isa. 57:15.   **38.** Matt. 5:34.   **39.** Rev. 20:11.   **40.** Isa. 34:4; 2
Pet. 3:10; Rev. 6:13.   **41.** Rev. 12:7–10.   **42.** Cf. Rev. 12:10,12.   **43.** 2
Pet. 3:10,12.   **44.** Rev. 21:1.

millennial age. If the "new earth" is a new creation of God after the final judgment, the literal interpretation of these prophecies can only with difficulty be applied to the new earth.

There can be no question, however, about the need of a palingenesis of this earth, and this is clearly taught (cf. where *paliggenesia* is translated "in the new world,"[45]). The only question is to identify what belongs to the messianic age and what belongs to the age to come. If we believe that ages overlap, as the Parousia includes both advents of Christ, this problem is partially resolved.

The New Jerusalem.   John has given us the most details in his description of the New Jerusalem.[46] It is a city, but not such as those which have been built by fallen humankind. It is a holy city, "coming down out of heaven from God."[47] It therefore can be taken as the ultimate fulfillment of the promise made to Abraham, or in the words of the author of Hebrews, "For he looked forward to the city which has foundations, whose builder and maker is God,"[48] called "the heavenly Jerusalem."[49]

The city is described as "coming down from heaven," using the present participle suggesting that it is poised above earth.[50] It is extremely large, "twelve thousand stadia," or about 1500 miles (2500 kilometers), and "its length and breadth and height are equal."[51] This obviously is not the Jerusalem we know on earth, for 1500 miles would cover an area extending from Iran to Crete and from the Black Sea to Luxor. But what about the "height" of the city. Is it a cube, a colossal apartment house, 1500 miles high? I shudder at the thought! What about a pyramid, like that on the Seal of the United States (on the back of the dollar bill)? To stand on the sides of a pyramid whose height is equal to its base would be most difficult. And the river that flows through the city[52] would become a mighty torrent, tearing out the banks on which the tree of life is located. What about a sphere? It could hardly be described as "foursquare," but its length, breadth, and height would be equal, and if it is "hanging down" from heaven, like a small satellite above the earth, the spherical shape would be logical.

---

45. Cf. also Rom. 8:19–23.   46. Rev. 21:2–22:5.   47. Rev. 21:2.
48. Heb. 11:10.   49. Heb. 12:22.   50. Rev. 3:12; 21:2,10.   51. Rev. 21:16.   52. Rev. 22:1,2.

The city was radiant "like a most rare jewel."[53] It had a "great, high wall, with twelve gates."[54] The wall "was built of jasper" and the city "was pure gold, clear as glass,"[55] with foundations "adorned with every jewel."[56] The gates "were twelve pearls, each of the gates made of a single pearl, and the street of the city was pure gold, transparent as glass."[57] It seems that the Revelator is having difficulty describing in earth language the heavenly city. Why this city needs a great, high wall and gates, when its "gates shall never be shut by day" and there is no night,[58] is not explained. Certainly it is not an "iron curtain," to keep its people inside, and, while "nothing unclean shall enter,"[59] the open gates cannot keep them out.

The interpretation must surely go beyond city planning and architecture and materials. There is no temple in the city, for the Lord God the Almighty and the Lamb constitute the temple. After all, the temple, like the tabernacle, was merely a symbol representing the presence of God, a type to be replaced by its antitype which is God. When the real is present, there is no need for symbols.[60] There is no need for sun or moon (it doesn't say they do not exist), "for the glory of God is its light,"[61] and this splendor, "the glory of God,"[62] provides the light in which the nations shall walk. The river that flows "through the middle of the street of the city"[63] has its source in the throne of God and of the Lamb.[64] It is "the water of life"[65] and the tree of life grows on its banks,[66] providing fruit continually, and its leaves are "for the healing of the nations."[67]

Best of all, the Lord's servants, beholding his face ("the beatific vision"), will render the highest form of service. They shall worship him.[68] On the gates of the city were inscribed "the names of the twelve tribes of the sons of Israel," and on the foundations "the twelve names of the twelve apostles of the Lamb."[69] When John would have fallen at the feet of the angel who showed him the holy city, the angel said: "You must not do that! I am a fellow servant with you and your brethren the prophets, and with those who keep

53. Rev. 22:11.   54. Rev. 22:12.   55. Rev. 22:18.   56. Rev. 22:19.
57. Rev. 22:21.   58. Rev. 22:25.   59. Rev. 22:27.   60. 1 Cor. 13:10;
Heb. 9:11–14.   61. Rev. 21:23.   62. Rev. 21:11.   63. Rev. 22:2.
64. Ezek. 47:1,6–12.   65. Rev. 22:1.   66. Rev. 22:2.   67. Rev. 22:2.
68. Rev. 22:3,4.   69. Rev. 21:12,14.

the words of this book." Israelites, apostles, prophets, and angels, "all who wash their robes"[70] have the right to enter that holy city and worship God.[71]

The Kingdom of God

In his chapter on the resurrection, Paul says, "Then comes the end, when he [Christ] delivers the kingdom to God the Father after destroying every rule and every authority and power."[72] According to some (many?) Bible scholars, the picture given in the closing chapters of Revelation refers to this "end." The expression is sometimes used that we have moved from time to eternity.[m] We speak of the period between Creation and the End as the "space-time continuum," meaning that God created space and time, and these will come to an end. God himself is not subject to either, being infinite (without spatial limits) and eternal (without temporal limits). The differentiation between time and eternity, however, arises more from Greek philosophy than from biblical teaching.

We should therefore raise the question whether, God having created space and time, and having through his Son taken on human likeness, there is an end of time and space.[n] It is possible that the term "ages of the ages"[73] refers to an endless succession of ages, during which God and his saints are active in many parts of his universe. What, then, is "the kingdom" that the Son delivers to the Father?

Meanings of "Kingdom of God."   G. Campbell Morgan, with his gift of alliteration, interprets the word "kingdom" by three words: "rule, realm, result."[o] God as Creator of heaven and earth, as Sustainer and Judge, is always its king. But since he does not force his rule upon us in this age, he is king only of those who bow before him. Ultimately he wills to rule over all. As rule, his kingdom has been and is ever in effect. As realm, it is only as wide as we let it be. But the result will come into being when Jesus Christ has overcome all opposition, becoming King of kings and Lord of lords. At that time he will deliver over to the Father the kingdom in the perfection of his redemptive work.

---

70. Rev. 22:14.   71. Rev. 22:9.   72. 1 Cor. 15:24.   73. Ps. 84:4
(MT 5; LXX 83:5).

The New Jerusalem and the Kingdom of God.   John saw the throne of God and of the Lamb in the holy city.[74] Whether this is to be taken literally, along with verses such as "heaven is my throne, and earth my footstool,"[75] is a matter of interpretation that we must decide to the best of our ability in the light of scriptural revelation. At the very least, this sin-cursed, Satan-dominated planet and the beings in it will at last be made new, and God will be the supreme Ruler. We who belong to him will not only be his servants, but we shall reign with him.[76]

But perhaps even the New Jerusalem is but the entrance into unending ages. I personally do not look upon "eternal life" as something static, nor do I believe that God is planning to "retire" as soon as he gets this mess cleaned up. He is the God of the living, and we shall be like him. God created a vast universe, and, if certain scientific theories have an element of truth in them, the universe may be in a continual state of renewal.[p] We continually make our God too small, and our theological systems seek to fence him in. He is a great God, and great are the works of his hands. In the ages to come, we who now "see in a mirror dimly"[77] will have an eternity to study those works and to sing with the elders around the throne:

Worthy art thou, our Lord and God,
    to receive glory and honor and power,
for thou didst create all things,
    and by thy will they existed and were created.[78]

We give thanks to thee, Lord God almighty, who are and who wast,
    that thou hast taken thy great power and begun to reign.
The nations raged, but thy wrath came,
    and the time for the dead to be judged,
for rewarding thy servants, the prophets and saints,
    and those who fear thy name, both small and great,
and for destroying the destroyers of the earth.[79]

Great are thy deeds,
    O Lord God the Almighty!
Just and true are thy ways,
    O King of the ages!

---

74. Rev. 22:1.   **75.** Cf. Isa. 66:1.   **76.** Rev. 20:6.   **77.** 1 Cor. 13:12.
78. Rev. 4:11.   **79.** Rev. 11:17,18.

Who shall not fear and glorify thy name, O Lord?
For thou alone art holy.
All nations shall come and worship before thee,
for thy judgments have been revealed.[80]

The Spirit and the Bride say, "Come." And let him who hears say, "Come." And let him who is thirsty come, let him who desires take the water of life without price. . . . He who testifies to these things says, "Surely I am coming soon." Amen. Come, Lord Jesus![81]

NOTES

a. The terms are badly confused, according to the authorities that I have consulted. I am referring to those who hold the system that the human being is totally without need of any divine or superhuman aid to achieve a perfect order.

b. Jesus made use of this language; cf. Mark 9:48.

c. In this same context he makes the statement, "that with the Lord one day is as a thousand years, and a thousand years as one day" (2 Pet. 3:8).

d. This is a very important point for scriptural interpretation. We must always ask first: what is the speaker/writer trying to teach? If the purpose is *not* to teach astronomy or geology or anthropology or whatever, we should hesitate to construct dogmas concerning those subjects on such passages.

e. In addition to the creation story in Genesis, see the following sampling, only a part of the scriptural presentation of the doctrine: Exod. 20:12; 1 Sam. 2:8; 2 Kings 1:15; 1 Chron. 16:26; Neh. 9:6; Job 12:7; 26:7; Ps. 89:11 [MT 12]; Prov. 3:19; Eccl. 3:11; Isa. 37:16; 40:28; Jer. 10:12; Amos 9:6; Jonah 1:9; Zech. 12:1; Mark 13:19; Acts 4:24; Rom. 1:20; 1 Cor. 8:6; Eph. 3:9; Heb. 11:3; Rev. 4:11.

f. Such an interpretation obviates the discussion of geocentricity, for from our viewpoint the earth is the center of the universe, and the sun and moon do revolve about the earth. Moreover, there is no need to attempt a scientific definition of the "firmament." It is something like the ecliptic and can be described as a "scroll" (Isa. 34:4), against which we can trace the apparent motion of the sun, moon, and planets. The biblical people of course were, like other ancients, aware of stars and constellations (cf. Amos 5:8) and distinguished between the "fixed" stars and the "wanderers" (Greek *planetai*, cf. Jude v. 13).

g. There was also a "third" heaven (I do not intend to identify the rank; for this see 2 Cor. 12:2) from which the rains descend. It is unnecessary to contend, as has often been said in a disparaging way, that the biblical viewpoint is a "three-tiered" universe, for phenomenologically there *are* three heavens: that of the clouds; that of the sun, moon, and planets; and that of the stars. We can see the clouds moving against a relatively fixed sun or moon, and we can see the planets moving against the background

---

80. Rev. 15:3,4.   81. Rev. 22:17,20.

of the stars—phenomena which the ancients of Egypt and Babylonian (not to mention other peoples) observed.

h. This is the statement of a scoffer, but it doubtless reflects a common belief.

i. Some biblical scholars interpret these "stars" to mean governments of earth that collapse. I hesitate to accept this interpretation, although I admit that the passages are difficult.

j. The dogma of the "cleansing" of the heavenly sanctuary, put forth by E. G. White in *The Great Controversy*, (Mountain View, CA: Pacific Press, 1950 [1911 ed.]), p. 376, is, in my opinion, without biblical foundation.

k. C. E. Mason offers a novel interpretation, suggesting that there is an overlapping here with the earlier portion of these chapters referring back to the millennial age (*Prophetic Problems*, pp. 229–251). Mason's interpretation depends in part on his dispensational viewpoint; nevertheless, the theory that Revelation does not provide a strict chronological sequence is valid and the suggestion merits further study.

l. The angle would be about 65°. The Greek word *tetragonos* "four-cornered" is used of rectangles, squares, or cubes, but since the measurements are equal, the base would be a square.

m. C. E. Mason, for example, follows a discussion of Revelation 20 with a subheading, *"Plainly, at this point we are over into eternity!"* (*Prophetic Problems*, p. 230, italics his).

n. The expression "time shall be no more" is based on the KJV translation of Revelation 10:6, more accurately translated "there shall be no more delay" (cf. NSRB, NASB, NIV, and RSV).

o. Cf. G. C. Morgan, *The Teaching of Christ*, p. 207.

p. The statement that God completed his creation and rested on the seventh day may have reference simply to our solar system and our planet; cf. Genesis 2:1,2. Jesus' statement (John 5:17) tells us that God is still working.

ADDITIONAL READING

English, E. S. *Companion to the New Scofield Reference Bible*. New York: Oxford University Press, 1972. Pp. 154–156.

Lindsey, Hal. *There's A New World Coming*. Santa Ana, CA: Vision House, 1973; New York: Bantam, 1975.

Pache, René. *L'Au Delà*. Vennes sur Lausanne: Éditions Emmaüs, 1955.

Bibliography

Armerding, Carl E., and Gasque, W. Ward, eds., *Dreams, Visions, and Oracles: The Layman's Guide to Biblical Prophecy*. Grand Rapids, MI: Baker, 1977.

Arndt, W. F., and Gingrich, F. W. *A Greek-English Lexicon of the New Testament*. Cambridge: Cambridge University Press, 1957.

Baldwin, J. G. *Daniel* (TOTC). Grand Rapids, MI: Eerdmans, 1978.

Beasley-Murray, G. R. *Jesus and the Future*. London: Macmillan, 1954.

Beecher, W. J. *The Prophets and the Promise*. Reprint. Grand Rapids, MI: Baker, 1975.

Beet, Joseph Agar. *The Last Things*. New York: Methodist Book Concern, 1897.

Boutflower, C. *In and Around the Book of Daniel*. London: Society for Promoting Christian Knowledge, 1923.

Braaten, Carl E. *The Future of God*. New York: Harper & Row, 1969.

Brown, F.; Driver, S. R.; and Briggs, C. A. *Hebrew and English Lexicon of the Old Testament*. Oxford: Clarendon, 1907; reprint 1953.

Bruce, F. F. *The New Testament Development of Old Testament Themes*. Grand Rapids, MI: Eerdmans, 1968.

_____, ed. *Promise and Fulfillment*. Edinburgh: T. & T. Clark, 1963.

Christ and Glory. (Addresses delivered at the New York Prophetic Conference, November 25–28, 1918.) New York: "Our Hope," n. d.

Charles, R. H. *The Revelation of St. John* (ICC). 2 vols. New York: Scribner's, 1920.

_____. *The Apocrypha and Pseudepigrapha of the Old Testament*. 2 vols. Oxford: Clarendon, 1913.

Clements, R. E. *Old Testament Theology*. Atlanta, GA: John Knox, 1978. Pp. 79–103, 131–154.

Clines, D. J. A. "Darius." *ISBE* 1 (1979): 867–868.

Darmsteegt, P. Gerard. *Foundations of the Seventh-day Adventist Message and Mission*. Grand Rapids, MI: Eerdmans, 1977.

Dictionary of the Apostolic Church. 2 vols. Edited by J. Hastings. Reprint. New York: Scribner's, 1922.

Dictionary of Christ and the Gospels. 2 vols. Edited by J. Hastings. Reprint. New York: Scribner's, 1924.

Dougherty, R. P. *Nabonidus and Belshazzar*. New Haven, CT: Yale University Press, 1929.

Douglas, Herbert E. *The End: Unique Voice of Adventists About the Return of Jesus*. Mountain View, CA: Pacific Press, 1979.

Eichrodt, W. *Theology of the Old Testament.* 2 vols. Translated by J. A. Baker. London: SCM, 1961, 1967. 1:459–511; 2:93–230, 380–495.
English, E. S. *A Companion to the New Scofield Reference Bible.* New York: Oxford University Press, 1972.
Expositor's Greek Testament. 5 vols. Reprint. Grand Rapids, MI: Eerdmans, n. d.
Froom, Leroy E. *The Prophetic Faith of Our Fathers.* 4 vols. Washington, DC: Review and Herald, 1954.
Frost, Stanley. *Old Testament Apocalyptic.* London: Epworth, 1952.
Gaebelein, Arno C. *The Harmony of the Prophetic Word.* New York: Revell, 1907.
————. *The Revelation.* New York: "Our Hope," 1915.
————. *The Prophet Daniel.* New York: "Our Hope," 1936.
Harnack, Adolph. *History of Dogma.* 7 vols. Translated by Neil Buchanan. London: Williams & Norgate, 1896–1899. 1: 167–169; 2: 294–300.
Hastings, James, ed. *A Dictionary of the Bible.* 5 vols. New York: Scribner's, 1899.
Heinisch, P. *Christ in Prophecy.* Translated by W. G. Heidt. St. Paul, MN: Liturgical Press, 1956.
The Holy Bible. New International Version. Grand Rapids, MI: Zondervan, 1978.
Interpreter's Dictionary of the Bible. 4 vols. New York and Nashville, TN: Abingdon, 1962; Supplement, 1976.
International Standard Bible Encyclopedia. 5 vols. Chicago: The Howard-Severance Co., 1930; fully revised, 4 vols. Grand Rapids, MI: Eerdmans, 1979– .
Ironside, Harry A. *Lectures on Daniel.* 2d ed. New York: Loizeaux, 1920.
————. *Lectures on the Book of Revelation.* New York, Loizeaux, 1919; rev. ed. 1930.
Jeremias, Joachim. *Jesus' Promise to the Nations.* Naperville, IL: Allenson, 1958.
Klausner, Joseph. *The Messianic Idea in Israel: From Its Beginning to the Completion of The Mishnah.* Translated by W. F. Stinespring. London: Allen and Unwin, 1956.
Ladd, George E. *The Blessed Hope.* Grand Rapids, MI: Eerdmans, 1956.
————. *Crucial Questions about the Kingdom of God.* Grand Rapids, MI: Eerdmans, 1952.
————. *A Theology of the New Testament.* Grand Rapids, MI: Eerdmans, 1974.
LaSor, William Sanford. *Amazing Dead Sea Scrolls.* Chicago: Moody, 1956. Rev. ed. *The Dead Sea Scrolls and the Christian Faith,* 1962. Pp. 151–176.
————. *Great Personalities of the Old Testament.* Westwood, NJ: Revell, 1959. Pp. 164–173.
————. *Great Personalities of the New Testament.* Westwood, NJ: Revell, 1961. Pp. 175–184.
————. *The Dead Sea Scrolls and the New Testament.* Grand Rapids, MI: Eerdmans, 1972. Pp. 93–105.

LaSor, W. S.; Hubbard, D. A.; and Bush, F. W. *Old Testament Survey*. Grand Rapids, MI: Eerdmans, 1982. Chaps. 29, 30, 35, and 51.

Liddell, H. G. and Scott, R. Revised by Jones, H. S., and McKenzie, R. *Greek-English Lexicon*. 9th ed. 2 vols. Oxford: Clarendon, 1940.

Mason, Clarence E., Jr. *Prophetic Problems, with Alternate Solutions*. Chicago: Moody, 1973.

McConkey, James H. *The Book of Revelation*. Pittsburgh, PA: Silver, 1921.

Milligan, William. *St. Paul's Epistles to the Thessalonians*. London: Macmillan, 1908.

_____. *The Book of Revelation (Expositors' Bible)*. New York: Eaton & Mains, 1889. Pp. 1–110, 277–315, 335–359.

Moltmann, Jurgen. *The Theology of Hope*. London: SCM, 1967.

Moore, George Foot. *Judaism in the First Centuries of the Christian Era: The Tannaim*. 3 vols. Cambridge, MA: Harvard University Press, 1927.

Morgan, G. Campbell. *God's Methods with Man*. New York: Revell, 1898.

_____. *The Gospel according to Matthew*. New York: Revell, 1929.

_____. *The Teaching of Christ*. New York: Revell, 1913. Pp. 197–309.

_____. *The Crises of the Christ*. New York: Revell, 1903.

Muirhead, L. A. "Apocalypse." *DAC* 1: 71–81.

New American Standard Bible. LaHabra, CA: Lockman Foundation, 1963.

The New Bible Dictionary. Edited by J. D. Douglas. Grand Rapids, MI: Eerdmans, 1962.

The New Scofield Reference Bible. Edited by C. I. Scofield; editorial committee for the new edition, E. Schuyler English, chairman, et al. New York: Oxford University Press, 1967.

Pache, René. *Le Retour de Jesus Christ*. N.p., n.d. *The Return of Jesus Christ*. Translated by W. S. LaSor. Chicago: Moody, 1955.

Piper, Otto A. *God in History*. New York: Macmillan, 1939.

Plummer, Alfred. *An Exegetical Commentary on the Gospel according to S. Matthew*. London: Robert Scott, 1928.

Robinson, James A. T. *In The End, God*. New York: Harper & Row, 1968.

Rowley, H. H. *The Relevance of Apocalyptic*. London: Lutterworth, 1947.

_____, ed. *Studies in Old Testament Prophecy Presented to Professor T. H. Robinson*. Edinburgh: T. & T. Clark, 1950.

Rust, E. C. *Nature and Man in Biblical Thought*. London: Lutterworth, 1953.

Sauer, Erich. *From Eternity to Eternity*. Translated by G. H. Lang. Grand Rapids, MI: Eerdmans, 1954.

Schweitzer, Albert. *The Quest of the Historical Jesus*. New York: Macmillan, 1961.

Scofield Reference Bible. New ed. New York: Oxford University Press, 1917.

Seiss, Joseph A. *The Apocalypse*. 10th ed. 3 vols. New York: C. C. Cook, 1909.

Swete, Henry B. *The Apocalypse of St. John*. London: Macmillan, 1906.

Synave, P. and Benoit, P. *Prophecy and Inspiration*. New York: Desclée, 1961.

Theological Dictionary of the New Testament. 10 vols. Edited by G. Kittel. Translated by G. W. Bromiley. Grand Rapids, MI: Eerdmans, 1964–1976.

Thielecke, H. *The Evangelical Faith*. Vol. 3, *Theology of the Spirit*. Translated by G. W. Bromiley. Grand Rapids, MI: Eerdmans, 1982. Pp. 385–450.

Westermann, C. *Essays on Old Testament Hermeneutic*. Richmond, VA: Knox, 1963.

Vischer, W. *The Witness of the Old Testament to Christ*. London: Lutterworth, 1936.

von Rad, G. *Old Testament Theology*. 2 vols. Translated by D. M. G. Stalker. New York: Harper & Row, 1962, 1965. 1:306–459; 2:99–125, 278–315, 319–409.

Vos, Geerhardus. *The Pauline Eschatology*. Princeton, NJ: p.p., 1930. Pp. 72–93, 227–260.

Warfield, Benjamin B. "Prophecies of St. Paul." "The Millennium and the Apocalypse." In *Biblical Doctrines*. Collected articles published posthumously. New York: Oxford University Press, 1929. Pp. 601–640, 643–664.

Westcott, B. F. *The Epistles of St. John*. Reprint. Grand Rapids, MI: Eerdmans, 1966.

Wiseman, D. J. *et al*. *Notes on Some Problems in the Book of Daniel*. London: Tyndale, 1965.

Subject Index

Aaron, 83–84, 85, 113
Abarim, Valley of, 145
Abel, 30, 181
Abijam, 76
Abortion, increase of, as sign of end-time, 6
Abraham (Abram), 34, 40, 168, 176; as "chosen" or elect, 28, 37, 38, 41; covenant with, 38–39, 44–45, 75, 80, 152, 161, 201; resurrection view of, 177–78; Semitic or Hebrew identity of, 39
Abraham's bosom, 165, 176
Acts: demons in, 72; Parousia in, 104
Adam (Adamic couple): creation of, 24–25, 49; and evil, 25–28, 53, 60, 63; Fall of, 25–28, 32, 181; primal innocence of, 34
Advent (parousia), 94–95, 98, 130, 132, 134. See also Parousia; Second Coming
Afghanistan, 3
Agabus, prophecy of famine by, 14
Age, present, 23–35; boundaries of, in time, 24; contrast between a present and a future age, 15; end of, 14–15; human government in, 30–32; problems of interpreting, 23–24; role of creation, 24–25; role of Fall, 25–28; redemption for humankind in, 32–33; as revelatory age, 28–30; as Satanic, 24–28, 33
Ahab, 31
Ahura Mazda (Ormazd), 72
Alexander the Great, 68, 110
Amillennialism, 151, 160
Amos, 6, 187; and "Day of Yahweh," 136; eschatology in, 16; on God's judgment, 182; on ideal kingdom, 76, 93
Angelology, angels and, 16, 18, 71–72
Anger, divine, 183, 193
Angra Mainyu (Ahriman), 72
Antichrist, 6, 108–19, 146; Belial or Beast as, 108–10; characteristics of, 108; described by John, 112; he-goat and little horn visions, 110–11; identity

of, 116–17; as man of lawlessness, 111–12, 118; New Testament figures, 111–16; origin of idea, 108–11
Antinomianism, 51
Antiochus IV Ephiphanes, 110, 111, 117, 129, 140
Anti-Semitism, 146
Apocalyptic prophecy, 6, 113–14, 139–40, 141–42, See also Prophecy; individual prophets by name
Apostasy, Second Coming and, 101
Apostles' Creed, 91, 103–4
Arab-Israeli conflict, Armageddon and, 2–3, 8, 135, 146
Arabs: biblical treatment of, 46; claim to Palestine, 39
Arizona, Second Coming awaited in, 7, 90, 103
Armageddon, 135–49; contemporary interpretations of, 146; Daniel's prophecy, 140–41; as Day of the Lord, 136–37; defined, 135, 141; Ezekiel's prophecy, 137–40; Joel's prophecy, 142–43; location of, 148; New Testament teachings on, 143–46; in Revelation, 144–46; schedule for war, 148
Arminianism, 37
Ascension of Isaiah (noncanonical book), 94, 108–9
Assyria, 140, 156, 181
Astrology, 5
Athanasian Creed, 91
Atonement, Day of, 29
Augsburg Confession, 91–92, 171
Augustine, 160, 171, 181
Australia, 24

Baal, and baal worship, 51, 58
Babel, Tower of, 30, 35
Babylon, Babylonia, 69, 70, 76, 140, 152, 156; as agent of God's punishment, 181; as harlot, 115–16, and Antichrist, 114–16

"Babylonian Genesis," 49
Barr, J., 20–21
Beasts: as Antichrist, 112–13; in Daniel, 109–10; identification of, 114, 118; in Revelation, 141
Beelzebul (Beelzebub), 62, 71
Belial, Beliar, 108–9, 117
Bethlehem, 76
Bethsaida, 97
Birth stories, 83
Book of Common Prayer, 166
Bowman, J. W., 184
Bronze Age, 24
Bulletin of Atomic Scientists, 1
Bultmann, Rudolf, 166

Caesarea-Philippi, Peter's confession at, 82, 97
Cain, 30, 141
Calvary, 29
Calvinism, 37 See also Protestantism, doctrinal views of
Canaan and Canaanites, 31, 38, 51, 70, 182
Canon, concept of, 22
Capernaum, 97
Chastisement, as term for judgment, 183–84
Chiliasm, 87, 103, 104, 151, 162–63; development of doctrine, 160
China, People's Republic of, 135, 148
China Syndrome, 6
Chorazin, 97
Chosen people, concept of, 36–48; basis for election, 43–44; the elect, 38–41; and Jewish identity, 45–46; meaning of "chosen," 36–37; one or two chosen peoples, 44–45; purposes of election, 41–42
Christ, Second Coming of. See Second Coming
Church: beliefs in Messiah of, 82–84; as body of Christ, 25; effect of Tribulation on, 130–31; election of, 40–41; in Old Testament, 40; Paul's view of composition of, 52; use of prophecy by, 77
Circumcision, 44, 50
Common Market, 3–4, 8
Communism, 6, 139
Compenetration, 185
Condemnation, as term for judgment, 184
Constantinople, Council of (AD 381), 91

Corinthians (epistles), 52; Paul explains abode of dead in, 177; Paul on judgment in, 185, 187; resurrection idea in, 169–70
Council of Constantinople (AD 381), 91
Council of Nicea (AD 325), 91
Creation, 205, 206; biblical doctrine of new creation, 199–203; concept of, 21; essential goodness of, 198–99; location of heaven in, 199; place of, in history, 24–25, 160; relative import of male and female in, 25
Creedal statements, 91–92, 103–4
Cush, 147
Cyrus, 31
Czechoslovakia, 56

Daane, J., 47
Daniel: and Armageddon prophecy, 140–41; description of "Antichrist" in, 113; on God's kingdom, 77; kingdoms on earth, 31, 153–54; and Messianic kingdom, 84, 85, 86–87, 133; prophecies of, invoked by Jesus, 120, 122; prophecy of, and Great Tribulation, 122–24, 128–29, 133; purported fulfillment of prophecy, 3–4, 5; and resurrection, 168; Revelation compared with, 124–25; role of Satan in, 65; Son of Man term used in, 94; timing of calendar in, and end-time, 8, 110–11, 117, 123, 125, 128–29, 132, 133; visions of, 109–11, 117
David, 31, 87; ascription of genealogy to Jesus, 83; covenant with, and millennial system, 152; descendant of, as ideal king, 76, 78–79, 84, 85, 86, 113, 116, 153, 162; as elect, 28, 41; in Ezekiel's prophecy, 138, 139; and implied Second Coming, 93; kingship of, 75–77, 162
Day of Christ, Armageddon and, 136–37
Day of the Lord, 147; Armageddon and, 136–37. See also Yahweh, Day of
Dead Sea, 146, 191
Dead Sea Scrolls, 109, 117
Dembert, Lee, 8
Demons, as Satan's agents, 66, 71, 72
Devil, 60. See also Satan, Satanology and
Diadochoi (Alexander's successors), 110
Disciplinary suffering, 53, 54
Disobedience, disciplinary suffering and, 54

Dispensationalism, 35, 130–31, 151, 161, 163, 194
Divine grace, 33, 43–44, 47
Doctrine, dogma and, distinguished, 159
Dragon, as term for Satan, 61, 129
Dualism, 23, 67–68. See also Zoroastrianism

Earthquakes, as sign of end-time, 4
Eden, Garden of, 24, 33, 45, 53, 181; expulsion from, 23, 30, 32; Satanic presence in, 60
Edom, 138, 197
Egypt, 3, 39, 148; punishment of, 54, 181
Eichrodt, W., 193
Election, doctrine of, 28, 36–37, 49; basis of, 43–44; of Church, 40–41; of Israel, 38–41, 50–51; purpose of, 41–42
Elijah, 29, 31, 159
Emmaus, 83
End of world: defined, 11–14; explained, 11–22; in New Testament thought, 18–20; in Old Testament thought, 15–18; present signs of, 1–9. See also Eschatology
Endor, Medium of, 175
Enoch (noncanonical book), 26–27; apocalyptic passages in, 81, 144, 169, 188
Ephesians (epistle): absence of reference to Second Coming in, 92; warning against Satan in, 66
Esau, 37, 39, 46
Eschatology: as biblical doctrine, 7; Christian–Old Testament background of, 15–18, 21; defined, 11–12; distinguishing "apocalyptic" from "prophetic," 22; New Testament ideas, 18–20; temporal idea, 12. See also End of world
Esdraelon, 141, 144
Esther, 31
Eternity, concept of, 14
Ethiopia, 148
Euphrates River, 38
European Common Market, 3–4, 8
Eve, Fall of, 25–28. See also Adam (Adamic couple)
Evil, 32, 53. See also Sin
Exodus, redemption and Messianic prophecy in, 28, 84
Ezekiel, prophecy of, 16, 79, 162; Armageddon in, 135; compared with Dan-

iel's prophecy, 141; date formulas in, 137–38, 147; Gog-Magog prophecy, 137–40; on human free will, 43; on ideal kingdom, 76, 78, 84, 93, 153–55; promise of land in, 80; and resurrection, 168; as source of Satanology, 69–70
Ezra, 4 (apocryphal book), 109; resurrection idea in, 178

Faith, as basis of judgment, 189–90
Fall, role of, 25–28; and free will and evil, 43, 54
Family, breakdown of, as sign of end-time, 6
Famines, as signs of end-time, 4, 8, 14, 101, 125
Feinberg, C. L., 188
Fig tree, meaning of, in Matthew, 24
Fire, Lake of, 191–92
Fishing Net, Parable of, 186
Flood, 30, 126
Free will, paradox of divine grace and, 43–44

Galatians (epistle): absence of reference to Second Coming in, 92; Paul on judgment in, 187
Gaster, T. H., 67
Gehenna, Ge-Hinnon, 191
Genesis, Messianic prophecy in, 84
Gentiles: distinguished from Jews, 39–40; making God's will known to, 41–42; Paul's view of, 41; and redemption, 44–45
Germany, 147
Gerontology, 162
Gesenius, 147
Gethsemane, 41
Gilgamesh Epic, 26
Glorificatory suffering, 53, 55–56
God: "image of God" concept, 25; nature of, and election, 36–37; uniqueness of, 44
Gog, Magog and, 145, 146; in Ezekiel's prophecy, 137–40; Gog-Magog wars, 16, 18, 81, 84, 135; identification of, 3, 139, 147
Gomer, 57, 147
Government, human, 30–32, 132, 140; judgment and, 180–82; role of Satan in, 31–32, 64–65

Grace, divine, 33, 43–44, 47
Great Britain, Premillennialism in, 160
Greece, 123, 140. *See also* Alexander the
    Great
Griffin, Merv, 162
Guyana, 7
Gyges of Lydia, 139

Habakkuk, 94
"Hadad," 148
Hadadrimmon, 141
Hades, 165, 168, 176, 188, 191
Haggai, prophecy of, 144
Haman, 31
Hamitic peoples, 147
Hamon-gog, Valley of, 145
Hasmonean dynasty, 86
Heaven, 196–206; meaning of, 199–200
Hebrew language, revival of, as sign of
    end-time, 2
Hebrews (book), 72, 176; on Armaged-
    don, 144; eschatology in, 12, 19; on
    judgment, 187; on New Jerusalem, 201;
    portrayal of Jesus in, 64, 83; on resur-
    rection, 177–78; on Second Coming,
    94
Hell, 168, 190–91, 192
Heresy, Marcionite, 44
Hermeneutical method, 152, 155
Herzl, Theodore, 2
Hezekiah, 76
Hillel, 156
Hinnom, Valley of, 191
History: biblical view of, 23–24; redemp-
    tive character of, 28–29; Yahweh's role
    in, 28
Hitler, 66, 114
Hodge, Charles, 20, 178
Holiness, revelation through, 29–30
Holocaust, 2, 56
Horoscopes, dependence on, as sign of
    end-time, 5
Hosea: condemnation of Baal worship by,
    51; nature of future vision in, 16, 17,
    78; Paul's use of, on election, 41; and
    suffering, 54, 57
Humanist school, 196, 205
Hungary, 56
Hymenaeus, 68

Idealism, 170–71, 196
Idolatry, 31, 181, 182

Immortality, resurrection distinguished
    from, 165–66
Incarnation, Antichrist and, 108
India, 148
Intertestamental Period: abode of dead in,
    190–91; contribution of, to Christian
    eschatology, 18; defined, 21; Jewish
    thought during, 15; resurrection idea
    during, 168–69; terminology used in,
    74, 94, 109
Iran, 3
Iron Age, 24
Ironside, H. A., 113
Isaac, 168, 176, 178; covenant with, 39,
    152; as elect, 28
Isaiah: and doctrine of new heavens and
    new earth, 196–97; on election of Is-
    rael, 51; eschatology of, 16, 17; on
    God's judgment, 182; on God's "refine-
    ment" of man, 126–27; and ideal king-
    dom, 76, 78, 84, 93, 155; on Israel's
    failure to speak for God, 42; on
    purificatory suffering (Suffering Ser-
    vant), 55, 131; on resurrection, 168; as
    source of Satanology, 69; use of term
    shepherd by, 79; and Zion, 79, 87
Ishmael, 38, 39
Israel: depicted as child or spouse, 59;
    election of, 28, 41; kingship in, 30–31,
    74–77; promise of land to, 38–39; pro-
    phetic condemnations of, 41–42, 51–
    52, 54, 181; restoration of, 124, 138–
    39, 152, 153
Israel, State of, 2–3, 8, 39, 133, 135
Israeli, meaning of term, 46
Israelite, meaning of term, 39

Jacob, 16, 37, 168, 176, 182; covenant
    with, 39, 75, 152; as elect, 28; evoked
    by Isaiah's Suffering Servant, 55
James (book): concept of servant in, 50;
    on need for works to be saved, 189; Pa-
    rousia in, 95, 104; on Second Coming
    and Last Judgment, 101, 187; on source
    of evil, 32
Japan, 135, 148
Japhetic peoples, 147
Jehoiachin, 86
Jehoshaphat, Valley of, 142
Jeremiah, prophecy of, 128; in Daniel,
    123; eschatology of, 16, 17; on God's
    absolute power, 43; on God's judgment,

182; on ideal kingdom, 78, 79, 93; tribulation in, 124

Jerusalem, 137, 141, 158, 181; Messianic and apocalyptic significance of, 2, 79, 145, 146, 153, 154, 159

Jerusalem, New, 201–3, 204–5

Jesse, 78; root of, 17

Jesus: on Antichrist, 111; Armageddon in teachings of, 143; dealings with and teachings about Satan, 23, 27, 31–32, 60, 61–64; election and salvation of, 41, 45; and eschatology, generally, 11–12, 19–20; and institution of Church, 25, 40, 41, 42; Israel criticized by, 42, 51–52; Messianic claims of, 81–84, 93–94, 114, 123–24, 141, 157–58, 162; at Millennium and Last Judgment, 150, 186–87; nature of God and universe in teachings of, 44, 60–61, 168, 192; and Old Testament law, 16, 51. 104; Parousia of, 95, 99–102; redemptive sacrifice of, 29; and resurrection, 167, 169, 173, 176, 178; spiritual nature of message, 156–57; suffering and punishment in teachings of, 52, 55, 126, 131; on Tribulation, 120–22, 143; use of Daniel by, 123–24

Jews, Judaism and: as "chosen people," elect, 36, 38–41, 45–46, 50–51; Messianic concept of, 81, 84; and Millennium, 150; origin of name, 39–40. See also Old Testament; Intertestamental Period; Israel; Judah

Jezebel, 31

Jezreel, Plain and Valley of, 141, 143, 144, 145

Job, 109, 131; on essential goodness of creation, 198–99; new heavens and new earth doctrine, 198; and resurrection, 168, 178; Satan and, 63–64, 68, 71

Joel, prophecy of, 83, 102; and Armageddon, 142–43; eschatology in, 16–17, 19; influence of, on Jesus' teachings, 143; and new heavens and new earth doctrine, 198; on role of prophets, 42

John (book), 41, 202; Antichrist in, 112; beasts and demons in, 72, 112–13; and doctrine of new heavens and new earth, 197–98, 204; on effect of God's "refinement" of man, 127; eschatology of, 11, 19; and Great Tribulation, 131;

133; on Second Coming, 98, 101; terms used referring to judgment, 194

John (epistles), absence of reference to Second Coming in, 92

John the Baptizer, 83, 93, 94, 158, 174

Jonah, 186

Joseph, 39, 50

Joshua, 29, 61, 78–79

Josiah, 141

Jubilee year, 50

Judah, 39, 181; restoration of, 124, 138–39, 152, 153

Judaism. See Jews, Judaism and

Judas Iscariot, 63, 66

Jude, 50, 66, 144, 188

Judgment, 180–95; basis of, 189–90; as cardinal belief of Christianity and Judaism, 193; government and, 180–82; Jesus' teachings on Last Judgment, 186–87; Last Judgment doctrine, 185–90; Last Judgment in Old Testament, 185–86; number of judgments, 180, 188–89; Paul's teachings on, 187; as process and act, 19, 184–85, 189; role of Hell, 190–91; terms for, 180, 182–84

Justice, as term for judgment, 183

Justification, in New Testament, 183

Kaiser, W. C., Jr., 86

Keil, C. F., 147

Kent, Saul, 162

Kidron Valley, 142

King, kingship and, 41, 74–76

Kingdom, Parables of the, 97, 186

Kingdom of God, 13–14, 24, 30, 35, 203–5; establishment of, 103

Kissinger, Henry, as Antichrist, 114

Kittim, 132, 136

Klausner, J., 85, 87, 159, 162–63

Knowledge, increase of, as sign of end-time, 5

Kromminga, D. H., 103

Lake of Fire, 191–92

Lamech, taunt-song of, 30

Larger Catechism, 92

Last Supper, 19, 98

Last Judgment. See Judgment

Lawlessness, man of, 111–12, 118, 143

Lazarus and the Rich Man, Parable of, 169, 174, 176, 191

Levi, Rabbi, 162

Levi, Tribe of, 81, 84
Lighthouse Gospel Trust Foundation, 103
Lindsell, H., 46
Lindsey, H., 148
Lo-Ammi, 57
Lo-ruhama, 57
Lucifer, origin of term, 73
Luke, 16, 121, 173
Luther, Martin, 189–90. See also Protestantism, doctrinal views of
Lutheranism, Second Coming and, 91
Lybia, 148

Maccabees, 86
Magi, visit of, 83
Magog, land of, 3, 135, 137–40, 147. See also Gog, Magog and
Malachai, on God's "refinement" of man, 127
Man of sin, in Daniel, 140
Marcionite heresy, 44
Mark: on agents of Satan, 72; on tribulation, 121
Mary, prophecy to, 83
Mason, C. E., Jr., 118, 206
Materialism, 156, 171
Matthew: on suddenness of Second Advent, 132; on tribulation, 121; use of term chosen by, 37
Maupin, Bill, 103
Megiddo, Megiddon, 141, 144, 148
Mendenhall, G. E., 37
"Meshech" (Gog's realm), 135, 139, 147
Messiah, and Messianic idea, 2, 18, 21, 74–89, 90, 160–61, 162; Antichrist as false Messiah, 112, 117; Church's belief in, 82–84, 129, 157–58; inferences of, in Old Testament, 78, 113–14, 133, 138–39, 141, 152; Jewish hopes for Messianic kingdom, 21, 36, 74–81, 159; length of Messianic age, 87; Messianic claims of Jesus, 81–84; origin and development of term, 74, 78–79. See also Parousia; Second Coming
Messiah ben Aaron, 81
Messiah ben Joseph, 81
Micah: nature of future vision, 17; on ideal kingdom, 76; and promise of Davidic king, 93; use of term Zion in, 79–80
Middle East, importance of, as sign of end-time, 2–3

Midtribulation, 130, 134
Millennium, Millenarianism and, 90, 104, 150–64, 189; biblical basis for, 151–58; chiliasm, 151; development of the dogma, 159–60; Dispensationalism, 151, 161; meaning and origin of expression, 150–51; New Testament teaching on, 156–58; Old Testament teaching on, 152–56; physical changes in end-time, 154–55; Pre-, Post-, and Amillennialists, 151; reasons for earthly kingdom, 160–61; spiritual changes, 155–56; terms and definitions, 150–51
Milton, John, 63, 67
Mohammed, identified as Antichrist, 114
Moore, G. F., 167–68
Moral evil, 53
Morals, relativization of, as sign of end-time, 6
Mordecai, 31
Morgan, G. Campbell, 203
Moriah, Mount, 148
Moschi, Meshech identified as, 139
Moscow, Meshech identified as, 135, 139
Moses, 54, 75, 85, 113, 176; covenant with, 39, 45, 84; as elect, 41; eschatology of, 16
Mount of Olives, 83, 99, 142, 169
Mussolini, identified as Antichrist, 114

Nahum, Belial in, 109
Nathan, 75
Natural disasters, 4, 8, 14, 125
Natural evil, 53
Natural law, God's creation of, 184
Natural revelation, 29, 34–35
Nebuchadnezzar, 31, 65, 77, 140
Neco, Pharaoh, 141
Nero, 31, 66
New heavens and new earth, 196–206; biblical basis for doctrine, 196–99; biblical description of new creation, 199–203; Kingdom of God, 203–5; material universe and, 198–99; new earth, 200–201; New Jerusalem, 201–3
New Scofield Reference Bible, 188–89
New Testament: abode of dead in, 191; concept of "world," 14; contrast between present and future age, 15, 18–20; and creation of evil, 53; Day of the Lord in, 137; doctrine of sanctification in, 29–30; import of Fall for, 26; Jewish

content of, 15–16; justification doctrine in, 183; resurrection in, 165, 166,
167, 169–70; on Satan and demonic
forces, 61, 67, 71, 72; Second Coming
in, 8, 92; servant concept, 50; teachings on Armageddon, 143–46; teachings on Millennium, 156–58; and term
Messiah, 74
Nicea, Council of (AD 325), 91
Nicene-Constantinopolitan Creed, 91,
103, 104
Nile River, 38
Noah, 34, 186
Nuclear energy, 1–2, 5–6, 7
Numerology, and signs of end-time, 3, 8,
108, 114, 118

Obedience, 51–52
Old Testament, 21, 34, 37, 40, 87, 109;
and Armageddon, 140–43; death and
resurrection in, 167–68, 175, 190–91;
and development of Messiah concept,
74, 78, 85, 86, 113–14, 140–43; eschatology of, 15–18; evil and suffering
in, 53, 54, 58; Last Judgment doctrine
in, 185–86; law of, affirmed by Christian Church, 44–45; on Millennium,
152–56; Second Coming in, 8, 92–94
Olives, Mount of. See Mount of Olives
Olivet Discourse, 19, 101, 120–21, 125,
186
OPEC, 3
Origen, 159

Pache, R., 8, 113, 115
Paddan-Aram, 75
Palestine, 39, 124
Palm Sunday, 141
Parables: of the Fishing Net, 186; of the
Kingdom, 97, 186; of Lazarus and the
Rich Man, 169, 174, 176, 191; of the
Sower, 72; of the Talents, 186; of the
Vineyard, 52, 186; of the Wheat and
the Weeds, 72, 186
Paradise Lost (Milton), 63
"Parenthesis" in Church, 36, 46, 130
Parousia ("advent"), 94–95, 104, 111,
137, 201. See also Second Coming
Patmos, seer of, 4
Paul: 14, 31, 109, 111–12; Armageddon
in teachings of, 143–44; on the concept
of the servant and suffering, 50, 52, 56,

131; description of the Rapture by, 130;
eschatology and world-view of, 12, 13,
19, 199, 203; and Fall, 27; on free will
and divine grace, 43–44; and Gentiles,
39–40, 41; and Jesus' Davidic descent,
83; on Judaism and Old Testament law,
16, 38, 39–40, 44–45, 162; on judgment and salvation, 45, 127, 184, 185,
194, 199; on obedience to governmental authority, 32; on resurrection of
the dead, 19, 94, 102–3, 169–70, 173,
174–75, 176–77; on Parousia and Second Coming, 90, 95, 98–103; teachings
about Satan, 60, 62, 63, 64, 66, 67,
68, 71, 72, 127; use of "election" by,
37, 41, 46; validity of epistles, 104
Pearson, Dirk, 162
People of God. See Chosen people, concept of
Perean Ministry, 97
Perizzites, 182
Persia, 123, 140, 147, 152, 156, 167
Persian Gulf, 146
Peter, 31, 47, 95, 102; on Armageddon,
144; confession of, at Caesarea-Philip-
pi, 82, 97; declares fulfillment of Joel's
prophecy, 83; and doctrine of new
heavens and new earth, 197, 198; es-
chatology of, 12, 19; and installation of
Church, 40, 41; on Last Judgment,
188; Satan and, 64, 66; and Second
Coming, 98, 100, 101
Petra, Second Coming awaited in, 7, 148
Pharisees, 62, 97, 162; and resurrection,
168, 169
Philippians, on resurrection, 173
Philosophy, Greek, and doctrine of resur-
rection, 165
Pilate, 82
Plastic Age, 24
Poland, 56
Pope, Antichrist identified as, 108, 114
Postmillennialism, 151, 160
Posttribulation, 130–31
Potiphar, 50
Premillennialism, 151, 152, 160, 163;
number of judgments, 188; and resur-
rection, 172
Present age, 23–35, 60–73. See also Age,
present
Pretribulation, 130–31, 134
Process, judgment as, 19, 184–85, 189

Prophecy: Armageddon in, 137–43; early Church's use of, 77, 82–84; fulfillment of, by Jesus, 93–94; government in period of, 30–31; and ideal kingdom, in Old Testament, 152–56; Messianic prophecy, 77–79, 82–84, 93–94; on new earth, 200–201; Premillennialist interpretation of, 152; problem of identifications in, 113–14; role of, 30–31, 42; and signs of end, 1–6, 122–24. See also *individual prophets by name*

Protestantism, doctrinal views of, 37, 91–92, 108, 171

Psalms, 109, 168; on goodness of creation, 198; and Messianic kingdom, 84; nondoctrinal basis of, 178; reference to Zion in, 79, 87

Psalms of Solomon (apocryphal book), 81

Ptolemy dynasty, 111, 123, 124, 132, 140, 156

Punishment, 54. See also Suffering

Purgatory, 165

Purificatory suffering, 53, 54–55

Put, 147

Qumran, eschatological writings of, 18, 81. See also Dead Sea Scrolls

Rabbinic writings, 81, 87, 139

Rapture, 103, 130–31; and "Day of Yahweh," 136–37; Dispensationalist view of, 151; place of, in resurrection theory, 172

Redemption, 28–29, 199

Refinement, as purpose of Tribulation, 126–27

Result, New Testament view of end of world as, 19

Resurrection, 94, 103, 165–79; in deuterocanonical and apocryphal literature, 168–69; distinguished from immortality, 165–66; in New Testament, 169–70, 174; number of resurrections, 165, 171–75; objections to the doctrine, 170–71; Old Testament development of idea, 167–68; "out-resurrection," 173–75; in Paul's writings, 19, 94, 102–3, 169–70, 173, 174–75, 176–77; period between death and, 165, 175–77; summary statement of doctrine, 177; three-resurrection theory, 172; time of, 165; two-resurrection theory, 172, 175

Retribution, as term for judgment, 183

Revelation: as characteristic of present age, 28; and holiness of God, 29–30; in nature, 29, 34–35

Revelation (book): on Armageddon, 144–46; on battle led by Gog, 135, 139; death and resurrection in, 172, 191; and doctrine of new heavens and new earth, 84, 197–98, 199, 202; earthly kingdoms in, 65; on Last Judgment, 188; Millennialism in, 151–52; redemptive sanctification in, 30; Satan and demons in, 61, 66, 71, 72, 109–10, 112–13, 127, 141; and Second Coming, 101; timing of events in, 125, 128, 129–30, 139; tribulation in, 124–26, 128, 129–30

"Rimmon," 148

Righteousness, God's judgment and, 181–82

Romans (epistle): judgment in, 187; redemption of universe in, 199; Second Coming in, 104

Rome, 14, 91, 148, 156; as Antichrist headquarters, 146; and Daniel's prophecy, 3–4; identified with Babylon, 115, 116, 140; and New Testament concept of world, 14

Ros, Russia identified as, 147

"Rosh," 135, 139

Russia, 3, 146; identified as Ros, Rosh, 135, 139, 147. See also Union of Soviet Socialist Republics

Sadducees, and resurrection, 167, 169, 173, 178

Salvation, doctrine of, 44, 162

Samaria, 145

Samuel, 42, 74–75, 168, 175

Sanctification, doctrine of, in New Testament, 29–30

Sanders, J. A., 58

Saoshyant, 79

Sargon of Akkad, 2

Satan, Satanology and, 60–73, 147, 158; access to heaven of, 199, 200; agents of, 65–67, 71–72; at Armageddon, 146; destruction of, 103, 189; doctrine of, 18, 23, 27, 67–70; and evil, 53; gender of, 62, 71; last assault of, 127–28; method of operating, 63–64; in Old Testament, 18; origin and meaning of name, and synonyms, 24, 61–64, 71;

person and nature of, 67–70; powers and limits of, 64–65, 68–69; present age as "Satanic," 24–28, 33, 60–73; purpose of, 37, 62–63, 160; role in human governments, 31–32; Satanic world system, 60–67; as sign of end-time, 5; temptations of, 52, 157; tribulation through age of, 132

Saul, 31, 42, 75, 77, 175, 176

Schrenk, G., 47

Scofield, C. I., 188

Scofield Reference Bible, Dispensationalism in, 161

Second Advent. See Second Coming

Second Coming, 90–107, 142, 151, 161; assertion of, by all Christian groups, 91–94; and Coming of the Spirit, 102; contemporary anticipation of, 7, 90, 103, 148; creedal statements of, 91–92; and death of the believer, 102–3; duration of Christ's appearance, 96; incidence of, in Bible, 8; Jesus' teaching about his return, 96–98; and judgment, 187; manner of coming, 99–102; resurrection and, 175, 177; signs of, 100–101; terminology in Bible, 94–96; timing of, 90, 101–2

Seleucid dynasty, 111, 123, 124, 132, 140, 156

Sermon on the Mount, 96

Serpent, in Fall, 27–28, 34

Servant, concept of, 37, 49–59; Greek concept of, 49–50; Hebrew concept of, 50–51; implication of being Lord's servant, 50, 51–52; meaning of, 47; sufferings of, 52–56; wife as, 58; worship owed by, 52

Seventh-Day Adventists, 117

Sexual mores, as sign of end-time, 6

Sheol, 168, 169, 175

Sibylline Oracles (noncanonical book), 108, 109

Sidon, 186

Silas, 14

Sin, concept of, 18, 34. See also Evil

Sinai, 29

Six-Day War (1967), 2

666, meaning of, 3, 8, 108, 114, 116

Solomon, 85, 113; and construction of temple, 31; as elect, 41; on infinitude of heaven, 199–200; kingship of, 75–76, 78

Son of David, 30. See also David

Son of Man, 18, 187; Jesus' use of doctrine, 85, 96, 97, 100, 121, 186; in Intertestamental Period, 94; in Old Testament, 113, 122–23

Soul, immortality of, 166

Sower, Parable of the, 72

Stone Age, 24

Substance abuse, as sign of end-time, 6

Suffering: as God's problem, 57; of God's servants, 52–56, 131; in Great Tribulation, 126–28; kinds of, 53–56; and problem of evil, 53; as purpose of election, 42; solutions to, in Old Testament, 58

Suicide rate, as sign of end-time, 6, 8–9

Supererogation, 56

Syria, 3

Table of Nations, 30, 116

Talents, Parable of, 186

Tamuz, 148

Temple of Solomon, 75–76

Temptation, Satanic, 63

Terrorism, interpreted as wrath of God, 126

Testaments of the Twelve Patriarchs, 81, 109

Theocracy, in Israel, 75

Thessalonians (epistles), 158; concept of "world" in, 14; concern for Antichrist in, 111; concern for Second Coming in, 90, 102; Parousia in, 104; on resurrection, 173; use of revelation in, 95

Thirty-nine Articles of Religion, 103–4

Three Mile Island, 5

Timothy, 68

Titus, 95, 100

Tobolsk, "Tubal" and, 135, 139

Tower of Babel, 30, 35

Toynbee, A. J., 45

Translation, problems imposed by, 20

Tribulation, Great, 120–34; in Book of Revelation, 124–26; and Daniel's prophecy, 122–24; duration of, 120, 128–30; effect on Church, 130–31; Jeremiah's prophecy, 124; in Jesus' teaching, 120–22, 143; Midtribulation, 130, 134; nature and purpose, 126–28; Posttribulation, 130–31; Pretribulation, 130–31, 134; as "refinement," 126–27; in resurrection theory, 172; and Satan's last assault, 127–28; scriptural basis of, 120–26

Trinity, doctrine of, 34
"Tubal" (Gog's realm), 135, 139, 147
Tyre, 186; prince of, 69, 70

Union of Soviet Socialist Republics, 139.
    See also Russia
Universe, geocentricity and levels of, 205
    –6. See also Creation

Vandalism, interpreted as wrath of God,
    126
Vengeance, as term for judgment, 183
Vineyard, Parable of the, 52, 186
Vos, G., 178, 192

Wadi, ᶜAra, 144
Wars, as sign of end-time, 4, 101
Westminster Confession, 92
Westminster divines, 160
Wheat and the Weeds, Parable of, 72,
    186

White, J. W., 8
Will, human, 32–33
Works, as basis of judgment, 189–90
World War II, 160
Worship, as service owed by servant, 52
Wrath, divine, 126, 183
Wynne, E. A., 8

Yahweh, Day of, 136–37, 148

Zechariah, prophecy of, 153; and Ar-
    mageddon, 141–42; fulfillment of, 82,
    97; on God's "refinement" of man, 127;
    on ideal kingdom, 76–77, 78–79, 93
Zedekiah, 76
Zerubbabel, 79, 86, 162
Zion, 116, 153; incidence of term in Old
    Testament, 87; meaning of, 79, 87
Zionism, rise of, as sign of end-time, 2
Zoroastrianism, 68, 73, 74, 192

Index of Scripture Verses

OLD TESTAMENT

Genesis 1:1, 24, 68, 198, 199; 1:2, 21, 70, 199; 1:8, 199; 1:15, 199; 1:26, 198; 1:27, 25, 198; 1:28, 49; 1:31, 25, 68, 198; 2:1, 206; 2:2, 206; 2:9, 25, 27; 2:17, 25, 26, 49; 2:18, 25, 27; 2:19, 27; 2:25, 25; 3:1-15, 60; 3:3, 27; 3:4, 62; 3:4-5, 26; 3:4-6, 63; 3:5, 27, 34; 3:6, 26; 3:7, 26; 3:13, 43; 3:14, 26, 53; 3:14-19, 26; 3:15, 26, 27, 45, 53; 3:16, 26; 3:17, 26; 3:19, 26; 3:22, 26, 28, 34, 49; 3:23, 26, 49, 81; 3:24, 26, 28, 181; 4:8-12, 30; 4:10-12, 181; 4:13, 193; 4:18, 30; 4:23, 30; 4:24, 30; 5:5, 26; 5:8, 26; 5:11, 26; 5:14, 26; 5:17, 26; 5:19, 26; 5:21, 26; 5:24, 27; 5:31, 26; 6:2, 71; 6:5-6, 30; 6:7, 181; 6:11-13, 181; 6:13, 126; 10, 30; 10:2, 147; 10:2-5, 147; 10:6, 147; 10:13, 35; 11:4, 35; 11:6-8, 30; 12:1, 80; 12:1-3, 152; 12:2, 38, 40; 12:3, 28, 38, 41, 45; 12:5, 38; 12:7, 157; 13:14-17, 38; 13:16, 38; 15:5, 38; 15:7, 80; 15:16, 38; 15:18-20, 38; 15:18-21, 157; 17:1-8, 152; 17:5, 38; 17:6, 38, 75; 17:7, 38; 17:8, 38, 80; 17:19-21, 39, 17:20, 38; 18:18, 38, 41; 19:24, 191; 22:17, 38; 22:18, 38; 26:4, 38; 26:24, 38; 28:13, 39; 28:14, 38, 39; 32:28, 39; 34:30, 182; 35:11, 75; 35:12, 75; 37:35, 190; 39:37, 50; 40:15, 39; 45:8, 51; 45:9, 51; 46:3, 39; 49:1, 16; 49:4, 84; 50:24, 39; 90:6, 15

Exodus 3:6-8, 39; 3:15, 38; 3:18, 39; 6:8, 39; 8:32, 181; 12:12, 54, 181; 12:44, 50; 19:5, 41; 19:6, 41, 77, 84; 19:12-24, 29; 20:10, 50; 20:12, 205; 21:2, 50; 21:6, 58; 23:17, 51; 33:1, 39; 33:2, 39; 34:10, 40

Leviticus 16, 29; 19:2, 29; 25:40, 50; 25:44, 50; 26:41, 54; 26:42, 38

Numbers 34:1-12, 39; 35:31, 184

Deuteronomy 4:30, 16; 5:14-15, 50; 6:13, 50; 8:5, 54; 11:2-7, 54; 12:12, 50; 12:15-18, 50; 15:12ff, 50; 15:17, 15; 17:15, 75; 18:18, 84, 113; 28:36, 80; 28:64-67, 80; 31:17, 54; 31:29, 16

Judges 3:7, 181; 3:8, 181; 3:12, 181

Ruth 4:17, 78

1 Samuel 2:8, 21, 205; 7:7, 39; 8:4, 74; 8:5, 30, 74; 8:7, 75; 8:9, 30; 8:11-18, 75; 15:16, 75; 15:22, 42; 15:28, 31; 16:1ff, 75; 28:6-19, 175; 28:9, 175-76; 28:12-14, 168; 28:14, 168

2 Samuel 5:3, 31; 5:6-9, 79; 7, 75, 93; 7:2, 31; 7:4-29, 152; 7:12, 75, 152; 7:12-13, 75; 7:13, 31, 93, 152; 7:13ff, 15; 7:16, 93; 17:1, 41

1 Kings 8:27, 200; 8:30, 199; 12:19, 39; 14:10, 54; 14:21, 41; 15:3, 76; 17:1, 29; 21:13, 109

2 Kings 1:2, 71; 1:15, 205; 9:7, 50; 16:7, 140; 17:6, 181 17:7, 181; 18:1, 39; 18:3, 76; 21:12, 54; 23:29, 141; 23:30, 141

1 Chronicles 16:16, 38; 16:26, 205; 21:1, 61, 71; 28:5, 41; 28:6, 41; 28:7, 41; 28:10, 41; 29:11, 77

2 Chronicles 2:6, (MT 5), 200

Ezra 3:2, 86

Nehemiah 9:6, 205; 9:7, 41

Esther 2:5, 39

Job, 71; 1:6, 63-64, 68, 69; 1:6ff, 42, 61; 1:7, 68, 69; 1:7-12, 53; 2:1, 63-64, 68; 2:1ff, 42, 61; 2:6, 53, 68; 2:2, 68; 3:8, 61; 3:11-19, 168; 5:17, 54; 7:12, 61; 8:1-4, 52; 10:3, 198-99; 11:4-6, 52; 12:7, 205; 14:12, 198; 17:13, 190; 19:25, 168; 19:26, 168; 21:7, 53; 22:12-14, 200; 24:35, 198; 26:7, 205; 34:18, 109

Psalms 2, 116; 2:6, (MT 7), 79, 153; 2:7, 85; 2:9, 84, 129; 6:1, (MT 2), 54; 6:5, (MT 6), 168, 190; 8:2, 82; 8:5, 43; 9:17, (MT 18), 168; 16:10, 168, 190; 18:4, 14; 18:4-6, (MT 5-7), 190; 22:28, 77; 30:3, (MT 4), 190; 33:3, 84; 33:20, 25; 40:6-8, (MT 7-9), 58; 41:8, (MT 9), 109; 44:6, 14; 45:1, 86; 45:6, (MT 7), 77, 153; 45:7, (MT 8), 153; 45:9, 86; 47:9, 38; 49:15, (MT 16), 160; 53:6, 79; 72, 153; 78:70, 41; 82:6, 68; 84:4, (MT 5; LXX 83:5), 203; 88:3, (MT 4), 190; 88:4, (MT 5), 190; 89:4, 93; 89:11, (MT 12),

205; **89:29**, 93; **89:36**, 93; **102:25**, (MT 26), 186; **102:26**, (MT 27), 198; **105:6**, 38; **106:23**, 41; **118:26**, 94; **125:1**, 79; **132:13**, 41; **135**, 29; **145:1**, 77; **145:13**, 77; **148:6**, 198; **149:7**, 54

Proverbs **3:11**, 54; **3:19**, 205; **8**, 113; **15:11**, 190

Ecclesiastes **3:11**, 205; **5:2**, 29

Isaiah **1:2**, 42, 52; **1:2-26**, 182; **1:3**, 52; **1:16**, 182; **1:17**, 182; **1:21**, 115; **2:2**, 16; **2:2-4**, 79-80, 153; **2:13**, 136; **4:2**, 17, 78; **4:2-4**, 155; **4:5**, 155; **6:2**, 52; **6:3**, 52; **6:13**, 78; **7:1**, 140; **9:6**, 76, 93; **9:7**, 76, 93; **10:5**, 140; **10:20**, 17; **10:21-23**, 162; **11:1**, 78, 154; **11:4**, 112; **11:6**, 76; **11:6-9**, 154; **11:9**, 76, 154; **11:10**, 17; **11:11**, 17, 162; **11:12**, 162; **12:6**, 153; **13:6**, 136; **13:6-13**, 136; **13:9**, 136; **14:4**, 69; **14:12-15**, 69; **19:19**, 17; **19:24**, (MT 23), 17; **22:5**, 136; **23:17**, 115; **24:23**, 77; **26:19**, 168; **26:20**, (LXX), 94; **29:18**, 93; **29:19**, 93; **30:23-26**, 155; **34:4**, 197, 200, 205; **34:8**, 136; **35:5**, 93; **35:6**, 93; **37:16**, 205; **39:6**, 16; **40:1**, 55; **40:2**, 55; **40:11**, 79; **40:28**, 205; **40-50**, 55; **41:8**, 38, 51; **41:9**, 51; **41-55**, 85; **42:1**, 37, 41; **42:19**, 42; **43:1**, 37; **43:17**, 162; **43:6**, 37; **44:1**, 37; **44:24**, 68; **44:28**, 31; **45:1**, 31; **45:7**, 53; **45:18**, 68; **48:9**, 183; **48:10**, 127; **48:20**, 12; **49:5**, 55; **49:6**, 55; **50:5**, 42, 55; **50:6**, 55; **51:2**, 37; **51:6**, 197; **52:5**, 55; **52:8**, 55; **52:9**, 55; **52:10**, 55; **52:11**, 55; **52:13–53:12**, 85; **52:14**, 55; **52:15**, 55; **53**, 55; **53:4-7**, 55; **53:11**, 42; **53:12**, 42; **54:14**, 155; **54:17**, 50; **55:8**, 29; **55:13**, 27; **57:15**, 200; **60:1-16**, 153; **61:1**, 84, 93: **63:9**, 14; **63:16**, 32; **63:18**, 130; **64:8-9**, 32; **65:17**, 196; **65:18**, 196; **65:19**, 196-97; **65:20**, 198; **65:20-22**, 155; **65:21**, 197; **65:22**, 155; **65:23**, 197; **65:25**, 155, 197; **66:1**, 197; **66:22**, 197; **66:24**, 197

Jeremiah **1:4-10**, 29; **1:10**, 80; **1:13-16**, 181; **1:14**, 148; **1:15**, 126; **1:16**, 126; **2:13**, 153; **3:6**, 115; **3:8**, 115; **3:9**, 115; **3:16-18**, 17; **7:32**, 16, 17; **10:12**, 205; **11:2-12**, 182; **14:13-15**, 138; **18:2-6**, 43; **18:7**, 43, 80; **18:8**, 43; **18:9**, 43; **18:10**, 43; **22:18**, 51; **23:4**, 79; **23:5**, 78, 93; **23:6**, 93; **23:20**, 16; **25:11**, 123, 128; **29:10**, 128; **30:2**, 124; **30:3**, 17; **30:5**, 124; **30:7**, 124; **30:8**, 124; **30:9**, 78, 124; **30:24**, 16; **31:9**, 32; **31:10**, 79; **31:10-14**, 162; **31:28**, 80; **31:31-34**, 17,

155; **31:40**, 153; **33:14**, 78; **33:15**, 78; **35:8-22**, 182; **46:10**, 136; **46:10-12**, 136; **48:47**, 16; **49:39**, 16

Ezekiel **2:1-8**, 29; **7:10**, 136; **8:14**, 148: **11:12**, 147; **13:5**, 136; **13:17-19**, 126; **14:10**, 54; **18:2**, 43; **18:5-32**, 43; **18:32**, 43; **20:37**, 189; **23**, 59, 181; **23:11**, 181; **28:2-9**, 69; **28:2-10**, 69; **28:11-16**, 70; **28:11-19**, 69; **28:13-15**, 53; **29:3**, 61; **30:3**, 136; **30:3-5**, 136; **32:2**, 61; **33:21**, 137; **33:24**, 138; **33:21–39:29**, 138; **33:25-29**, 138; **34:2-6**, 138; **34:10**, 138; **34:11**, 79; **34:11-16**, 138; **34:12-15**, 93; **34:15**, 79, 153; **34:20**, 138; **34:23**, 76, 79, 93, 153; **34:24**, 76, 93, 138; **34:25**, 76, 158; **34:25-31**, 138; **34:27**, 76, 154-55; **34:29**, 76, 154-55; **34:30**, 76; **35**, 138; **35:10**, 40; **35:15**, 138; **36:5-7**, 138; **36:8–37:28**, 153; **36:20**, 138; **36:21**, 138; **36:24**, 155; **36:24-27**, 138; **36:25**, 155; **36:28**, 80, 155; **36:36**, 56; **36-39**, 80; **37**, 122, 138, 168; **37:2-6**, 168; **37:11**, 138, 168; **37:12**, 138; **37:19**, 138; **37:19-22**, 93; **37:21-25**, 80; **37:22**, 40, 138; **37:24**, 78, 79, 139, 154; **37:24-28**, 93; **37:25**, 79, 139, 154; **37:26**, 139; **37:27**, 139; **38**, 135, 137, 138, 139; **38:2**, 3, 139; **38:2-9**, 139; **38:3**, 139; **38:5**, 147; **38:6**, 148; **38:8**, 16, 154; **38:14**, 17, 137; **38:14-21**, 137; **38:15**, 139; **38:16**, 16; **38:18-23**, 17, 137; **38:19**, 144; **38:20**, 42, 144; **38:21**, 140; **38:22**, 140; **38-39**, 3, 146; **39**, 135, 137, 138; **39:4**, 145; **39:8**, 140; **39:9**, 140; **39:11**, 145; **39:12**, 140; **39:17-20**, 145; **39:21**, 154; **39:21-23**, 42; **39:78**, 80; **40:1**, 138; **40-48**, 153; **43:24**, 78; **47:1**, 202; **47:6-12**, 202; **48:35**, 153

Daniel **8:1-6**, 132; **2**, 65; **2:36-43**, 153; **2:38**, 31, 65; **2:39**, 65; **2:40**, 3; **2:42**, 4; **2:43**, 31, 148; **2:44**, 4, 65, 77, 148, 153; **2:45**, 31, 65, 153; **7**, 65, 113, 122; **7:2**, 122; **7:3**, 109, 145; **7:7**, 109; **7:8**, 109; **7:11**, 109; **7:12**, 109, 153; **7:12-14**, 65, 133; **7:13**, 84, 94, 100, 123, 133; **7:14**, 100, 123; **7:17**, 65, 109, 123, 153; **7:17-18**, 133; **7:18**, 109, 123, 153-54; **7:19**, 65, 109; **7:19-21**, 123; **7:20**, 109; **7:21**, 65, 128; **7:23**, 65; **7:24**, 4, 65, 109; **7:25**, 5, 65, 109, 110, 128, 129, 133; **7:25-27**, 112; **7:12**, 132; **8:3**, 110; **8:5-8**, 110; **8:8**, 110; **8:9**, 110, 117; **8:10**, 110; **8:11-14**, 110; **8:13**, 110; **8:14**, 128, 129; **8:17**, 123; **8:19**, 123; **8:21**, 110, 123; **8:22**, 110; **8:23**, 110, 123; **8:24**, 110,

128; 8:25, 117-18, 123; 8:26, 111, 123;
9, 123; 9:1, 124; 9:2, 123, 128, 154;
9:17, 110; 9:24, 123, 128; 9:25, 86-87,
133, 154; 9:25-27, 128; 9:26, 86-87, 110,
123, 133; 9:26-27, 123; 9:27, 110; 9:29,
123; 10:14, 123, 154; 11, 113, 123;
11-12, 140-41; 11:2, 123; 11:5, 123;
11:6, 123; 11:10, 136; 11:14, 136;
11:15, 136; 11:21, 123; 11:30, 132;
11:31, 110, 111, 117, 122, 123, 154;
11:35, 117, 140; 11:36, 5, 112, 124, 140;
11:36-45, 113, 123; 11:37, 112, 124;
11:40, 111, 117; 11:41-45, 148; 11:42,
148; 11:43, 148; 11:44, 148; 11:45, 148;
12:1, 111, 122, 123-24, 128, 133, 141,
154, 168, 172; 12:1-4, 117; 12:2, 111,
124, 168, 172; 12:4, 5, 110, 123, 132;
12:7, 129, 133; 12:9, 110, 123; 12:11,
110, 123, 129, 154; 12:12, 129; 12:13,
110, 123
Hosea 1:2, 57; 1:3, 57; 2, 59; 2:1-13, 115;
2:2-6, 52; 2:5, 57; 2:17, (MT 18), 51;
2:18-20, (MT 16-18), 17; 2:23, 41; 3:1,
57; 3:4, 78; 3:5, 16, 78; 4:15, 52; 5:2, 54;
10:10, 54; 23:17, 115
Joel 1:15, 136; 2:1, 136, 147; 2:2, 147;
2:10, 198; 2:11, 136; 2:15-21, 102;
2:20, 148; 2:28, (MT 3:1), 42, 156;
2:28-32, (MT 3:1-3), 83; 2:29, (MT
3:2), 42, 156; 2:30-31, (MT 3:3-4), 198;
2:31, (MT 3:4), 136; 2:32, (MT 3:5), 44;
2:33, 102; 3:1, (MT 4:1), 16-17; 3:2,
(MT 4:2), 17, 142; 3:9, 142; 3:14, (MT
4:14), 136, 142; 3:15, (MT 4:15), 142,
143; 3:16, 142; 3:17, 142; 3:18, (MT
4:18), 17
Amos 1:3–2:3, 29; 2:6, 182; 2:7, 182; 3:2,
182; 3:6, 53; 3:7, 28, 29, 50; 4:2, 116;
4:12, 6; 5:8, 205; 5:18, (LXX), 137;
5:18-20, 136; 6:2, 29; 6:7, 87; 7:8, 39;
7:9, 39; 8:2, 12; 8:3, 137; 8:9, 137; 8:11,
17, 137; 8:13, 137; 9:6, 205; 9:7, 29;
9:11, 76, 93, 154; 9:12, 154; 9:13, 17
9:13-15, 76; 9:14, 152; 9:15, 152
Obadiah v. 15, 136
Jonah 1:9, 205
Micah 5:2, (MT 1), 93; 5:2-4, (MT 1-3),
76, 154; 3:10, 87; 4:1, 16, 93; 4:1-3,
79-80, 153; 4:2, 93; 4:3, 155; 4:6, 17
Nahum 1:15, 109
Habakkuk 2:3, 94
Zephaniah 1:7-8, 136; 1:14, 154; 1:14-16,
136; 1:14-18, 136; 2:7, 39; 2:9, 39, 154;
3:8, 154; 3:9, 154; 3:14, 39; 3:14-20,
154

Haggai 1:1, 86; 2:6, 144; 2:7, 144; 2:21,
144; 2:22, 144; 2:23, 144
Zechariah 3:1, 61; 3:1-2, 71; 3:8-10, 79;
6:12, 79; 6:13, 79; 8:23, 39; 9:9, 76, 82,
93, 97, 141; 9:10, 93, 141; 9:6, 76-77;
9-14, 148; 11:17, 141; 12:1, 205; 12:2,
141, 142; 12:3, 136; 12:3-8, 17; 12:4,
142; 12:5, 142; 12:6-9, 153; 12:7ff, 31;
12:8, 76, 142; 12:11, 141; 13:1, 31, 142;
13:2, 127, 142; 13:9, 127; 14, 141-42;
14:1, 136; 14:1-3, 136-37; 14:2, 142;
14:3, 142; 14:4, 142; 14:5, 142; 14:8,
142, 153; 14:9, 142; 14:16, 142; 14:17,
153
Malachi 1:2, 39; 1:2-3, 37; 1:3, 39; 3:1,
127; 3:2, 127; 3:3, 127

NEW TESTAMENT

Matthew 1:12, 86; 1:17, 83; 2:1-16, 157;
2:2, 39, 83; 3:2, 157; 3:9, 38; 4:1-11, 53;
4:2, 62; 4:3, 63, 68; 4:4, 62; 4:6, 63, 68;
4:8, 32, 53, 57, 63, 65; 4:9, 52, 63; 4:10,
50; 4:11, 58; 4:23-25, 158; 5:17, 16,
157; 5:18, 157, 198; 5:22, 191; 5:34,
158, 200; 6:13, 53, 58; 7:1, 185; 7:2,
185; 7:21, 190; 7:22, 97, 137; 7:23, 97;
8:11, 157; 8:14-17, 158; 8:29, 68; 8:31,
66, 71; 9:27-30, 81; 10:15, 137; 10:25,
62; 10:28, 68, 191; 11:3, 94; 11:5, 166;
11:20-27, 97; 11:22, 186; 12:18, 37;
12:23, 157; 12:24, 62; 12:28, 62; 12:32,
15; 12:38-42, 97, 186; 13, 19; 13:17, 19;
13:18-23, 19; 13:22, 14; 13:25, 62;
13:29, 62; 13:36-43, 128; 13:37-42, 97;
13:38-39, 72; 13:39, 14, 19, 62;
13:39-42, 186; 13:41, 19, 126, 185;
13:41-43, 173; 13:42, 19, 126, 185, 192;
13:43, 19; 13:49, 19, 126, 173, 186;
13:50, 19, 126, 173, 186; 15:1-6, 156;
16:16, 82; 16:17, 82; 16:18, 40; 16:21,
82, 97; 16:27, 97, 99; 18:8, 192; 18:9,
191; 18:15-17, 185; 19:30, 11; 20:30,
76; 21:1-9, 141; 21:1-10, 82; 21:15, 76,
82; 21:16, 82; 21:23, 82; 21:28-43, 82;
21:33-41, 186; 21:43, 52, 98; 21:45, 82;
22:23-32, 169; 22:30, 78, 178; 22:31,
174; 22:32, 38, 44, 168; 22:41-45, 98,
162; 23:39, 141; 24, 19, 101, 120, 121,
125; 24:3, 83, 95, 98, 120; 24:5, 111;
24:6, 19, 101, 143; 24:7, 53, 101; 24:8,
53; 24:9, 101, 120, 121; 24:10, 101;
24:11, 101; 24:12, 101; 24:14, 14, 19,
101, 120, 122; 24:15, 110, 117, 121, 142;

24:21, 101, 120-21, 143; 24:24, 111, 112, 143; 24:29, 101, 121; 24:29-32, 19; 24:30, 95, 98, 99, 101, 121, 143, 186; 24:31, 186; 24:32, 8; 24:32-35, 122; 24:33, 122; 24:34, 122; 24:36, 122; 24:36-39, 186; 24:37, 34; 24:40-44, 132; 24:42, 98; 24:42-44, 100; 24:44, 98; 24:45-51, 132; 25:5, 132; 25:13, 100; 25:14-30, 186; 25:30, 186; 25:31, 98, 100; 25:31-46, 173, 186; 25:32, 189; 25:34, 14; 25:40, 187; 25:45, 187; 25:46, 192: 26:29, 19, 98; 26:64, 157; 26:65, 157; 26:66, 157; 27:19, 39; 28:9, 169

Mark 1:23-26, 158; 3:14, 41; 3:15, 41; 3:22, 62; 3:26, 12; 4:15, 72; 4:16, 72; 4:18, 72; 4:20, 72; 6:14, 174; 9:43, 191; 9:44, 192; 9:48, 192, 205; 10:45, 53; 12:19, 167; 12:25, 178; 13, 101, 120; 13:4, 120; 13:14, 110; 13:19, 121, 205; 13:24, 121; 13:26, 96; 13:28-31, 122; 13:32, 100; 14:61, 82, 157; 14:62, 82, 84, 157; 14:63-65, 82

Luke 1:32, 83, 157; 1:33, 83, 157; 1:54, 157; 1:55, 157; 1:68, 83; 1:68-75, 157; 1:69, 76, 83; 2:1, 14; 2:4, 157; 2:10, 157; 2:11, 76, 83, 157; 2:13, 52; 2:14, 52; 2:38, 158; 4:6, 65; 4:18-22, 158; 4:33-37, 158; 4:41, 81; 6:46, 51, 190; 7:19f, 94; 7:20, 93; 7:20-22, 158; 7:21, 71, 93; 7:22, 93; 9:26, 100; 9:51, 97; 9:51-18:34, 97; 10:13, 186; 10:14, 186; 10:18, 73; 10:19, 61; 10:23, 97; 10:24, 97; 11:15, 62; 11:29-32, 97; 12:30, 13; 12:40, 97; 12:43, 97; 16:14, 176; 16:19-31, 191; 16:22-26, 176; 16:23, 191; 16:28, 176; 16:31, 169, 176; 17:10, 56; 17:20, 97; 17:21, 97; 17:22-30, 97; 17:27, 34; 18:8, 5; 19:28, 97; 19:29-38, 97; 20:35, 173, 175, 178; 20:36, 175; 20:37, 176; 20:38, 176; 21, 120; 21:7, 120; 21:23, 121; 21:24, 2, 101, 130, 158; 21:25, 121; 21:27, 96; 21:29-33, 122; 21:32, 53; 22:3, 63; 22:16, 98; 22:31, 53, 58, 63; 22:32, 64; 23:43, 176; 24:16, 169; 24:21, 83; 24:31, 169; 24:42, 169; 24:43, 169

John 1:29, 157; 1:49, 157; 1:51, 96; 2:19, 167; 2:22, 113; 3:3, 157; 3:16, 180; 3:17, 180, 184; 3:18, 184; 4:3, 113; 4:14, 153; 4:25, 157; 4:26, 157; 5:8, 167; 5:17, 206; 5:21, 174; 5:22, 186, 194; 5:24, 180, 184; 5:25, 172; 5:27, 186; 5:28, 170; 5:28-29, 172; 5:29, 172; 5:30, 186; 5:39, 92-93; 5:43, 111; 6:14,

94; 6:15, 156; 6:38-40, 97; 6:39, 137; 7:49, 162; 8:44, 53, 62; 9:39, 189, 194; 10:16, 45; 11:24, 166; 11:48, 156; 12:1, 174; 12:9, 174; 12:17, 174; 12:31, 62, 65, 188-89; 12:48, 184; 13:13-16, 51; 13:13-17, 190; 13:17, 63; 13:33, 98; 14:3, 98, 102; 14:12, 158; 14:16, 98; 14:16-18, 102; 14:17, 98; 14:18, 98; 14:25, 98, 102; 14:26, 102; 14:30, 13, 62; 15:2, 190; 15:8, 42; 15:10, 190; 15:12, 42; 15:16, 41, 42; 15:18, 61; 15:19, 61; 15:20, 57; 15:26, 98; 16:5, 98; 16:7-11, 102; 16:11, 62, 189; 16:16, 98; 16:22, 98; 16:28, 98; 16:29, 98; 16:33, 131; 17:14, 30; 17:15, 40, 53, 58; 18:33, 82; 18:36, 32; 18:37, 82, 157; 18:38, 157; 19:3, 93; 19:19, 82; 20:15, 169; 20:26, 169; 20:27, 169; 21:22, 98

Acts 1:6, 83, 93, 100, 157; 1:6-8, 19; 1:6-11, 102; 1:7, 100; 1:8, 11; 1:9, 169; 1:11, 20, 99, 171; 1-12, 104; 2:16, 19; 2:16-21, 83; 2:17, 19; 2:17-21, 198; 2:23, 53; 2:23-31, 168; 2:30-36, 158; 2:36, 83; 3:7, 167; 3:15, 167; 3:21, 157; 4:24, 205; 4:29, 50; 7:2, 44; 7:8, 38; 11:28, 14; 13:22, 167; 14:22, 131; 17:6, 14, 118; 17:7, 158; 17:11, 92-93; 17:18, 72; 17:24, 13; 17:31, 185, 187; 26:23, 174; 28:20, 83; 28:23, 83

Romans 1:1, 50; 1:3, 83; 1:4, 174; 1:20, 205; 1:23, 166; 1:26, 6; 1:27, 6; 2:5, 137; 2:9-11, 182; 2:16, 104; 2:17-24, 39, 182; 2:24, 182; 3:23, 56; 3:24, 56; 4, 34; 4:1-25, 38; 4:9-12, 44; 4:16, 38; 4:17, 38; 5:1, 183; 5:3, 131; 5:7-10, 183; 6:6, 53; 6:13, 174; 8:1, 180, 184; 8:3, 183; 8:4, 183; 8:9-11, 102; 8:13, 58; 8:16, 56; 8:17, 36, 42, 56; 8:17-25, 104; 8:18, 42; 8:18-22, 160; 8:18-23, 98; 8:18-24, 102; 8:19-22, 13; 8:19-23, 199, 201; 8:21, 27; 8:22, 27; 8:27, 64; 8:28-30, 104; 8:33, 41, 184; 8:34, 184; 8:35-39, 104; 9:13, 37; 9:15, 41; 9:22-24, 44; 9:25, 41; 9-11, 45, 83, 157; 10:4, 12; 10:13, 44; 10:18, 14; 11:1, 40; 11:13, 40; 11:17, 45; 11:18, 45; 11:24, 45; 11:25-26, 104; 11:28, 37; 11:32, 41; 12:1, 183; 12:2, 183; 12:19, 183; 13:1, 32; 13:1-3, 118; 13:4, 32; 13:9, 58; 13:11, 167; 13:11-14, 104; 14:10, 187; 15:8-13, 104; 16:26, 14

1 Corinthians 1:8, 187; 1:20, 13; 1:21, 13; 2:11, 13; 2:12, 13; 3:13, 127; 3:15, 127; 5, 185; 5:5, 68; 5:7, 28; 5:9-10, 13; 5:12, 13; 6, 185; 6:2, 179; 6:3, 179; 8:6, 205;

10:11, 19; 10:19-21, 66; 11:26, 98;
11:31, 185, 189; 11:32, 189; 12, 25;
12:5, 52; 12:9, 52; 12:10, 52; 12:21-26,
52; 12:27, 52; 13:10, 202; 13:12, 204;
15, 169, 174; 15:12, 174; 15:12-19, 169;
15:20, 169, 174; 15:20-27, 94; 15:21,
174; 15:22-24, 173; 15:24, 144, 173,
203; 15:24-26, 19; 15:24-28, 187;
15:26, 173; 15:27, 19, 173; 15:42, 166,
174; 15:42-54, 170; 15:44, 170; 15:50,
166; 15:52, 19; 15:52-54, 166; 15:53,
166

2 Corinthians 1:3, 56; 1:4, 56; 1:5, 56; 1:6,
56; 2:6, 54; 3:17, 29; 3:18, 29; 4:4, 62,
64; 5:1-8, 177; 5:10, 187, 189; 6:15, 109;
7:4, 131; 7:6, 95; 7:7, 95; 11:13-15, 67;
11:14, 63; 12:2, 130, 205; 12:3, 176;
12:4, 176; 12:7, 66

Galatians, 92; 1:5, 15; 2:16, 46; 3, 34; 3:8,
38; 3:15, 44; 3:16-18, 157; 3:17, 38;
3:18, 44; 3:28, 58; 4:3, 53; 4:8, 53; 4:9,
53; 5:5, 92; 5:19-24, 187; 5:20, 66; 5:22,
194; 5:23, 194; 6:1, 185; 6:2, 185; 6:7,
183, 184; 6:8, 183; 6:16, 39

Ephesians, 92; 1:4, 41; 1:7, 41; 1:10, 41;
2:1, 45; 2:2, 62, 166; 2:5, 45; 2:8, 189;
2:12, 41, 45; 2:13, 45; 2:16, 45; 2:18,
45; 3:9, 205; 3:21, 15; 4:7-10, 176; 4:30,
92; 5:5, 92, 126; 5:6, 126, 187; 5:21-33,
58; 5:27, 127; 5:29-31, 45; 6:11, 143;
6:12, 66, 127, 143; 7:2, 65

Philippians 1:6, 137; 1:10, 137, 187; 1:12,
56, 95; 1:21-24, 103, 176-77; 1:29, 42;
2:7, 50; 2:14-16, 58; 2:15, 14; 3:11,
167, 174-75; 3:20, 100; 3:21, 100

Colossians 1:18, 178; 1:24, 55, 56; 3:6,
187; 3:12, 36, 41

1 Thessalonians, 104; 1:9, 102; 1:10, 102;
3:5, 62; 4:3, 29; 4:13, 175; 4:13-5:11,
90; 4:16, 99, 173; 4:16-18, 103; 4:17,
130, 173; 5:1, 100; 5:2, 100, 137; 5:3,
143; 5:5, 173; 5:9, 131, 173, 187

2 Thessalonians, 104; 1:5-8, 143, 183; 1:7,
95; 1:7-10, 187; 2, 113; 2:1-11, 90;
2:1-12, 111; 2:3, 6, 101, 111, 143; 2:3-4,
5; 2:3-7, 143; 2:4, 6, 111, 112; 2:7, 112;
2:7-12, 6; 2:8, 95, 112, 143; 2:9, 95, 112;
2:10, 112

1 Timothy 1:5, 12; 1:17, 166; 1:20, 68;
6:16, 166

2 Timothy 1:10, 95, 166; 1:12, 187; 3:1,
101; 3:2, 6; 3:2-7, 101; 3:16, 184; 4:1,
95, 187; 4:8, 187

Titus 1:1, 41; 2:13, 100; 3:3, 53

Philemon, 92

Hebrews, 72; 1:1, 83; 1:2, 12, 19; 1:8, 14;
1:8-9, 86; 1:10, 198; 1:11, 197, 198; 2:5,
14; 2:6, 38; 2:14, 68; 3:1-4:10, 84; 3:3,
83; 3:6, 83; 4:14-5:10, 84; 5:5, 83;
6:20-10:25, 84; 7:11, 113; 7:25, 64;
8:6, 44, 83; 9:11-14, 202; 9:23, 44;
9:26-28, 35; 9:27, 187; 9:28, 96, 104,
187; 10:5-9, 58; 10:14, 55; 10:26-31,
187; 10:37, 94; 11:3, 205; 11:7, 34;
11:10, 201; 11:17-19, 178; 11:39, 176;
11:40, 176; 12:5, 54; 12:6, 54; 12:6-8,
184; 12:7, 54, 189; 12:22, 158, 201;
12:26, 144; 12:28, 144

James, 104; 1:1, 50; 1:13, 43; 2:20, 189;
4:1, 32; 4:2, 32; 5:3, 187; 5:7, 95, 187;
5:8, 101; 5:9, 188

1 Peter 1:2, 41; 1:5, 12; 1:6, 55; 1:7, 55, 95;
1:12, 70; 1:13, 95; 1:20, 12, 19; 2:4, 36;
2:4-10, 144; 2:9-10, 36; 3:7, 144;
3:10-12, 144; 3:17, 188; 3:18, 176, 188;
3:19, 176; 3:20, 34; 3:22, 188; 4:1, 54;
4:2, 54; 4:7, 101, 144; 4:12, 144; 4:14,
55; 4:17, 55, 188; 5:8, 64; 5:10, 54

2 Peter 1:16, 95; 2:1, 144; 2:4, 66, 194;
2:4-10, 188; 2:5, 34; 3:3, 101; 3:4, 101;
3:7, 137, 197; 3:8, 205; 3:8-10, 188; 3:9,
183; 3:10, 100, 197, 200; 3:12, 197, 200;
3:13, 197

1 John 2:18, 11, 12, 19, 101, 108, 112;
2:19-28, 101; 2:22, 112; 3:2, 127, 170;
5:4, 112

2 John, 92; v. 7, 108, 112; v. 13, 41

3 John, 92

Jude v. 1, 50; v. 6, 66, 144, 188, 189; v. 13,
205; v. 14, 144, 188; v. 15, 188; v. 18,
144, 188; v. 19, 144; v. 25, 15

Revelation, 72; 1:1, 125; 1:4, 94; 1:5, 41,
84, 174; 1:6, 41; 1:7, 99; 1:18, 188, 191;
2:11, 191; 2:12, 188; 2:18, 188; 3, 131;
3:7, 188; 3:10, 131; 3:12, 201; 3:14,
188; 4:1, 131; 4:1-19:11, 101; 4:8-11,
52; 4:11, 204, 205; 5:5, 84; 5:9, 84;
5:9-10, 32; 5:10, 84; 6:1, 125; 6:4, 125;
6:6, 125; 6:8, 125, 191; 6:9, 125; 6:12,
125; 6:12-14, 197-198; 6:13, 125, 200;
6:16, 125, 126; 7:4, 132; 7:8, 125; 7:9,
132; 7:14, 125, 131; 7:15-17, 132; 7:21,
125; 8, 125; 8:7-13, 2; 9, 125; 9:16, 135;
9:20, 66; 9:27, 125; 11:2, 125; 11:4,
129; 11:5, 129; 11:7, 133; 11:15, 125;
11:17, 204; 11:18, 204; 12, 61, 129;
12:4, 129; 12:5, 129, 130; 12:6, 129;
12:7, 65-66, 125; 12:7-9, 73; 12:7-10,
200; 12:7-12, 127; 12:9, 26, 61, 66, 110,
112, 145; 12:10, 61, 64, 200; 12:12, 200;

12:14, 129; 13, 61, 65, 118; 13:1, 109,
112; 13:1-10, 113; 13:2, 112, 114; 13:4,
69, 110; 13:5, 114, 125, 130; 13:5-7, 5;
13:5-8, 110; 13:6, 114; 13:7, 114;
13:11, 108, 110, 112; 13:11-13, 112;
13:11-17, 118; 13:11-18, 3; 13:12, 52,
113; 13:12-15, 69; 13:13, 69; 13:14,
114; 13:15, 69, 114; 13:16, 114; 13:17,
114; 13:18, 3, 114; 15:1, 125, 126; 15:3,
205; 15:4, 205; 16, 61, 65; 16:1, 125,
126; 16:6, 132; 16:12, 135, 145, 148;
16:13, 118, 145; 16:14, 126, 135, 145;
16:15, 126; 16:16, 135, 144; 16:17, 126;
16:18, 4; 16:19, 114, 115; 17, 115; 17:1,
115; 17:2, 115; 17:3, 115; 17:5, 115;
17:6, 115; 17:7, 115; 17:9, 115; 17:10,
115; 17:12, 4; 17:13, 4, 115; 17:14, 115;
17:15, 115; 17:16, 115; 17:17, 4; 17:18,
115; 17-18, 5; 18, 115; 18:3, 115; 18:4,
115; 18:10, 115; 18:11, 115; 18:20, 116;
19, 145; 19:11, 145; 19:11-16, 158;
19:11-21, 112; 19:13, 84, 126, 145;
19:13-15, 32; 19:14, 145; 19:15, 126,
145; 19:16, 32, 84, 126, 145; 19:17, 145;
19:18, 145; 19:19, 145, 189; 19:20, 5,
118, 141, 189, 191; 20, 61, 65, 188, 206;
20:1-10, 60; 20:2, 61, 158, 189; 20:2-7,
151-52; 20:3, 133, 158, 189; 20:4, 84,
131, 179; 20:4-6, 175; 20:4-15, 172;
20:5, 158, 170, 189; 20:5-13, 172; 20:6,
172, 175, 204; 20:7, 139, 146; 20:7-10,
1-3, 189; 20:8, 84, 135, 139, 146, 147;
20:8-10, 144; 20-9, 84; 20:10, 118, 191,
192; 20:11, 197, 200; 20:11-15, 185,
189; 20:12, 190; 20:13, 190, 191; 20:14,

189, 191, 192; 20:15, 190, 191; 21:1, 84,
144, 192, 197, 199, 200; 21:2, 29, 158,
201; 21:2–22:5, 201; 21:3, 158; 21:4,
158; 21:5, 192; 21:8, 88, 126, 191, 192;
21:10, 201; 21:12, 202; 21:14, 202;
21:16, 201; 21:23, 202; 21:24, 158;
21:26, 158; 21:27, 30, 190; 22:1, 201,
202, 204; 22:2, 202; 22:3, 52, 202; 22:4,
202; 22:9, 203; 22:11, 202; 22:12, 202;
22:14, 202-3; 22:15, 66, 126; 22:17,
205; 22:18, 202; 22:19, 202; 22:20, 101;
22:21, 202; 22:25, 202; 22:27, 202

APOCRYPHA

4 Ezra, 178; 7:28, 87; 11, 109; 12, 109
Wisdom of Solomon 3:4, 166
2 Maccabees 7:23, 169; 12:43, 169; 12:44,
169
4 Maccabees 14:5, 166

NONCANONICAL BOOKS

Ascension of Isaiah 2:4, 108; 11:1, 94
Dead Sea Scrolls, 109
Enoch 1:9, 144, 188; 22:1-14, 190; 48:10,
81; 51:1, 169; 52:4, 81; 67:4ff, 191;
71:15, 21
Psalms of Solomon 17:36, 188
Sybilline Oracles 2:167, 108
Testaments of the Twelve Patriarchs, 109; T.
Dan 5, 81; 5:10, 117; 5:11, 117; T. Levi
8, 81; 18, 81; T. Reuben 6, 81